CW00553149

Teaching Entrepreneurship

*To entrepreneurial educators everywhere; thank you for your spirit,
imagination, and curiosity*

Teaching Entrepreneurship

A Practice-Based Approach

Heidi M. Neck

Ph.D., Jeffry A. Timmons Professor of Entrepreneurial Studies, Babson College, USA

Patricia G. Greene

Ph.D., Paul T. Babson Chair in Entrepreneurial Studies, Babson College, USA

Candida G. Brush

DBA, F.W. Olin Distinguished Chair in Entrepreneurship, Babson College, USA

Edward Elgar

Cheltenham, UK • Northampton, MA, USA

© Heidi M. Neck, Patricia G. Greene and Candida G. Brush 2014

All rights reserved. No part of this publication may be reproduced, stored in a retrieval system or transmitted in any form or by any means, electronic, mechanical or photocopying, recording, or otherwise without the prior permission of the publisher.

Published by
Edward Elgar Publishing Limited
The Lypiatts
15 Lansdown Road
Cheltenham
Glos GL50 2JA
UK

Edward Elgar Publishing, Inc.
William Pratt House
9 Dewey Court
Northampton
Massachusetts 01060
USA

A catalogue record for this book
is available from the British Library

Library of Congress Control Number: 2013958021

This book is available electronically in the ElgarOnline.com Business Subject Collection, E-ISBN 978 1 78254 056 4

ISBN 978 1 78254 055 7 (cased)
ISBN 978 1 78254 069 4 (paperback)

Typeset by Servis Filmsetting Ltd, Stockport, Cheshire
Printed and bound in Great Britain by T.J. International Ltd, Padstow

Contents

Figures, tables and boxes

FIGURES

TABLES

BOXES

1. Teaching entrepreneurship as a method that requires practice

Entrepreneurship is neither science nor art. It is a practice. (Peter Drucker)

The message of our book is quite simple. We want to advance entrepreneurship education for all types of students using an action-based method rooted in a specific set of practices. From our extensive experience training a global cadre of entrepreneurship educators (four-year college professors, community college professors, and adjuncts), we have observed that the mindset of most educators is discipline specific and rooted in process models. Though the entrepreneurship process orientation is the most common approach seen in entrepreneurship education today, we posit that it is neither the most realistic nor the most effective approach for the current environment, which is characterized by increasingly high levels of uncertainty.

While entrepreneurship education has not significantly changed in at least two decades, the global emphasis on the relevance and potential impacts of entrepreneurship has dramatically increased and is cited as a potent economic force (Kuratko, 2005). As educators we are lagging, and our role in the world cannot be undervalued. The late Jeff Timmons[1] said that entrepreneurship is "not just about new company, capital and job formation, nor innovation, nor creativity, nor breakthroughs. It is also about fostering an ingenious human spirit and improving humankind."

At the same time as we have seen this change in the phenomenon of entrepreneurship around the world, business education in general has come under scrutiny (Trank and Rynes, 2003; Mintzberg, 2004; Bennis and O'Toole, 2005; Datar, Garvin, and Cullen, 2010), and content is becoming a commodity. Entrepreneurship education is not without its share of criticism given the dearth of research on its impact (Kuratko, 2005). As a result our role, our classrooms, and our teaching approaches are being challenged – and rightfully so. Now more than ever our role as educator is to unleash the entrepreneurial spirit of our students, cultivate a mindset of practice, and build environments in which practice can occur. In turn our students can lead more entrepreneurial lives because of their newly found bias for action, appreciation for learning through action, and comfort with ambiguity. Yet the big question remains: How should entrepreneurship be learned?

As we lag a bit in education legitimacy, entrepreneurship's academic legitimacy continues to grow because of scholars heeding calls to action with respect to research domains and important questions (Brush et al., 2003; Kuratko, 2005). Membership in the entrepreneurship division of the Academy of Management now tops 2400 – one of the largest divisions in the academy. The number of abstracts submitted to the Babson College Entrepreneurship Research conference now exceeds 750. There are 71 refereed journals devoted to entrepreneurship, over 100 U.S. university-based centers, and more than 400 endowed chairs. We are also fortunate to have largely buried the "Can entrepreneurship be taught?" debate, even though this continues to be a favorite question posed by popular press journalists. Legendary educator Peter Drucker (1985) said "Entrepreneurship is not magic, it is not mysterious and it has nothing to do with genes. It is a discipline. And, like any discipline, it can be learned."

Since the late 1980s entrepreneurship education has exploded across the globe. All AACSB-accredited schools are teaching entrepreneurship at some level (Katz, 2003). In the United States alone there are 2200 courses being offered at 1600 colleges and universities (Katz, 2003). It is one of the fastest growing subjects among undergraduate institutions (Myrah and Currie, 2006) and a primary source of growth for MBA programs (MBA Roundtable, 2012). China's premier, Li Kequiang, has promised unprecedented support for entrepreneurship education (Bastin, 2014). The Malaysian government launched the Higher Education Entrepreneurship Development Policy in 2010 (http://www.mohe.gov.my/portal/en/pelajar/program-keusahawanan.html) with a goal of graduating college students with a greater ability to think and act entrepreneurially as a "catalyst for the achievement of economic transformation of the country from a middle to high income economy." Banco de Chile is funding a five-year program to train Chilean educators in Babson's approach to entrepreneurship. And Babson's Symposium for Entrepreneurship Educators indirectly touches over 7000 students per year by training a global cadre of faculty. More locally the private sector is jumping on board. For example, Goldman Sachs has funded and supported a program for the growth of 10 000 Small Businesses through entrepreneurship education delivered to business owners through community colleges across the United States and in the UK, as well as 10 000 Women, which has actually reached its 10 000th participant. Large foundations such as Kauffman and Coleman support education initiatives on multiple levels, and the Network for Teaching Entrepreneurship (NFTE) is making significant impact with its initiatives at the primary and second-ary levels of education.

Entrepreneurship education is exploding, and new approaches are needed not only to keep up with demand but also to keep up with the changing nature of entrepreneurship education – which is precisely the reason why we have written *Teaching Entrepreneurship*! This book approaches teaching entrepreneurship from a new practice-based perspec-tive. We are not advocating a particular course or curriculum; rather, we are advancing the notion that entrepreneurship is a method composed of a portfolio of practices. And these practices can happen in any course, on any campus, with any student! To better understand why we embarked on the journey of this book, it is important to have a historical perspective of the entrepreneurship field from both a research and a teaching perspective. The two are highly intertwined, and it is not prudent to discuss research without teaching and vice versa; therefore our historical discussion is fol-lowed by a consideration of the conundrum of theory versus practice in education, a point of particular concern for us given the perceived practi-cality of the field of entrepreneurship. We then introduce entrepreneurship as a method, discuss the role of practice in theory, and introduce the five practices of entrepreneurship education highlighted throughout the book.

THE EVOLUTION OF ENTREPRENEURSHIP EDUCATION: FROM INDIVIDUAL TO PROCESS TO METHOD

The role of the entrepreneur in economic theory dates back to the early 1940s, yet until 1970 very few business schools offered courses in entrepre-neurship (Vesper and Gartner, 1997). The 1970s were a time of transition for small business ownership in the U.S. overall. The number of small businesses had been declining across the country since the industrial revo-lution. However, in 1972 the decrease leveled off, and for the following decades the numbers of small businesses again began rising (Greene, 1993). Many reasons have been proposed for the change, some economic, some sociological. One perspective, proposed by Vesper and Gartner (1997), speculates that technological advances, such as the personal computer, created new markets and an array of opportunities emerged. The pace of change and the ease of entry created a wave of entrepreneurship that has yet to subside. Parallel to these structural changes, in the early 1970s "connotations of the term 'entrepreneur' began to shift from notions of greed, exploitation, selfishness, and disloyalty to creativity, job creation, profitability, innovativeness, and generosity" (Vesper and Gartner, 1997,

p. 406). Entrepreneurs began to be recognized not only as a driving force of the economy, but also as very positive and contributing members of society. These changes have continued until now. In the present day, according to the Global Entrepreneurship Monitor, high status for being an entrepreneur is perceived among 72 percent of entrepreneurs practicing in 69 economies, and 68 percent believe entrepreneurship is a good career choice (Xavier et al., 2012).

Early research efforts focused on the traits of entrepreneurs. Researchers attempted to identify a certain set of characteristics that differentiated entrepreneurs from non-entrepreneurs (e.g. McClelland, 1965; Collins and Moore, 1970; DeCarlo and Lyons, 1979; Brockhaus, 1980; Cooper and Dunkelberg, 1981). Brockhaus and Horwitz (1986) reviewed the trait literature and concluded that there are four major personality traits of entrepreneurs: need for achievement, internal locus of control, high risk-taking propensity, and tolerance for ambiguity. Since this time, however, there has been very little consensus in the trait literature or further scientific evidence that the four traits are from either nature or nurture. These early research efforts were present in most entrepreneurship textbooks, with opening chapters discussing "who" the entrepreneur is and what kind of personality profile "he" possesses. Many years ago Low and MacMillan (1988) argued that any attempt to profile the typical entrepreneur was inherently futile, yet the research, to our dismay, continues. Miner (1996) proposed four psychological personality patterns of entrepreneurs: personal advisors, empathetic super-salespeople, real managers, and expert idea generators. Also, most recently, Shane posited the role and presence of an entrepreneurial gene (Mount, 2010), taking the nature-versus-nurture discussion to new extremes. Fisher and Koch (2008), in their book *Born Not Made*, bring us backwards arguing there is a personality profile, but their profile is heavily influenced by risk-taking propensity. Why do we still believe that all entrepreneurs are extreme risk takers?

In response to the traits approach Gartner (1988) argued for a behavioral approach to the study of entrepreneurship. For Gartner, entrepreneurship is ultimately about the creation of organizations (new venture creation), where many influences interact in the emergence process. The entrepreneur is only a part of the process; therefore, the activities undertaken by the entrepreneur in the context of new venture creation should be examined. As a result, research should focus on what the entrepreneur does – not who he or she is. Yet behaviors across samples of entrepreneurs are very idiosyncratic, so it became difficult to generalize this research for teaching purposes. To prove this point, a study comparing textbook content to the behaviors of nascent entrepreneurs concluded that there was very little overlap (Edelman et al., 2008). But researcher calls to move away from traits to behaviors did ultimately move entrepreneurship education away from the focus on one type of individual to a view of entrepreneurship as a process (Bygrave and Hofer, 1991).[2] As the process approach made its way into entrepreneurship classrooms, entrepreneurship became a linear activity of identifying an opportunity, developing the concept, understanding resource requirements, acquiring resources, developing a business plan, implementing the plan, managing the venture, and exit (Morris, 1998). In our opinion, entrepreneurship became just another version of management – a process of leading, controlling, planning, and evaluating, with the difference being its application to new organizations. Today the process orientation has a stronghold in entrepreneurship education. We conducted a review of 45 entrepreneurship textbooks currently on the market, and approximately 80 percent emphasize the process of entrepreneurship. Process topics included opportunity evaluation, business planning, marketing planning, resource acquisition, managing the business, and exit.

The entrepreneurship-as-process approach was heavily influenced by the proliferation of strategy scholars entering the field, and a debate between strategic management and entrepreneurship scholars ensued (Shane and Venkataraman, 2000; Hitt et al., 2001a, 2001b; Zahra and Dess, 2001; Meyer et al., 2002). Both fields felt the need to create distinction, and for entrepreneurship the space for this distinction was created by Venkataraman (1997). He called for researchers and educators in entrepreneurship to confront the question "What is the distinctive contribution of our field to a broader understanding of business enterprise?" He continued, "To the extent that our answer to this question is unclear, delayed and overlaps with other sub-fields, our legitimacy and our very survival in the world of business research and education is seriously threatened" (Venkataraman, 1997, p. 119). Shane and Venkataraman's (2000) seminal article introduced a definition of entrepreneurship that was distinctive: "the identification, evaluation, and exploitation of opportunities" (Shane, 2012, p. 12). This definition has become the most used and cited definition in the field (Aldrich and Cliff, 2003).

Acceptance of this scholarly pursuit by academicians led to the reemergence of studying individual entrepreneurs (but, thankfully, not from a traits perspective). Instead, the entrepreneurial cognition approach to studying entrepreneurship gained and continues to gain traction. Rather than distinguishing entrepreneurs based on personality traits, cognition researchers were uncovering patterns in how entrepreneurs think and began hypothesizing that specific ways of thinking were sources of competitive advantage and individual differentiation (Mitchell et al., 2000, 2002). Entrepreneurial cognition is defined as "the knowledge structures that people use to make assessments, judgments, or decisions involving opportunity evaluation, venture creation, and growth" (Mitchell et al., 2002, p. 97).

While most of the cognition work focused on *why* individuals make decisions pertaining to entrepreneurial action and related such decision making to deeply held knowledge structures and beliefs (Krueger, 2007), another stream of cognition-based research emerged that sought to address barriers to entrepreneurship – or the *how* part of entrepreneurship that related to the starting point for persons wishing to undertake entre-preneurial endeavors. To this point, largely missing from the discussion was "consideration of the origin of initial resource strengths, and how they contribute to, or determine, value-creating activities" (Brush et al., 2001). In other words, the question was no longer can an individual be an entre-preneur but rather how an individual can become entrepreneurial, create opportunities, and act on them. The work of Saras Sarasvathy (2001, 2003, 2008), a student of Nobel laureate Herbert Simon, introduced the field to a controversial new theory – effectuation.

Sarasvathy's dissertation research incorporated think-aloud, verbal protocols with 45 expert entrepreneurs. The experimental methodology required subjects to "think aloud" as they made decisions and solved a set of ten typical problems that occur in a start-up (Sarasvathy, 2008, p. 23).[3] Her resulting theory of effectuation emerged in contrast to its inverse, causation.

> Causal models begin with an effect to be created. They seek either to select between means to achieve those effects or to create new means to achieve preselected ends. Effectual models, in contrast, begin with given means and seek to create new ends using non-predictive strategies. In addition to altering conventional relationships between means and ends and between prediction and control, effectuation rearranges many other traditional relationships such as those between organism and environment, parts and whole, subjective and objective, individual and social, and so on. In particular, it makes these rela-tionships a matter of *design* rather than one of *decision*. (Sarasvathy, 2008, p. 16)

Understanding how entrepreneurs view the world and how they learn, the entrepreneurial mindset suddenly became important – really impor-tant! Sarasvathy (2008) empirically discovered that effectual entrepreneurs see the world as open to a host of different possibilities, fabricate as well as recognize new opportunities, make rather than find markets, accept and leverage failure, and interact with a variety of stakeholders – all for the purposes of creating the future rather than trying to predict the future (Schlesinger et al., 2012).

The discovery of patterns in how entrepreneurs think (Sarasvathy, 2008) combined with additional research from Babson (Costello et al., 2011; Greenberg et al., 2011; Neck and Greene, 2011; Noyes and Brush, 2012; Schlesinger et al., 2012) encouraged us to think about moving entrepreneurship education to the next level. Building off effectuation theory (Sarasvathy, 2008), we believe that entrepreneurship can no longer be taught as a process but rather must be taught as a *method* (Venkataraman et al., 2012). The method of entrepreneurship requires the development of a set of practices. Through these practices we can help students think more entrepreneurially, which in turn can develop students who can act more entrepreneurially.

As you can see from this historical view, the method is not devoid of theory. As a matter of fact, theory in our view plays a stronger role in entrepreneurship education than ever before. Theories related to entrepreneurial cognition are just our jumping-off platform for establishing the need for entrepreneurship as a method. The practices that constitute the method are steeply entrenched in theory from a multitude of disciplines that we will discuss throughout the book.

THE THEORY VERSUS PRACTICE CONUNDRUM

If we look at the history of education, theory actually ruled first. Indeed, practice has been getting a bad rap since Plato's Theory of Forms. Brockbank and McGill (2007) provide a helpful description of Plato's early dualistic approach between the intellectual and aesthetic work of the ruling class and the others, the ruled, who engage in manual work. The manual workers were decidedly seen as lesser. This particular philosophical emphasis, grounded largely in Plato and Aristotle, also, however, presents us with the beginning of the theory–practice conflict. Both Plato and Aristotle "championed the primacy of the intellect over practice" and set the tone, a theme picked up later in the work of Descartes. While this model is still a significant influence on our traditional model of higher education, upon reflection, the path was not as straight and clear as sometimes reported. One crack in the road is Aristotle's contribution about the importance of learning by doing, with his example centering on the learning of virtue (Brockbank and McGill, 2007, p. 19). In fact, while this either/or approach has since been labeled as a "category mistake" (Ryle, 1983 in Brockbank and McGill, 2007, p. 19) that privileges the "mind domain" over the domain of the body, the mistake is actually attributed to an early philosophical dilemma concerning how to think about the soul. Of most concern for us is that "This polarization and differentiation of mind and matter has remained intact and lives today in the persistence of dualism in academic life, with skills, 'knowing how,' practice and affect being undervalued, while cognition, 'knowing that' and impersonal modes of communication are championed through the academy" (Ryle, 1967 in Brockbank and McGill, 2007, p. 20).

While the dominance of the importance of theory is strongly supported by the early philosophers, the critical importance of practice has emerged more strongly over the last half-century, largely driven by the work of Pierre Bourdieu, who called out Plato on this very subject, claiming that Plato had tipped the balance by negatively describing the logic of practice (Bourdieu, [1980] 1990):

> But the most formidable barrier to the construction of an adequate science of practice no doubt lies in the fact that the solidarity that binds scientists to their science (and to the social privilege which makes it possible and which it justified or procures) predisposes them to profess the superiority of their knowledge, often won through enormous effort, against common sense, and even find in that superiority a justification for their privilege, rather than to produce a scientific knowledge of the practical mode of knowledge and of the limits that scientific knowledge owes to the fact that it is based on a privilege. (Bourdieu, [1980] 1990, p. 28)

There is a continuing and growing quandary in entrepreneurship education: What are the role of theory and the role of practice in the entrepreneurship classroom? The battle for power and position between theory and practice is one that has been oft discussed in teaching discussions and publications. Wren et al. (2007) updated research conducted in 1977 (Wren et al., 1980) and again in 1989 (Wren et al., 1994) on the emphasis of theory versus application among management educators. Using a sample of 525 members of the Academy of Management, they reported that the 1970s were a decade of theory but the 1980s were a decade of application. It is surprising then that their most recent research (2005 data) saw a trend reversal back to the theory. Wren et al. (2007) discussed:

> In many instances, the 2005 respondents indicated that theory was even more pervasive in our pedagogy than was reported in the 1977 data ... Although theory is emphasized more in undergraduate courses, the aforementioned trend toward more theory is similarly occurring in graduate courses. This lends further credibility to the notion that theories are emphasized to a greater extent than the usefulness of those theories in practice at all levels of our management instruction. As some have suggested, it appears as though the trend in our pedagogy has been more directed toward the exercise of theory and analysis than toward training our students in thinking, analysis, and application skills. (p. 490)

The debate for us is not surprising given that entrepreneurship is one of the most applied of all business disciplines, and many argue, us included, that, in order to *learn* entrepreneurship, one must *do* entrepreneurship. Our position, however, is that doing entrepreneurship does not exclude theory. On the contrary, effective *doing* of entrepreneurship requires a set of *practices* and these practices are firmly grounded in theory. The students, however, do not see the theory – it is invisible and hidden in the practice. We call this actionable theory (Neck and Greene, 2011; Corbett and Katz, 2012).

The poles of the continuum can be considered to be, on one side, the theory-based faculty member, perhaps with no "real" entrepreneurship experience, and guided by a belief and commitment to promulgating frameworks with a sincere belief that they will guide practice (e.g. the business plan) and, on the other end, the practitioner with a visceral disdain for what is perceived to be an ivory tower approach. The desired end advanced in this book is a synthesis. The matrix in Figure 1.1 is a useful guide to considering the theoretical-based options (or lack thereof) for teaching entrepreneurship today.

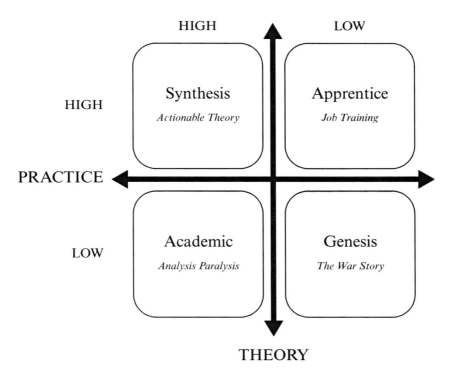

Figure 1.1   Theory–practice matrix

Entrepreneurship education was born in Genesis. We had no research, no theory, and, therefore, very few options for teaching entrepreneurship except hearing the war stories. One of our favorite stories comes from the late Jeff Timmons (1941–2008):

> One of the challenges faced by faculty with real world experience is whether and how to utilize those experiences in the classroom. There are basically two schools of thought on this subject: 1) "Tell"; and (2) "Whatever you do, do not tell war stories." As you would guess these two groups are not seen frequently together in the faculty dining area. In fact, the entrepreneurs and business people are often admonished in advance by some regular faculty with a severe warning: no war stories. However, one must put this advice in perspective. Donald Brown, a highly successful real estate entrepreneur from Washington, DC, spent many years teaching one semester each year at HBS. Students considered him to be a highly effective professor. His insight on the advice of sage regular faculty colleagues at HBS "to avoid telling war stories" is priceless: "I finally figured out," Don noted in his talk, "that *they* did not have any war stories to tell!"[4]

Timmons had a point, and in 1984 he brought practitioners together with academics to solve the either/or issue and learn together the most effective ways at the time to teach entrepreneurship. The Price-Babson Symposium for Entrepreneurship Educators was born and continues today. However, today's entrepreneurship professor often has both entrepreneurial experience and academic experience – it is more the norm than the exception. We call it Genesis now because it represents the beginning of entrepreneurship education when war stories were really all we had. There is a limit to learning from war stories and very little practice is involved – we can say the same to some extent about case studies.

The Apprentice cell represents training of very specific tasks. It is a vocational perspective where skill development takes precedence over critical thinking and where understanding and developing theory is not important. The Academic cell supports theory but at the expense of action (e.g. the business plan), while the Synthesis cell provides the opportunity for informed application. Our book, and the practices that are highlighted, is devoted to a deep dive into the Synthesis cell – where invisible theory meets practice. Here we introduce a practice-based approach for teaching entrepreneurship. Let us not forget the famous words of Kurt Lewin, "There is nothing so practical as a good theory."

ENTREPRENEURSHIP AS A METHOD

We support entrepreneurship as a method because process implies one will get to a desired outcome if prescribed steps are followed. Furthermore, the word "process" assumes known inputs and known outputs as in a manufacturing process. In writing about this previously we used a car manufacturing analogy (Neck and Greene, 2011). Think about building a car on an assembly line. Great thought and engineering are involved in designing the process, where the required parts that enter the manufacturing process are known, the specifications of how the parts are to be assembled, and what the car will look like (exactly) as it comes off the line. The process is quite predictable. Can we really expect entrepreneurship to be such a process? Is entrepreneurship really that predictable? As we previously addressed, educators have traditionally accepted a process view – a view dominated by a linear, staged approach to new venture creation: identify an opportunity, develop the concept, determine resource requirements, acquire resources, develop a business plan, implement the plan, manage the venture, and exit (Morris, 1998).

Entrepreneurial environments are unpredictable, uncertain, and ambiguous, and require a specific mindset, which is in stark contrast to the environments we teach in. A method of entrepreneurship allows our students to navigate the discipline. A method represents a body of skills or techniques that help students develop a set of practices that implore them to think and act more entrepreneurially. We believe that introducing entrepreneurship as a method of practices is just as important as, if not more important than, the content so often seen in the textbooks. As we mentioned earlier, information is a commodity today; therefore, "we need to teach methods that stand the test of dramatic changes in content and context" (Neck and Greene, 2011, p. 62).

Approaching entrepreneurship as a method means teaching a way of thinking and acting built on a set of assumptions using a portfolio of practices to encourage creating. The method forces students to go beyond understanding, knowing, and talking. It requires using, applying, and acting. The method requires continuous practice. Therefore, our underlying assumptions of the method include (Neck and Greene, 2011, p. 62):

1. It applies to novices and experts: the assumption is that the method applies across student populations and works regardless of experience level. What is important is that each student understands how he or she views the entrepreneurial world and his or her place in it.
2. The method is inclusive, meaning that the definition of entrepreneurship is expanded to include any organization at multiple levels of analysis. Therefore, success is idiosyncratic and multidimensional.
3. The method requires continuous practice. The focus here is on doing and then learning, rather than learning and then doing.
4. The method is for an unpredictable environment.

Entrepreneurship as a method	Entrepreneurship as a process
A set of practices ◄·····················►	Known inputs and predicted outputs
Phases of learning ◄·····················►	Steps to complete
Iterative ◄·····················►	Linear
Creative ◄·····················►	Predictive
Action focus ◄·····················►	Planning focus
Investment for learning ◄·····················►	Expected return
Collaborative ◄·····················►	Competitive

Source: Adapted from Neck and Greene (2011).

Figure 1.2   Method versus process

Figure 1.2 contrasts teaching entrepreneurship as a method and as a process. As we show in this book, the method view requires a different approach to teaching and learning. The method view is not about a class, a course, or even an entrepreneurship curriculum. Our view is concerned with inculcating a spirit of entrepreneurial thinking and acting into every student so that students may create their future regardless of context.

THE FIVE PRACTICES OF ENTREPRENEURSHIP EDUCATION

Billett (2010) in a robust, edited volume delves into practice theory and how learning through practice is operationalized (or not) in education settings. Practice-based learning is often seen as the stepchild living next door to the ivory tower. Billett (2010) notes that experiences from practice are "seen as adjunct to an educational provision that is organized and structured in colleges or universities or through programs offered by professional bodies and other agencies, rather than [learning] experiences that are both legitimate and effective in their own right" (p. 21). Within the realm of practice theory, practice is defined as "the enactment of the kinds of activities and interactions that constitutes the occupation" (Billett, 2010, p. 22). There is a long tradition of research that supports learning through practice. Because of the philosophical foundations of practice, we would be remiss to ignore Aristotle, who said: "For the things we have to learn before we can do them, we learn by doing them." Given such a rich tradition Billett (2010) notes that there is nothing new about learning from practice, but he is surprised that learning through practice is positioned in contrast to the traditional educational experiences offered in higher education (Rogoff and Gauvain, 1984).

We are promoting the practice-based approach as a model of learning to support entrepreneurial action. Unlike the Apprentice cell (Figure 1.1), we are not promoting the pure practice models that ensure competence in a specialized occupation such as medicine, law, or even a position in a symphony orchestra. On the contrary, our goal is focusing on synthesis that encourages the practice of actionable theory. Rather than a narrow view of learning through practice which requires particular knowledge to enact the practice, we align with a broader perspective:

> [Learning] can be enhanced by particular kinds of pedagogic activities which, as instanced, required the practitioner to represent their tacit learning in some way. This requirement creates an imbedded practice that has significant pedagogic qualities in so far as it generates the kinds of knowledge structures that make explicit what was tacit, and generates richer understanding about practice, but from and through practice, not on behalf of it. (Billett, 2010, p. 29)

A noted criticism of practice theorists is that they often treat practice as a singular and distinct construct while overlooking the complexity, diversity, and range of practice (Dall'Alba and Sandberg, 2010). This is precisely why we cannot simply say that entrepreneurship is a practice and must submit that entrepreneurship is a method composed of a portfolio of practices. In addition to learning *through* practice, we leave room for learning *about* practice. Both contribute to skillful performance (Dall'Alba and Sandberg, 2010).

The complexity of practice theory cannot be overstated, and our book cannot give justification to its rich history in the social sciences, especially in the fields of sociology and anthropology. Rouse (2006), analyzing the work of seminal practice theorists (e.g. Foucault, 1972; Bourdieu, 1977, [1980] 1990; Giddens, 1984; Pickering, 1992; Turner, 1994; Schatzki, 1996; Rouse 2002), identified several themes in practice theory that relate to our work and support entrepreneurship as a method or even metapractice. In other words, entrepreneurship is a set of practices that describe and give information about the method of entrepreneurship. Combined, our practices create a method of thinking and acting entrepreneurially.

1. Practices are meaningful performances governed by social rules and norms. Each practice highlighted in our book is governed by theory from multiple disciplines within and outside of business administration.
2. Practices become the background of culture formation and the platform for social structure construction. The practices of entrepreneurship discussed in the following chapters can create a culture of entrepreneurship among students, in classrooms and beyond.

3. Practices are dependent on human agency and social interaction. Through sustained practice habits are formed that expand existing knowledge structures and encourage new ways of acting. Thus entrepreneurship is learned through practice.
4. Practices create shared meaning through "shared presuppositions, conceptual frameworks, vocabularies, or 'languages'" (Rouse, 2006, p. 515). Entrepreneurship education, through a practice-based approach, becomes a community of learning that is student-centered.

Just as we have been talking about what practice is, it is just as important to talk about what practice is not as it relates to our approach. An interesting line of inquiry emerging in the management and entrepreneurship literatures, but borrowed from cognitive science, is the concept of deliberate practice to achieve expert performance (Ericsson et al., 1993). Deliberate practice is devoting a large number of focused hours to intense practice to achieve mastery of a skill. For example, Chase and Simon (1973) studied chess players and estimated that mastery was achieved only after 10 000 to 50 000 hours of practice. More recently Campitelli and Gobet (2011) estimated that chess players need only 3000 hours of deliberate practice and found that other variables such as season of birth, cognitive ability, and being left-handed contributed to mastery. Deliberate practice has been applied to entrepreneurship as a way to show how some entrepreneurs outperform others. Baron and Henry (2010) proposed that expert performance resulting from deliberate practice could differentiate successful entrepreneurs from the less successful. They argued that deliberate practice by entrepreneurs could enhance cognitive resources while also increasing motivation, self-efficacy, and self-control. But a characteristic of deliberate practice is prolonged periods of highly focused practice such as those seen with chess players, athletes, and musicians. Baron and Henry (2010) admitted that prolonged periods of practice may not work for start-up entrepreneurs, nor is it clear what specific skills they would deliberately practice over and over.

To resolve this dilemma of extreme amounts of devoted time, Baron and Henry (2010) delve into the entrepreneurial learning literature. They introduce two types of learning: experiential learning and vicarious learning (Kolb and Kolb, 2005). For example, quarterbacks can learn while playing football (experiential learning) or they can learn by watching tapes of other quarterbacks (vicarious learning). Baron and Henry (2010) note:

> Applying this general principle of vicarious learning to entrepreneurship, we suggest that an important route to building expert performance in situations where time pressures and other environmental conditions provide little oppor-

tunity for hours of overt focused practice is offered by *exposure to a large number of pertinent, realistic, and highly relevant examples.* (p. 57)

The solution to the time dilemma required of deliberate practice, in our opinion, is not a solution at all. Rather, the approach offered by Baron and Henry is nothing new in entrepreneurship education – the use of examples and case studies as modes of vicarious learning – and is not moving entrepreneurship education forward. Students are relegated to the role of involved spectators (Higgins and Elliott, 2011). However, this does lead us to an important question related to the practice-based approach we are proposing. How does our practice-based approach differ from Kolb's popular notion of experiential learning?

Kolb (1984) defines experiential learning as knowledge created through the transformation of experience. He emphasizes a focus on the process of learning rather than outcomes of learning as well as the knowledge created and recreated through experiences. In other words, experiential learning emphasizes the experience, feedback from or interaction with others on the experience, and self-reflection on the experience (Kolb, 1984; Jennings and Wargnier, 2010).

Our practice-based approach complements that of Kolb and other experiential learning theorists. Our approach is mostly concerned with learning within the practice as well as learning through practice. Thus, the only way to learn within the practice is through experience. In each of our practices of entrepreneurship education learning, innovation, communication, interpretation, and history are present – the essential elements of experiential learning (Higgins and Elliott, 2011). In sum, the entrepreneurship method as a series of practices can only be learned through experiential approaches.

With an understanding of why we elect to view entrepreneurship as a method as well as a better understanding of what we mean by practice intertwined with the importance of theory, we can now turn to the core of our book – the practices subsumed in the method. Our concept of practice relates to the acquisition of skills, knowledge, and mindset through deliberate hands-on, action-based activities that enhance development of entrepreneurial competencies and performance. Given the complex and multifaceted nature of entrepreneurship, a single practice is not possible. Therefore, we introduce five specific practices of entrepreneurship education (Figure 1.3) that represent our earlier notion of synthesis (Figure 1.1) as the integration of theory and practice – actionable theory. The five practices include: the practice of play; the practice of empathy; the practice of creation; the practice of experimentation; and the practice of reflection.

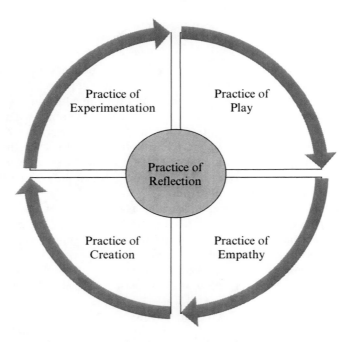

Figure 1.3   The practices of entrepreneurship education

ORGANIZATION OF THE BOOK

Our book is organized into two parts. Part I details the definitional and theoretical foundations for each of the practices. Chapter 2 introduces the *practice of play*. The practice of play relates to the development of a free and imaginative mind, allowing one to see a wealth of possibilities, a world of opportunities, and a pathway to more innovative ways of being entrepreneurial. Chapter 3 borrows heavily from psychology, neuroscience, and design thinking and introduces the *practice of empathy*. Empathy is defined as "a social and emotional skill that helps us feel and understand the emotions, circumstances, intentions, thoughts, and needs of others, such that we can offer sensitive, perceptive, and appropriate communications and support" (McLaren, 2013, p. 11). Chapter 4 introduces the *practice of creation*, which discusses the role of creativity in entrepreneurship education as well as delves into the world of creation in contrast to prediction. Chapter 5 characterizes the *practice of experimentation*, drawing from medical sociology and other theory. Experimentation is trying something, seeing what the results are, learning from the results, and then trying it again. Chapter 6 discusses our final practice – the *practice of reflection*. Reflection encourages students to codify their learning experiences, especially in high-action environments. This is perhaps the most integrating of all the practices, because there is evidence that practicing reflection can enhance each of the other practices (Schön, 1983).

Where Part I emphasizes the theoretical foundations of our practices, Part II includes a series of 42 experiential exercises, organized by practice, that can help students develop each of their entrepreneurship practices within a classroom environment. Chapters 7–11 include exercises related to play, empathy, creation, experimentation, and reflection respectively. Each exercise includes an extensive teaching note that describes the exercise, learning outcomes, classroom plan, summary points, readings for theoretical foundations, and teaching tips. Our focus on classroom activities is intentional. We recognize the importance, more now than ever, of co-curricular activities, but we also know how faculty struggle with engagement inside the classroom. Therefore, we are meeting a need of our colleagues to address practical engagement in the classroom based on rigorous (yet invisible) theory.

In concluding, Chapter 12 includes our final thoughts and addresses assessment. There is a popular myth that entrepreneurship education does not progress owing to the limitations and constraints demanded by accreditation. There is fear among faculty and administrators that using a practice-based approach will not meet the traditional assurance of learning standards mandated by AACSB and other accrediting bodies. We debunk the myths and fears and argue that a practice-based approach can be a viable pathway to meet the current standards required of business schools. How do we know this? Because we interviewed the President and CEO of AACSB, John Fernandes, and he told us so!

NOTES

1. Jeff Timmons (1941–2008) is considered one of the founding fathers of entrepreneurship education. A distinguished professor at Babson from 1982, Jeff played a central role in Babson College's status in entrepreneurship education. His commitment to higher education and to entrepreneurship was a statement of his belief in humanity. He believed goodness and achievement were inherent in everyone. Jeff also believed that entrepreneurship classes were a perfect vehicle to redefine and amplify purposeful study and action that would lead to a better life and a better world.
2. During the same time that the process approach was emerging, Aldrich (1990) and Aldrich and Wiedenmeyer (1993) introduced the "rates" approach grounded in the ecology of organization formation. "Rates" researchers focused on the environmental conditions generating variation in the number of foundings over time. The rates

approach has great application to public policy but has not made its way into most
entrepreneurship classrooms – or at least in a substantive way beyond the presentation
of start-up, growth, and failure statistics.
3. See Sarasvathy (2008, pp. 19–43) for a detailed discussion on the rigor and efficacy of her
research methodology.
4. This quote came from a note Jeff Timmons wrote for the Price-Babson SEE program
titled "War Stories: To Tell or Not to Tell?" The date it was originally written is unknown.

REFERENCES

Aldrich, H.E. 1990. Using an ecological perspective to study organization found-
ing rates. *Entrepreneurship Theory and Practice*, 14(3), 7–24.
Aldrich, H.E., and Cliff, J.E. 2003. The pervasive effects of family on entrepre-
neurship: Toward a family embeddedness perspective. *Journal of Business
Venturing*, 18, 573–96.
Aldrich, H.E., and Wiedenmeyer, G. 1993. From traits to rates: An ecological
perspective on organizational foundings. *Advances in Entrepreneurship, Firm
Emergence, and Growth*, 1, 145–95.
Baron, R.A., and Henry, R.A. 2010. How entrepreneurs acquire the capacity to
excel: Insights from research on expert performance. *Strategic Entrepreneurship
Journal*, 4, 49–65.
Bastin, M. 2014. Entrepreneurship education needed in China. *Forbes.com*,
http://www.ft.com/cms/s/2/80529984-876b-11e3-9c5c-00144feab7de.
html#axzz2sZuH2YYd.
Bennis, W., and O'Toole, J. 2005. How business schools lost their way. *Harvard
Business Review*, 98(5), 96–104.
Billett, S. (ed.). 2010. *Learning through Practice: Models, Traditions, Orientations
and Approaches*. London: Springer.
Bourdieu, P. 1977. *Outline of a Theory of Practice*. Cambridge, UK: Cambridge
University Press.
Bourdieu, P. [1980] 1990. *The Logic of Practice*. Stanford, CA: Stanford University
Press.
Brockbank, A., and McGill, I. 2007. *Facilitating Reflective Learning in Higher
Education*, 2nd edn. New York: Open University Press.
Brockhaus, R.H. 1980. Risk taking propensity of entrepreneurs. *Academy of
Management Journal*, 23(3), 509–20.
Brockhaus, R., and Horwitz, P. 1986. The psychology of the entrepreneur.
In D. Sexton and R. Smilor (eds.), *The Art and Science of Entrepreneurship*
(pp. 25–48). Cambridge, MA: Ballinger.
Brush, C.G., Greene, P.G., and Hart, M.M. 2001. From initial idea to unique
competitive advantage: The entrepreneurial challenge of constructing a resource
base. *Academy of Management Executive*, 15(1), 64–78.
Brush, C.B., Duhaime, I.M., Gartner, W.B., Stewart, A., Katz, J.A., Hitt,
M.A., Alvarez, S.A., Meyer, G.D., and Venkataraman, S. 2003. Doctoral
education in the field of entrepreneurship. *Journal of Management*, 29(3),
309–31.
Bygrave, W.D., and Hofer, C.W. 1991. Theorizing about entrepreneurship.
Entrepreneurship Theory and Practice, 16(2), 13–22.

Campitelli, G., and Gobet, F. 2011. Deliberate practice: Necessary but not sufficient. *Current Directions in Psychological Science*, 20(5), 280–85.

Chase, W.G., and Simon, H.A. 1973. Perceptions in chess. *Cognitive Psychology*, 4, 55–81.

Collins, O.F., and Moore, D.G. 1970. *The Organization Makers*. New York: Appleton-Century-Crofts.

Cooper, A.C., and Dunkelberg, W.C. 1981. A new look at business entry: Experiences of 1805 entrepreneurs. In K.H. Vesper (ed.), *Frontiers of Entrepreneurship Research*. Wellesley, MA: Babson College.

Corbett, A.C., and Katz, J.A. (eds.). 2012. *Advances in Entrepreneurship, Firm Emergence and Growth*, Vol. 14: *Entrepreneurial Action*. Bingley, UK: Emerald Group Publishing.

Costello, C., Neck, H., and Williams, R. 2011. *Elements of the Entrepreneur Experience*. Babson Park, MA: Babson Entrepreneur Experience Lab.

Dall'Alba, G., and Sandberg, J. 2010. Learning through and about practice: A lifeworld perspective. In S. Billett (ed.), *Learning through Practice: Models, Traditions, Orientations and Approaches* (pp. 143–62). London: Springer.

Datar, S.M., Garvin, D.A., and Cullen, P. 2010. *Rethinking the MBA: Business Education at the Crossroads*. Boston, MA: Harvard Business Press.

DeCarlo, J.F., and Lyons, P.R. 1979. A comparison of selected personal characteristics of minority and non-minority female entrepreneurs. *Journal of Small Business Management*, 17, 22–9.

Drucker, P. 1985. *Innovation and Entrepreneurship*. New York: Harper & Row.

Edelman, L.F., Manolova, T.S., and Brush, C.B. 2008. Entrepreneurship education: Correspondence between practices of nascent entrepreneurs and textbook prescriptions for success. *Academy of Management Learning and Education*, 7(1), 56–70.

Ericsson, K.A., Krampe, R.T., and Tesch-Römer, C. 1993. The role of deliberate practice in the acquisition of expert performance. *Psychological Review*, 100, 363–406.

Fisher, J.L., and Koch, J.V. 2008. *Born Not Made: The Entrepreneurial Personality*. Westport, CT: Praeger.

Foucault, M. 1972. *The Archeology of Knowledge*. New York: Harper & Row.

Gartner, W.B. 1988. Who is an entrepreneur? is the wrong question. *American Journal of Small Business*, 12(4), 11–32.

Giddens, A. 1984. *The Constitution of Society*. Berkeley: University of California Press.

Greenberg, D., McKone-Sweet, K., and Wilson, H.J. (eds.). 2011. *The New Entrepreneurial Leader: Developing Leaders Who Will Shape Social and Economic Opportunities*. San Francisco: Berrett-Koehler.

Greene, P.G. 1993. A theoretical and empirical study of self-employed women. Dissertation, University of Texas at Austin.

Higgins, D., and Elliott, C. 2011. Learning to make sense: What works in entrepreneurial education? *Journal of European Industrial Training*, 35(4), 345–67.

Hitt, M.A., Ireland, R.D., Camp, M., and Sexton, D.L. 2001a. Integrating entrepreneurship and strategic management actions to create firm wealth. *Academy of Management Perspectives*, 15(1), 49–63.

Hitt, M.A., Ireland, R.D., Camp, M., and Sexton, D.L. 2001b. Strategic entrepreneurship: Entrepreneurial strategies for wealth creation. *Strategic Management Journal*, 22(6–7), 479–91.

Jennings, C., and Wargnier, J. 2010. Experiential learning: A way to develop agile minds in the knowledge economy? *Development and Learning in Organizations*, 24(3), 14–16.

Katz, J. 2003. The chronology and intellectual trajectory of American entrepreneurship education 1876–1999. *Journal of Business Venturing*, 18(2), 283–300.

Kolb, A.Y., and Kolb, D.A. 2005. Learning styles and learning spaces: Enhancing experiential learning in higher education. *Academy of Management Learning and Development*, 4(2), 193–212.

Kolb, D.A. 1984. *Experiential Learning: Experience as the Source of Learning and Development*. Englewood Cliffs, NJ: Prentice Hall.

Kuratko, D.F. 2005. The emergence of entrepreneurship education: Development, trends, and challenges. *Entrepreneurship Theory and Practice*, 29(5), 577–97.

Krueger, N.R. 2007. What lies beneath? The experiential essence of entrepreneurial thinking. *Entrepreneurship Theory and Practice*, 31(1), 123–38.

Low, M.B., and MacMillan, I.C. 1988. Entrepreneurship: Past research and future challenges. *Journal of Management*, 14(2), 139–61.

MBA Roundtable. 2012. *Curricular Innovation Study*, http://www.mbaroundtable.org/curricular_innovation_study.

McClelland, D. 1965. Need achievement and entrepreneurship: A longitudinal study. *Journal of Personality and Social Psychology*, 1, 389–92.

McLaren, K. 2013. *The Art of Empathy: A Complete Guide to Life's Most Essential Skill*. Boulder, CO: Sounds True.

Meyer, G.D., Neck, H.M., and Meeks, M. 2002. The entrepreneurship–strategic management interface. In M.A. Hitt and D. Ireland (eds.), *Strategic Entrepreneurship* (pp. 19–44). Oxford, UK: Blackwell.

Miner, J.B. 1996. *The 4 Routes to Entrepreneurial Success*. San Francisco: Berrett-Koehler.

Mintzberg, H. 2004. *Managers, Not MBAs: A Hard Look at the Soft Practices of Managing and Management Development*. San Francisco: Berrett-Koehler.

Mitchell, R.K., Smith, J.B., Seawright, K.W., and Morse, E.A. 2000. Cross-cultural cognitions and the venture creation decision. *Academy of Management Journal*, 53(5), 974–93.

Mitchell, R.K., Busenitz, L., Lant, T., McDougall, P., Morse, E.A., and Smith, B. 2002. Toward a theory of entrepreneurial cognition: Rethinking the people side of entrepreneurship research. *Entrepreneurship Theory and Practice*, 27(2), 93–104.

Morris, M.H. 1998. *Entrepreneurial Intensity: Sustainable Advantages for Individuals, Organizations, and Societies*. Westport, CT: Quorum.

Mount, I. 2010. Nature vs. nurture: Are great entrepreneurs born . . . or made? *Fortune Small Business*, December 09/January 10, 25–6.

Myrah, K., and Currie, R. 2006. Examining undergraduate entrepreneurship education. *Journal of Small Business and Entrepreneurship*, 19(3), 233–53.

Neck, H.M., and Greene, P.G. 2011. Entrepreneurship education: Known worlds and new frontiers. *Journal of Small Business Management*, 49(1), 55–70.

Noyes, E., and Brush, C. 2012. Teaching entrepreneurial action: Application of creative logic. In A.C. Corbett and J.A. Katz (eds.), *Entrepreneurial Action: Advances in Entrepreneurship and Firm Emergence and Growth* (pp. 253–80). Bingley, UK: Emerald Group Publishing.

Pickering, A. 1992. *Science as Practice and Culture*. Chicago: University of Chicago Press.

Rogoff, B., and Gauvain, M. 1984. The cognitive consequences of specific experiences: Weaving versus schooling among the Navajo. *Journal of Cross-Cultural Psychology*, 15(4), 453–75.
Rouse, J. 2002. *How Scientific Practices Matter: Reclaiming Philosophical Naturalism*. Chicago: University of Chicago Press.
Rouse, J. 2006. Practice theory. In *Handbook of the Philosophy of Science*, Vol. 15: *Philosophy of Anthropology and Sociology*, ed. Stephen Turner and Mark Risjord (pp. 499–540). Amsterdam: North-Holland.
Ryle, G. 1967. Teaching and training in education. In R.S. Peters (ed.), *The Concept of Education*. London: Routledge & Kegan Paul.
Ryle, G. 1983. *The Concept of Mind*. Harmondsworth: Penguin.
Sarasvathy, S.D. 2001. Causation and effectuation: Toward a theoretical shift from economic inevitability to entrepreneurial contingency. *Academy of Management Review*, 26(2), 243–63.
Sarasvathy, S.D. 2003. Entrepreneurship as a science of the artificial. *Journal of Economic Psychology*, 24, 203–20.
Sarasvathy, S.D. 2008. *Effectuation: Elements of Entrepreneurial Expertise*. Cheltenham, UK and Northampton, MA, USA: Edward Elgar Publishing.
Schatzki, T. 1996. *Social Practices: A Wittgensteinian Approach to Human Activity and the Social*. Cambridge, UK: Cambridge University Press.
Schlesinger, L., Kiefer, C., and Brown, P. 2012. *Just Start: Take Action, Embrace Uncertainty, Create the Future*. Cambridge, MA: Harvard Business School Press.
Schön, D. 1983. *The Reflective Practitioner: How Professionals Think in Action*. New York: Basic Books.
Shane, S. 2012. Reflections on the 2010 AMR decade award: Delivering on the promise of entrepreneurship as a field of research. *Academy of Management Review*, 37(1), 10–20.
Shane, S., and Venkataraman, S. 2000. The promise of entrepreneurship as a field of research. *Academy of Management Review*, 25(1), 217–26.
Trank, C.Q., and Rynes, S.L. 2003. Who moved our cheese? Reclaiming professionalism in business education. *Academy of Management Learning and Education*, 2(2), 189–205.
Turner, S. 1994. *The Social Theory of Practices: Tradition, Tacit Knowledge, and Presuppositions*. Chicago: University of Chicago Press.
Venkataraman, S. 1997. The distinctive domain of entrepreneurship research. *Advances in Entrepreneurship, Firm Emergence and Growth*, 3, 119–38.
Venkataraman, S., Sarasvathy, S.D., Dew, N., and Forster, W.R. 2012. Reflection on the 2010 AMR decade award: Whither the promise? Moving forward with entrepreneurship as a science of the artificial. *Academy of Management Review*, 37(1), 21–33.
Vesper, K.H., and Gartner, W.B. 1997. Measuring progress in entrepreneurship education. *Journal of Business Venturing*, 12(5), 403–21.
Wren, D.A., Atherton, R.M., and Michaelsen, L.K. 1980. Theory and applications in management pedagogy: An empirical study. *Journal of Management*, 6(1), 21–31.
Wren, D.A., Buckley, M.R., and Michaelsen, L.K. 1994. The theory/applications balance in management pedagogy: Where do we stand? *Journal of Management*, 20(1), 141–57.
Wren, D.A., Halbesleben, J.R.B., and Buckley, M.R. 2007. The theory–

application balance in management pedagogy: A longitudinal update. *Academy of Management Learning and Education*, 6(4), 484–92.

Xavier, S.R., Kelley, D., Kew, J., Herrington, M., and Vorderwülbecke, A. 2012. *Global Entrepreneurship Monitor: 2012 Global Report*. Global Entrepreneurship Research Association, www.gemconsortium.org.

Zahra, S., and Dess, G.C. 2001. Entrepreneurship as a field of research: Encouraging dialogue and debate. *Academy of Management Review*, 26(1), 8–10.

PART I

The practices of entrepreneurship education:
the theory

2. The practice of play

How incredible would it be for a professor to say "Pull out your laptops, load up *Investhor: Lord of Wall Street*, and begin your midterm?" (Greene, 2009)

"Play it again, Sam!" OK, devoted cinephiles know that Humphrey Bogart really did not say this in *Casablanca*, but it is the ubiquitously quoted line and we're going with it – especially because the idea of playing something over and over again fits with the idea of a practice and subsequently teaching entrepreneurship as a method. The practice of play is about developing a free and imaginative mind, allowing one to see a wealth of possibilities, a world of opportunities, and a pathway to more innovative ways of being entrepreneurial. In fact, play has been pointed to as a necessary twenty-first-century skill (Pink, 2005).

THE CONCEPT OF PLAY

Jesse Schell, in his book *The Art of Game Design* (2010), dedicates a portion of a chapter to "A rant about definitions," calling out what he sees to be an overly large commitment of energy to definitional precision, while at the same time recognizing that having your own definition in mind is quite helpful in framing the discussion or, ultimately, the action. Useful for our purposes, Schell calls out the "murky" terms in the field of game design, emphasizing "experience," "play," and "game" as defined differently by different people. Our interest for advancing entrepreneurship education is in exploring the differences between "play" and "game," with ultimately some consideration of "fun."

The Dutch historian, Johan Huizinga, is one of the earliest people to devote careful thought to the concept of play, going so far as to suggest that instead of *Homo sapiens* we should actually be known as *Homo ludens*, or "Man the Player" (Huizinga, 1944). Huizinga defines "play" as:

[A] free activity standing quite consciously outside "ordinary" life as being "not serious," but at the same time absorbing the player intensely and utterly. It is an activity connected with no material interest, and no profit can be gained by it. It proceeds within its own proper boundaries of time and space according to fixed rules and in an orderly manner. (Huizinga, 1944, p. 13/Kindle).

The space of play becomes a particularly beguiling notion, with Huizinga's notion of "magic circle" often repeated among other theorists. Overall, his approach to play is broad and inclusive, ranging from the romping of dogs (including rules about nipping ears) to contests and performances. In an earlier work, one of us considered this definition as establishing the archetype of *play*, positioning it as the "opposite of productive work" (Greene, 2011). However, at the same time this definition notably still includes a sense of structure, exemplified by the reference to "fixed rules" and "orderly manner." In fact, the inclusion of rules almost makes the definition feel more like "game" than "play." Going beyond the question of rules or place, Huizinga places play as outside of ordinary events, with enjoyment as an important outcome. He describes play as superfluous and, importantly, voluntary, saying that "Play to order is no longer play," asserting that the only urgent need that play should fulfill is that of enjoyment (Huizinga, 1944, p. 175/Kindle).

Jean Piaget, child development psychologist, provided another notable contribution to the understanding of play. He actually started on the concept of games, and moved into the consideration of play as part of his study of developmental processes. Therefore, his study is largely on play in childhood. Even so, it is interesting to note the criteria he proposes as to what makes up "play." Play is disinterested and spontaneous (in opposition to work requirements); it is for pleasure; it is relatively unorganized, it is proposed as free from conflicts (positioned as more about internal conflicts than external ones), and it may contain an element of "overmotivation" (Piaget, 1962). Piaget proposes categories of play: exercise play, symbolic play, games with rules, and games of construction, with this last category representing the transition between symbolic play and non-playful activities or "serious" adaptations (Piaget and Inhelder, 1969).

Writing about the same time as Piaget, Kraus (1971) looked back and summarized work done by psychologists, sociologists, and educators, largely to consider the relationship of play to a variety of types of human development, including physical, social, emotional, and cognitive aspects (Rieber, 1996; Brougère, 1999). Kraus (1971) uses the early theories of play that follow as a foundation for advancing his study of play in the context of leisure and recreation:

- **surplus energy theory**: play is motivated by the need to burn up excess energy (Schiller, 1875; Spencer in Lehman and Witty, 1927, p. 13);
- **recreation theory**: play as a way of conserving or restoring energy (Lazarus);

- **instinct-practice theory**: play as a way of practicing life skills (Groos, 1901);
- **catharsis theory**: play as a "safety valve" for releasing pent-up emotions (Groos, 1901; Carr in Lehman and Witty, 1927, p. 19);
- **recapitulation theory**: play as a linkage of evolutionary stages, reliving the history of the human race (Hall, 1920);
- **relaxation theory**: play as a form of physical and emotional release that is necessary for social order (Patrick, 1916).

Kraus suggests that none of these theories could stand on their own, and proposes his own definition of play:

> [Play is] regarded as an activity carried on within leisure for purposes of pleasure and self-expression. It tends to be active and to be carried on in a spirit of competition, exploration, or make-believe. Customarily, play is regarded as a child's activity, although an adult may also engage in play and under some circumstances may find play in his [*sic*] work. (Kraus, 1971, p. 266)

Bateson (2006), with a slightly different twist, explores play as part of the evolution of communication. Bateson states: "It appears that play is a phenomenon in which the actions of 'play' are related to, or denote, other actions of 'not-play.' We therefore meet in play with an instance of signals standing for other events" (p. 317). Bateson pushes this approach somewhat, suggesting that many actions of play are indeed representative of ordinary events (not-play), but taking place in a different arena and with different expected outcomes. Consider the following:

> The challenge in thinking about play, however, is that we (the adults) tend to associate this kind of play with childhood, a time of freedom and imagination where minutes turned into hours, backyards transformed into magical faraway kingdoms, living rooms were reconfigured into tent cities, swimming pools became uncharted waters littered with sunken treasure, and stuffed animals sat at attention waiting for the assignment from the young seven-year-old teacher (Neck, 2010, p. 41).

In any of these scenarios we can see a connection to ordinary events – just some more loosely connected than others. Pushing to the looser connections raises potentially interesting questions about the relationship between play, creativity and innovation. In some ways, types of play and those connections to ordinary life might even be considered on a continuum, leading us to think about various types of play.

GAMES AS CONTEXT FOR PLAY

Much of the conversation in the educational literature actually focuses more on "game" than "play." As with "play," there are a variety of definitions of "games." One of the more explicit definitions is that "A game is a rule-based formal system with a variable and quantifiable outcome, where different outcomes are assigned different values, the player exerts effort in order to influence the outcome, the player feels attached to the outcome, and the consequences of the activity are optional and negotiable" (Jules, in Koster, 2005, p. 12). Other definitions particularly support the emphasis on "rule-based play" (Suits, 1978; Salen and Zimmerman, 2003; de Freitas, 2006).

It is understandable why the line between game and play is so porous. When we look at general game characteristics, the chief ones that emerge are:

- Games consist of highly abstract models of real things.
- They are generally quantified.
- They focus on presenting things to be absorbed into our unconscious (rather than the conscious and logical). (Koster, 2005, pp. 76, 116)

While moving between consideration of play and game may get confusing, Schell (2010) provides an extremely useful way of building from definitions of multiple concepts (play, fun, toy, and games). When summarized, "play" and "games," particularly regarding application to education and practice, lie at the intersections of rules, engagement, and fun.

While a game by definition is rules based, play also has rules. Huizinga explicitly connects play with games through rules: "All play has its rules . . . Indeed, as soon as the rules are transgressed the whole play-world collapses. The game is over" (Huizinga, 1944, p. 238).

Related to the question of rules is the question of the voluntary nature of play. One suggested difference between play and games is that play is voluntary and superfluous, filling no basic need except enjoyment (Huizinga, 1944, p. 175). This voluntary nature does raise the question of how play becomes an educational practice and indeed makes us very aware of the different types of teaching approaches needed to advance this practice. Rules give a framework where engagement can happen. When engaged within a framework there is an understanding of "the game," and more fun can be experienced.

Engagement is a key quality that makes play enjoyable (Csikszentmihalyi,

BOX 2.1   DEFINING TOWARDS FUN

For play:

- Play is the aimless expenditure of exuberant energy. (Friedrich Schiller)
- Play refers to those activities which are accompanied by a state of comparative pleasure, exhilaration, and power, and the feeling of self-initiative. (J. Barnard Gilmore)
- Play is free movement within a more rigid structure. (Katie Salen and Eric Zimmerman)
- Play is whatever is done spontaneously and for its own sake. (George Santayana)

For fun:

- Fun is pleasure with surprises.

For toy:

- Toy is an object that you play with.
- A good toy is an object that is fun to play with.

For games:

- Games are an exercise of voluntary control systems, in which there is a contest between powers, confined by rules in order to produce a disequilibrial outcome. (Elliot Avedon and Brian Sutton-Smith)
- [A game is] an interactive structure of endogenous meaning that requires players to struggle toward a goal. (Greg Costikyan)
- A game is a closed, formal system, that engages players in structured conflict, and results in an unequal outcome. (Tracy Fullerton, Chris Swain, and Steven Hoffman)

This all adds up to the following:

- Fun is pleasure with surprises.
- Play is manipulation that satisfies curiosity.

> - A toy is an object you play with.
> - A good toy is an object that is fun to play with.
> - A game is a problem-solving activity, approached with a playful attitude.
>
> (Schell, 2010, pp. 24–38)

1990). When someone is playing, that person is able to concentrate only on a limited "stimulus field" where he or she is transcended to a new environment where existence is limited to the moment and problems outside of the stimulus field are outside of consideration. Csikszentmihalyi called this state of being "flow" and described it as often experienced through play. He states:

> Flow denotes the holistic sensation present when we act with total involvement. It is the kind of feeling after which one nostalgically says: "that was fun," or "that was enjoyable." It is the state in which action follows upon action according to an internal logic which seems to need no conscious intervention on our part. We experience it as a unified flowing from one moment to the next, in which we feel in control of our actions, and in which there is little distinction between self and environment: between stimulus and response; or between past, present and future. (Csikszentmihalyi, 1990, p. 41)

We see Csikszentmihalyi's flow as equating to Huizinga's intense and utter absorption. It is a complete engagement. It is a highly desirable state for optimal learning.

Most definitions of play include a sense of enjoyment or at least imply that it is a pleasurable experience. Definitions of games generally do not explicitly include this, although some game theorists do suggest that it is an enviable attribute. In fact, during a recent game design class one of us took, the instructors specifically said that games do not have to be fun, but they do have to be engaging (Burak, 2013). But, like our other two major concepts "play" and "game," "fun" means different things to different people, with types of fun ranging across and between things such as sense-pleasure, make-believe, drama, obstacle, social framework, discovery, self-discovery and expression, and surrender (M. LeBlanc, in Koster, 2005). Expanding our view, and that of our students, for what constitutes "fun" motivates the practice of play. Of course, fun is also included for its pedagogical contribution. "Fun and humor stimulate creativity as the brain moves from a cognitive, rule-bound state to a more fluid, relaxed state where the whole body is engaged in problem solving" (Prouty, 2000 in Hromek and Roffey, 2009, p. 630). Overall, laughter, humor, and light-heartedness are credited with both health and professional benefits (Pink, 2005).

THE ROLE OF GAMES IN THE PRACTICE OF PLAY

Early games were designed to teach children survival skills while entertaining them (Shubik, 2009). The introduction of using games for training and education (didactic application) is largely tracked to war games (de Freitas, 2006), particularly around the time of World War II (Cohen and Rhenman, 1961; Shubik, 2009; Verzat et al., 2009). Since then, intentionally playing games has become an extensive part of the world of business, as well as for various kinds of education, nonprofit, and government organizations targeting social change. Two of the major areas where this can be seen are in the use of video games for purposeful education, called serious games, and, to a much more limited extent while staying quite interesting, the use of alternative reality games.

The first use of the term *Serious Games* is attributed to Carl C. Abt's book of the same name in 1970 (Annetta, 2008). In general, serious games are an outcome of "the convergence of education and gaming technologies, positioned as part of an evolution of learning" (Annetta, 2008, p. ix), with defining criteria that include a focus on governance by rules and specific outcomes that include the "pleasure of play" (Lastowka, 2009, p. 380; Greene, 2011). Early game pioneers tried to capture these characteristics. "Game play is about problem solving, applying ingenuity, anticipating the programmers' challenges, and their humour, in a tough cycle of observe, question, hypothesize, test" (Heppell, 2006, p. 4).

What is actually included in the genre of "serious games" is still somewhat ambiguous (Greene, 2011), with an emerging inventory of related terms being developed, moving the field towards a goal of a more shared and consistent terminology. Sawyer and Smith's (2008) examples to date include: educational games, simulations, virtual reality, alternative-purpose games, edutainment, digital game-based learning, immersive learning simulations, social impact games, persuasive games, games for change, games for good, synthetic learning environments, and game-based "X." One suggestion for an overarching term is that of *immersive learning simulations*, a categorization which includes those interactive learning tools that are representative of a real life situation and combine aspects of simulations, learning, and competition (Schooley et al., 2008). Another approach that we find more helpful, as we think about not only types but what makes up a serious game, is "the use of games or gaming dynamics not simply to entertain the player, but rather to inspire a particular action, effect some type of attitudinal change, or instill a particular lesson in the service of an organizational goal" (Keitt and Jackson, 2008, p. 3).

These attributes, or what makes up these games, are actually among our primary concerns. Merrilea Mayo, former director of Future Learning Initiatives at the Ewing Marion Kauffman Foundation, identified several game features that contribute to enhanced learning environments. By analyzing video game research from various authors she concluded that video games foster self-efficacy, collaboration, user-directed exploration, and continuous feedback. The gaming features are also seen to contribute to enhanced creativity. Improving self-efficacy leads to a greater belief in one's ability; collaboration requires group-based problem solving; user-directed exploration incites tolerance for ambiguity and curiosity; and continuous feedback provides real time learning to apply as one progresses through the game. It makes for a virtuous circle of practicing play as the game, or series of games, is played over and over.

Part of the growth in this area is due not only to the intersection of gaming technology and education, but also to the sheer size of the video game industry and the ever growing population of gamers. This has to do with not only the consideration of who might like to play, but also who is now making the decision about how work is done and how people are trained to do that work. In many respects, higher education, and entrepreneurship education specifically, is very late to the gaming party! Box 2.2 highlights some of the relevant gaming statistics today.

While mainstream video gaming numbers are intriguing from a societal perspective and help us understand the general video game industry, it is the serious game market that is of particular interest to us as educators. The market for simulation-focused learning was nearly $2.4 billion in 2012 and projected to grow to $6.6 billion in 2017. Revenues for packaged mobile education games reached $307.5 million in 2012, expected to reach $459.9 million by 2017.[1] The U.S. Army has created its own video group unit with the intent of investing up to $50 million for game training systems.[2] The intersection of education and social change with gaming is awe inspiring. For example, the game called *Half the Sky Movement* raises awareness and funds for global girl empowerment. Within six months the game reached 1 million registered players on Facebook! The game play has triggered more than 230 350 free book donations, raised over $145 100 for fistula surgeries, and contributed $410 450 in direct and sponsored donations.[3]

There are other changes in the industry producing these games. Serious games are being used as effective employee training and productivity tools. Intel provides an online arcade as a game training center for its

BOX 2.2 VIDEO GAMING QUICK FACTS

- Fifty-eight percent of Americans play video games.
- Consumers spent $20.77 billion on video games, hardware, and accessories.
- Purchases of digital content, including games, add-on content, mobile apps, subscriptions, and social networking games, accounted for 40 percent of game sales.
- The average game player is 30 years old and has been playing games for 13 years.
- The average age of the most frequent game purchaser is 35 years old.
- Forty-five percent of all game players are women. In fact, women over the age of 18 represent a significantly greater portion of the game-playing population (31 percent) than boys age 17 or younger (19 percent).
- 800 million people worldwide are regular players.

Source: Entertainment Software Association, 2012.

latest processors. Playing games related to security, visuals, connectivity, efficiency, partnerships, and performance allows participants to earn game points and training credits (arcade.intel.com). The Hilton Garden Inn was the first hotel brand to offer training on customer service through a "graphically-intense, 3-D, first-person video game" played on the Sony PlayStation gaming system. Representatives from the hotel chain report being enthused not only about the training per se, but also about the potential for this approach to enhance their recruiting efforts for next-generation team members to whom the gaming environment is particularly inviting (virtualheroes.com/projects/Hilton-ultimate-team-play). U. S. Army chaplains use gaming technologies to replicate the types of "trauma-oriented environments" in which chaplains may be called to serve (http://www.ecsorl.com/solutions/spiritual-triage-army-chaplain-school). Finally, IBM makes a business model case for the use of training games in a quantifiable way, reporting outcome possibilities including a 20 percent margin improvement, complete with a 12–18 percent increase in capacity, a 12 percent reduction in employees, and a 10–30 percent capital reduction (IBM White Paper).

GAMES FOR LEARNING AND EDUCATION

The use of video games for teaching has become the subject of much research in a number of different fields, largely in different types of cognitive sciences. Part of the discussion is led by the changing nature and understanding of not only how generations learn, but also how they want to work (Tapscott, 1998, 2009; Beck and Wade, 2004; Pink, 2005; Gee, 2007; Palfrey and Gasser, 2008; Edery and Mollick, 2009; Reeves and Read, 2009; Greene, 2011). For example, James Gee, a leading theorist in the field of learning in and through video games, is a linguist, with early work focused on language, learning, and literacy (Gee, 2007). For Gee, people learning to play video games are engaging in a semiotic exercise, in essence learning a new literacy complete with all the accompanying visual symbols. Gee cites Jean Lave, the social situation cognition theorist, quoting her in "learning is not best judged by a change in minds" (the traditional school measure), but by "changing participation in changing practices." For both these theorists, the movement is toward a form of learning that essentially moves from the use of "particular tools and techniques for learning" to ways "in which participants and practices change" (Gee, 2007, p. 203). "[T]he term 'learning mechanism' diminishes in importance, in fact, it may fall out altogether, as 'mechanisms' disappear into practice" (Gee, 2007, p. 203). One of the advantages Gee sees in playing these games is the contribution of practice; people can play before they are competent and continue to play (practicing) to develop their skills.

All of these advances suggest that our increased understanding of how people learn is supporting the emerging and proposed changes in how we teach, and certainly there is growing interest and acceptance in educational or serious games. As John Geiger describes it, "The play, the interaction, the rules, the value system in the games" combine with the other needed parts of the trajectory, "the pedagogy, the instruction, and making sure the learning outcome is met" (Geiger, in Greene, 2011, p. 268). The approach is not without its opponents, or at least those who question some of the attributes of the approach. Concerns abound, largely at the level of younger children, about the overall influence of computer games, especially given a perception of violence and aggression (Foster and Mishra, 2009). The additional issue is the increasing concern about an approach to education that more heavily relies on "edutainment" (de Castell and Jenson, 2003), a concern that raises questions about learning objectives, processes, and outcomes. Early research in this area looked at what play meant in terms of definition, structures, functions, and outcomes as well as the role of actual pleasure and enjoyment (de Castell and Jenson), but much of this research was focused on younger children (Winnicott, 1971; Brougère, 1999; Corbeil, 1999). However, play as a practice is important as a motivation for learning because it moves that motivation to the intrinsic category – the students play (learn) because they want to do so. It becomes voluntary and engaging.

There are many types and kinds of computer games available for use in teaching. One approach is to purchase, license, or even develop a game specifically for the discipline. Publishing houses are starting to offer computer games as a related educational asset to certain textbooks. Another version is to repurpose off-the-shelf games, buying existing games and modifying as necessary to help students learn the agreed-upon lessons. A third option is to have the students play an existing game, while designing the debrief (takeaways) around the desired learning objectives (Greene, 2011).

> Within that scope lies limitless practical potential to use video games for the betterment of the individual, yet much depends on the creativity and motivation of the end user, to make that crucial MacGuyveresque shift of perspective. Not everything can be listed on the box, and a tool can only do so much on its own. (Waugh, 2008 in Greene, 2011, p. 261)

Greene provides a set of examples:

> Examples of this include using *The Sims Open for Business* to teach the creation of entrepreneurial culture (Greene and Brush, 2009) and *SimCity* for civil engineering and government (Van Eck, 2006). Others include *Civilization, CSI*, and *RollerCoaster Tycoon* for teaching history, forensics, and physics respectively. Once considered "slightly eccentric" or the domain of "specialist companies," Serious Games are now becoming much more mainstream, a trend attributed back to that "increasingly sophisticated and affordable technology" (Damon, 2009). (Greene, 2011, p. 270)

At this point it is also important to think about the role of simulations. "Simulations are growing in importance because they address the radically different needs of next-generation employees" (Schooley et al., 2008). However, we need to think clearly about the nature of a simulation; it is generally what you make of it. A simplest form of a simulation is a representation or model of some part of reality (Lederman, 1984). Simulations may be a version of a computer game, or may be a simple set of physical and cognitive activities (such as an in-box exercise). Some simulations are made into games, largely through the addition of roles, interaction between the roles, rules about those interactions, and some criteria for determining who wins (Ruben and Lederman, 1982).

Another way to think about simulations is as providing the context for role-play. Role-plays can be an effective way to practice play, taking on other identities and moving into a fantasy of how you would lead, plan, react, and so on. A simulation, perhaps at its best, provides content and context to provide a more meaningful experience (Enspire Learning, 2007).

While a great deal of emphasis in this chapter has been on video and computer games and simulations, largely owing to the many questions that exist in the field, other types of games should absolutely be noted and considered as well. For example, the alternative reality game (ARG) has a niche following. This type of game is a socio-fantasy type of game, while having the potential for constructivism as well. These games are generally targeted toward teaching complex content while potentially motivating changes in behavior. In their overarching study of ARGs, Enspire Learning (2007) define this genre of gaming as " interactive experiences that make use of modern technologies and modes of communication to frame game events" and provide characteristics that include the following:

- Puzzle-solving or scavenger hunt as gameplay.
- Narrative explored through a variety of widely used technologies (email, webpages, source code, phone communication and voice mail, television, published novels, physical mail, trading cards, live meetings).
- In-game characters are directly controlled by the game architects, as opposed to programmed adversaries in a video game.
- Players have the power to alter the direction of the game.
- Blurred line between reality and gamespace: maintaining the fantasy that the experience is not really a game.
  - The whole world is gamespace (no artificial boundaries).
  - No stated or apparent artificially imposed rules of the game: any available means (within normal legal, societal, and moral boundaries) of progressing the game is fair.
  - Real time – no artificially constructed time divisions.
  - Game elements function outside of the game context: if a phone number or URL is used in the game, it works in the real world.

ARGs are emerging in both the business and the educational world. In 2008 ARGs were named one of the top 20 breakthrough ideas by the *Harvard Business Review* and celebrated in a blog by Jane McGonigal, one of the main advocates of ARG use. Examples of current uses of ARGs include *Conspiracy for Good*, which engage players to volunteer for nonprofit organizations, and *Skeleton Chase* and *Cryptozoo* (by Indiana University and the American Heart Association respectively) teach about getting people more physically active (http://www.argn.com/).

In sum, all types of games are considered in the practice of play, everything from physical games (creating and flying paper airplanes as part of an innovation exercise) to board games (reframing *Settlers of Catan* to learn about regional resources and populations) to video games (using The SIMS to teach culture creation). As educators we are only limited by our own imagination.

GAMES AND PLAY IN ENTREPRENEURSHIP EDUCATION: CONCLUDING THOUGHTS

Entrepreneurship educators have for some time been recognized as innovative teachers, partly because of the younger age of the discipline, and partly because of the sense of novelty, innovation and creativity that pervades entrepreneurship content and ultimately influences the approach to delivery as well. There are many uses and examples of playing and games found within entrepreneurship education, yet there is a great deal of room for considering not only more, but how.

The opportunity to play games to learn about entrepreneurship begins with the younger generation and spans a range of types of play. The National Federation for Independent Businesses (NFIB) provided *Johnny Money the Game* through their Young Entrepreneur Foundation up until December 2010. Another example of an approach to youth entrepreneurship is seen in SunDrum, part of the Center for Integral Economics in Canada. SunDrum uses a multi-prong approach to work with young people to learn to solve social problems through social purpose businesses, using pedagogical approaches of "art, stories and culture to inspire, and games and play to teach."[4]

In college, instructors are testing all types of play and games to advance student understanding and competences around entrepreneurial mindsets and skillsets, and a number of examples are included in the exercises included in Part II of this book. As we continue to think and learn about the role of play and games, there are a set of questions that emerge for incorporating play into an entrepreneurship curriculum:

1. What are the learning objectives for the exercise, course, etc.? As with any pedagogy, the desired outcomes need to be carefully thought out and planned, leaving room for both student and instructor to grow and maybe even be surprised.
2. What is the appropriate type of game? While computer games, mobile apps, ARGS, and so on offer a wide range of opportunities, more traditional games remain a positive option.
3. What are the rules? Are there rules? What happens if someone breaks

the rules? Sometimes in entrepreneurship education it is a good thing to have the discussion of the role of rules. Whose rules are they and do they really have to be followed? Are they rules or industry standards? Is going a different direction a positive move, or disastrous?

4. What is the desired level of engagement? Is it possible to have the students so immersed that they do accept (even if tacitly) responsibility for their own learning?

5. What is the role of fun? Is it an important attribute to promote creativity?

6. What is the role of place in play? A final consideration is the potential contribution of providing "playful spaces" (de Souza e Silva and Hjorth, 2009, pp. 604–05) to further push the boundaries of the "magic circle" of play.

Raph Koster (2005) on his theory of fun said that fun is just another word for learning. He also said that "fun is a neurochemical reward to encourage us to keep trying" (p. 19). We are not sure where formal education stopped becoming fun, but it has. Classrooms facilitating the learning of entrepreneurship and encouraging students to think and act entrepreneurially require a playful, engaging, challenging, and enjoying experience. We want you, as an educator, to honestly answer some of these questions:

● Are students walking out of your class frequently to "go to the restroom"?
● Are students more interested in their laptops or smartphones than what's going on in the real world of your classroom?
● Are students asking questions you have already answered?
● Are they arriving to class unprepared?
● Do they avoid eye contact with you?
● Does your classroom go silent when you ask for volunteers?
● Do you hear laughter less than three times in every class session (at the right time)?
● Do you not look forward to going to class?

If you answered yes to any of the questions above, the diagnosis is simple. You lack play in your entrepreneurship class. The remedy? Start building a practice of play for both yourself and your students. It is not just an interesting or alternative approach – it is really necessary.

NOTES

1. http://blogs.edweek.org/edweek/marketplacek12/AmbientInsight_SeriousPlay2013_WW
    _GameBasedLearning_Market.pdf
2. www.theesa.com/gamesindailylife/education/asp
3. http://www.gamesforchange.org/
4. http://www.indiegogo.com/projects/sundrum-youth-social-entrepreneurship

REFERENCES

Annetta, L.A. 2008. Video games in education: Why they should be used and how they are being used. *Theory into Practice*, 47, 229–39.

Bateson, G. 2006. A theory of play and fantasy. In K. Salen and E. Zimmerman (eds.), *The Game Design Reader: A Rules of Play Anthology* (pp. 314–29). Cambridge, MA: MIT Press.

Beck, J.C., and Wade, M. 2004. *Got Game*. Boston, MA: Harvard Business School Press.

Brougère, Gilles. 1999. Some elements relating to children's play and adult simulation/gaming. *Simulation and Gaming*, 30(2), 134–46.

Burak, A. 2013. Games for Impact Workshop, School of Visual Arts, New York.

Castell, S. de and Jenson, J. 2003. Op-ed: Serious play. *Journal of Curriculum Studies*, 35(6), 649–65.

Cohen, K., and Rhenman, E. 1961. The role of management games in education and research. *Management Science*, 7(2), 131–66.

Corbeil, P. 1999. Learning from the children: Practical and theoretical reflections on playing and learning. *Simulation and Gaming*, 30(2), 163–80.

Csikszentmihalyi, M. 1990. *Flow: The Psychology of Optimal Experience*. New York: Harper & Row.

Damon, N. 2009. Let the games begin. *Training Magazine* (Reed Business Information UK).

Edery, D., and Mollick, E. 2009. *Changing the Game: How Video Games Are Transforming the Future of Business*. Upper Saddle River, NJ: FT Press.

Enspire Learning. 2007. *This Is Not a Game: Using Alternate Reality Games in Corporate Training*. Austin, TX: Enspire Learning.

Foster, A., and Mishra, P. 2009. Games, claims, genres and learning. In R.D. Ferdig (ed.), *Handbook of Research on Effective Electronic Gaming in Education* (pp. 33–50). Hershey, PA: Information Science Reference.

Freitas, Sara de. 2006. Learning in immersive worlds: A review of game-based learning. Prepared for the JISC e-Learning Programme, JISC, UK.

Gee, J.P. 2007. *What Video Games Have to Teach Us about Learning and Literacy*. New York: Palgrave Macmillan.

Greene, P.G. 2009. Personal interviews, June–September.

Greene, P.G. 2011. Serious games: To play or not to play. In C. Henry and A. de Bruin (eds.), *Entrepreneurship and the Creative Economy: Process, Practice and Policy*. Cheltenham, UK and Northampton, MA, USA: Edward Elgar Publishing.

Greene, P.G., and Brush, C.G. 2009. The creation of culture in emerging organizations. USE Conference, October, Helsingør, Denmark.

Groos, K. 1901. *The Play of Man*. New York: Appleton-Century.

Hall, G.S. 1920. *Youth*. New York: Appleton-Century.

Heppell, S. 2006. Foreword. In S. de Freitas, Learning in immersive worlds: A review of game-based learning. Prepared for the JISC e-Learning Programme, JISC, UK.

Hromek, R., and Roffey, S. 2009. Games as a pedagogy to promote social and emotional learning: "It's fun and we learn things." *Simulation and Gaming*, 40(5), 626–44.

Huizinga, J. 1944. *Homo Ludens: A Study of the Play-Element in Culture*. Boston, MA: Beacon Press.

Keitt, T.J., and Jackson, P. 2008. *It's Time to Take Games Seriously*. August 19. Cambridge, MA: Forrester Research.

Koster, R. 2005. *A Theory of Fun for Game Design*. Paraglyph Press. Scotsdale, AZ.

Kraus, R. 1971. *Recreation and Leisure in Modern Society*. New York: Appleton-Century-Crofts, Meredith Corporation.

Lastowka, Greg. 2009. Rules of play. *Games and Culture: A Journal of Interactive Media*, 4(4), 379–95.

Lederman, L.C. 1984. Debriefing: A critical re-examination of the post-experience analytic process with implications for its effective use. *Simulations and Games*, 15, 415–31.

Lehman, H.C., and Witty, P.A. 1927. *The Psychology of Play Activities*. New York: A.S. Barnes.

Neck, H.M. 2010. Idea generation. In B. Bygrave and A. Zacharakis (eds.), *Portable MBA in Entrepreneurship* (pp. 27–52). Hoboken, NJ: Wiley.

Palfrey, J., and Gasser, Urs. 2008. *Born Digital: Understanding the First Generation of Digital Natives*. New York: Basic Books.

Patrick, G.T.W. 1916. *The Psychology of Relaxation*. Boston, MA: Houghton Mifflin.

Piaget, J. 1962. *Play, Dreams, and Imitation in Childhood*. New York: Norton.

Piaget, J., and Inhelder, B. 1969. *The Psychology of the Child*. New York: Basic Books.

Pink, D.H. 2005. *A Whole New Mind*. New York: Penguin Group.

Reeves, B., and Read, J.L. 2009. *Total Engagement: Using Games and Virtual Worlds to Change the Way People Work and Businesses Compete*. Boston, MA: Harvard Business Press.

Rieber, Lloyd P. 1996. Seriously considering play: Designing interactive learning environments based on the blending of microworlds, simulations, and games. *Educational Technology Research and Development*, 44(2), 43–58.

Ruben, B.D., and Lederman, L.C. 1982. Instructional simulation gaming: Validity, reliability, and utility. *Simulations and Games*, 13(2), 233–44.

Salen, K. and Zimmerman, E. 2003. *Rules of Play: Game Design Fundamentals*. Cambridge, MA: MIT Press.

Sawyer, B., and Smith, P. 2008. Serious game taxonomy. Presentation. February 19.

Schell, J. 2010. *The Art of Game Design: A Book of Lenses*. Burlington, MA: Elsevier.

Schiller, F. von. 1875. *Essays, Aesthetical and Philosophical*. London: George Bell.

Schooley, C., Moore, C., Schadler, T., and Catino, S. 2008. *For Stickier Learning,*

Try a Dose of Serious Gaming. September 19. Cambridge, MA: Forrester Research.

Shubik, M. 2009. It is not just a game! *Simulation and Gaming*, 40(5), 587–601.

Souza e Silva, A. de, and Hjorth, L. 2009. Playful urban spaces: A historical approach. *Simulation and Gaming*, 40(5), 602–25.

Suits, B. 1978. *The Grasshopper*. Toronto: University of Toronto Press.

Tapscott, D. 1998. *Growing Up Digital*. New York: McGraw-Hill.

Tapscott, D. 2009. *Grown Up Digital*. New York: McGraw-Hill.

Van Eck, R. 2006. Digital game-based learning: It's not just the digital natives who are restless . . . *EDUCAUSE Review*, 41(2) (March/April).

Verzat, C., Byrne, J., and Fayolle, A. 2009. Tangling with spaghetti: Pedagogical lessons from games. *Academy of Management Learning and Education*, 8(3), 356–69.

Waugh, E. 2008. SGS keynote: Sawyer, Smith on serious gaming for life. *Gamasutra.com*, February 18.

Winnicott, D.W. 1971. *Playing and Reality*. London: Tavistock.

3. The practice of empathy

When we see the other's reality as a possibility for us, we must act to eliminate
the intolerable, to reduce the pain, to fill the need, to actualize the dream.
When I am in this sort of relationship with another, when the other's reality
becomes a real possibility for me, I care. (Noddings, 1984, p. 14)

Imagine you are flying on an airplane from Boston to San Francisco.
Your focus is on your computer because you have a pending work deadline. As a frequent flier you are very accustomed to working on an airplane, typically able to block out distractions, disconnect, and get work
done. You always choose the window because it feels more private. Sitting
next to you is a young couple with a newborn baby, about six months
old. The young mother is in the middle seat and the father on the aisle.
Holding the baby is a shared responsibility and you've seen the baby
being passed back and forth several times during the first two hours of
the flight and you think how lucky you are that the baby has been quiet
and calmly playful most of the time. But soon the inevitable happens. The
baby begins to cry. The cry turns into a wail and the pitch is deafening.
You see tears streaming down the face of the child, his tiny face and head
red from his intense crying. You watch as the parents try to pacify the
baby. Holding and rocking don't seem to work. A bottle forced into the
child's tiny mouth fails miserably. The crying continues, sometimes fading
a bit but only to escalate again. At first you just feel aggravated because
the flight is long and you have work to do. The mother makes eye contact
with you but she quickly looks away. Your aggravation begins to subside
and empathy sets in. Not only do you relate to the parents, who are going
through the experience of trying to quiet the baby, but you also have a
need to actually comfort the crying child. You want to hold and try to
quiet the crying baby!

Whether we experience this first-hand, see it in a video, or read about
it in a book, this feeling of wanting to hold the baby is empathy. It is our
innate ability to relate, know, and understand the emotions of others.
Neuroscientists Jean Decety and Philip Jackson define empathy as "the
naturally occurring subjective experience of similarity between the feelings expressed by self and others without losing sight of whose feelings
belong to whom" (Decety and Jackson, 2004, p. 71). A potentially more

actionable definition is shared by self-proclaimed "empath" and social scientist, Karla McLaren: "Empathy is a social and emotional skill that helps us feel and understand the emotions, circumstances, intentions, thoughts, and needs of others, such that we can offer sensitive, perceptive, and appropriate communications and support" (McLaren, 2013, p. 11).

We are born with the natural ability to empathize, and it develops over time through interactions with others (Decety and Jackson, 2004) and can be enhanced through training and intentional experiences (Kouprie and Visser, 2009). The exact nature and definition of empathy are complicated, complex, and debated in many disciplines including psychology, biology, neuroscience, philosophy, and theology (Preston and de Waal, 2002). Yet there is some agreement that empathy is the combination of observation, memory, knowledge, and reasoning that allows humans (and even other mammals) to share the emotional experience of others as well as understand that experience on a very deep level (Ickes, 1997; Decety and Jackson, 2004).

The relationship of empathy to entrepreneurship education is threefold. First, students who desire to become entrepreneurs need to empathize with practicing entrepreneurs to develop a better understanding of the essence of living and being an entrepreneur. Entrepreneurship may not always be a career; for many it's a lifestyle that is different from most. Second, the ability to connect with others in meaningful, more empathic ways is essential for networking, leadership, and team building. Third, entrepreneurs create value from the creation and execution of "something" – a new product, service, venture, or process. Entrepreneurs are problem identifiers and problem solvers. Core to this assumption, however, is that entrepreneurship students develop a skillset that allows them to identify unmet needs of various stakeholders. Identifying needs begins with empathy. Whether it is feeling what it is really like to be an entrepreneur, connecting with stakeholders in order to build a new organization, or creating new products and services, the practice of empathy is required.

This chapter promotes the importance of entrepreneurship students being taught through and about the development of empathetic practices as a crucial entrepreneurship skillset, and we begin with a review of the concept of empathy. We then move to address design thinking and the particular role that empathy plays in design, exploring current design thinking approaches. We conclude the chapter with different techniques that can be used to help students actually practice empathy.

THE ORIGINS OF EMPATHY

Empathy has a storied past. In fact, it has only been in the last 15 years that empathy research has found more applied connections with business (Kouprie and Visser, 2009). If you think entrepreneurship researchers have a problem defining entrepreneurship, then we suggest you delve into the debates on the definition of empathy. Empathy has been a topic of research and discourse for over 100 years. Conversants range across a multitude of disciplines including theology, philosophy, many branches of psychology, and more recently neuroscience (Preston and de Waal, 2002), and everyone seems to have a different definition.

Its origin dates back to 1873 in art history to the German word *Einfühlung*, which translates to "feeling into" (Wispé, 1987) and was later labeled *empathy* (Titchener, 1909). *Empathy*, a Greek derivation, means "to suffer with" (Carter et al., 2009). *Einfühlung*, from an art perspective, implies that the artist projects herself upon an object to the point where it becomes difficult to separate the artist from the object portrayed in the art (Titchener, 1909). Moving away from art history, psychologist Theodore Lipps (1903) used the German concept to explain projection and imitation as a pathway to understanding the mental states and cognitive processes of others. As researchers started to examine the psychology of empathy, Theodor Reik (1949) recognized empathy as a diagnostic tool for psychoanalysis – a counseling technique. Decety and Jackson (2004) discuss Reik's process that implied that empathy is a process-based skill that allows the empathizer to enter the mind of another, understand that mind, but then be able to disconnect. The process includes (Decety and Jackson, 2004, p. 74):

- **identification**: allowing oneself to become absorbed in the contemplation of that person;
- **incorporation**: making the other's experience one's own via internalizing the other;
- **reverberation**: experiencing the other's experience while attending to one's own cognitive and affective associations to that experience;
- **detachment**: moving back from the merged inner relationship to a position of separate identity, which permits a response to be made that reflects both understanding of others and separateness from them.

However, even with all the definitional inconsistency and debate, we can identify some conclusive findings across these varied disciplines. In an extensive, multidisciplinary review Preston and de Waal (2002) show empirical support that empathy exists in many species and is also developed over time. The presence of empathy has been documented in the study of rats (e.g. Church, 1959; Rice, 1964), monkeys (e.g. Masserman et al., 1964; de Waal, 1996), apes (e.g. O'Connell, 1995), human infants (e.g. Zahn-Waxler et al., 1983), human children (e.g. Krebs, 1970; Lamb and Zakhireh, 1997), and human adults (e.g. Sawyer, 1966; Stinson and Ickes, 1992). Across all of these groups the research empirically supports that empathy increases with "familiarity (subject's previous experience with the object), similarity (perceived overlap between the subject and object, e.g. species, personality, age, gender), learning (explicit or implicit teaching), past experience (with situation of distress), and salience (strength of perceptual signal, e.g. louder, closer, more realistic, etc.)" (Preston and de Waal, 2002, p. 3). In other words, becoming empathetic requires practice and experience.

The opening story about the crying baby on a plane was an attempt to illustrate empathy with a seemingly simple story. However, neuroscientists Decety and Ickes (2009, pp. 15–21) argue that there are actually eight different psychological states or phenomena that all tend to be labeled *empathy*, and you can probably recognize each of them in our opening story:

1. knowing another person's internal state, including his or her thoughts and feelings;
2. adopting the posture or matching the neural responses of an observed other;
3. coming to feel as another person feels;
4. intuiting or projecting oneself into another's situation;
5. imagining how another is thinking and feeling;
6. imagining how one would think and feel in the other's place;
7. feeling distress at witnessing another person's suffering;
8. feeling for another person who is suffering.

In their critical examination of empathy research, Decety and Ickes (2009) discuss the above eight areas of empathy not only to highlight the disagreement among researchers but also to illustrate the complexity of the concept.

We cannot do justice to the depth and breadth of the literature and research on empathy here. Volumes have been written on the subject, and the amount of thought given to the phenomenon is both breathtaking and overwhelming. As a result, it is time for us to focus on the most salient view of empathy for our purposes. Our goal is to help students develop their practice of empathy; therefore, we now focus on a toolkit that will help students to do just this. This toolkit is called *design thinking*.

DESIGN THINKING

The growing popularity of the design firm IDEO, the creation of offshoot boutique design firms, new books and articles relating design thinking to strategy and innovation, and increased enrollments at design schools have all contributed to the mainstream assimilation of design thinking into our business vocabulary. But the genesis of thinking about design as part of business education must be attributed to the late Nobel laureate Herbert Simon in his influential book *The Sciences of the Artificial* (first published in 1969, with his most recent, third edition published in 1996).

According to Simon (1996) the natural sciences are concerned with how things *are*, while design is concerned with how things *ought to be*. This logic implies that creation of new ventures, strategy, teams, products, services, and operations requires human design. Design can be intentionally chosen, and objects are subsequently manipulated to remove and leverage constraints rather than be controlled by them, as is often the case in the scientific world. In essence, with a design approach we are constructing artifacts to achieve a desired end state and answering the "What if?" and "How might we?" questions of the day. Simon advances the role of design in professional education:

> Everyone designs who devises courses of action aimed at changing existing situations into preferred ones. The intellectual activity that produces material artifacts is no different fundamentally from the one that prescribes remedies for a sick patient or the one that devises a new sales plan for a company or a social welfare policy for a state. Design, so construed, is the core of all professional training; it is the principal mark that distinguishes the profession from the sciences. Schools of engineering, as well as schools of architecture, business, education, law, and medicine, are all centrally concerned with the process of design. (Simon, 1996, p. 111)

Simon's important work provides us with the jumping-off point for positioning design thinking as important to business education, laying the foundation for the integration of the design view with the more traditional normative science and analytical views that are increasingly considered to handcuff most business students today (Dunne and Martin, 2006). Design thinking allows others to access the tools of designers in order to solve a wide array of problems that have not been solved using more traditional, linear problem-solving techniques (Brown and Katz, 2009). They argue that design thinking in contrast to management thinking requires a combination of the *cognitive, attitudinal*, and *interpersonal* aspects generally recognized as characteristic of successful designers.

From a cognitive perspective, design thinking requires inductive reasoning (what is) and deductive reasoning (what should be), and introduces the lesser-known abductive reasoning (what might be) (Dunne and Martin, 2006). Entrepreneurship students, through traditional management education, are generally strong on deductive and inductive but have little practice in developing their abductive reasoning skills – the essence of design thinking and ultimately a prime tool for opportunity creation and/ or identification. Thus, through the development of abductive reasoning, students are better equipped actually to generate new ideas that can then be tested and analyzed with the more traditional inductive and deductive approaches. From an attitudinal perspective, designers view constraints not as limitations or barriers but as leverage points for more innovative solutions (Kline and Rosenberg, 1986; Bhatta et al., 1994; Sarasvathy, 2003). This moves the approach to being open to exploring the ways in which a designer not only discovers "new problem constraints" but also uses them "to generate new problem spaces" (Bhatta et al., 1994, p. 2).

Finally, the interpersonal perspective relates to empathy – understanding and relating to the people you are designing for. This third part, the empathic part, created a special branch of design called user-centered or human-centered design. Norman (1988) is attributed with coining the term and states that user-centered design is "a philosophy based on the needs and interests of the user, with an emphasis on making products usable and understandable" (Norman, 2002, p. 213). Traditional survey research of customers is not producing high levels of innovation but rather incremental innovation because customers don't always know what they need (Leonard and Rayport, 1997; Kouprie and Visser, 2009). Let us not forget the legendary Henry Ford quote: "If I had asked my customers what they wanted they would have said a faster horse." User-centered design requires designers to have empathy to better understand the lives of users and identify latent needs in order to create what they need, even if the user does not recognize it yet. Think iPad!

As the term "design thinking" has replaced "design" (notably largely in domains outside of design), the "user" takes many forms (customers, clients, employees, other stakeholders). These expanded uses of design thinking move us from the traditional view of design as making something look nice or work better to design thinking as a way to tackle more complex problems, as a differentiator, and as a way of creating new opportunities.

Design thinking involves different spaces or phases that interact with one another in a recursive and often chaotic fashion. However, these phases are talked about in a variety of ways. The world-famous design firm IDEO identifies three phases: inspiration, ideation, and implementation (Brown, 2008), while the Institute of Design at Stanford uses a five-phase approach: empathize, define, ideate, prototype, and test. The co-founder of Jump Associates, Dev Patnaik, uses a similar approach to IDEO, yet identifies the spaces as empathize, create, and test. They are all variations on the same theme, and they all have implications for entrepreneurship – design thinking is a tool to create and exploit new opportunities.

We see design thinking as a primary tool to advance the practice of empathy and improve our approach to teaching entrepreneurial behaviors. Any kind of entrepreneurial undertaking begins with the opportunity, and "people discover unseen opportunities when they have a personal and empathic connection with the world" (Patnaik, 2009, p. 13). Through empathy we are better able to identify unmet needs. Then we create solutions to meet those needs and quickly test the solutions in the real world with real people. The learning from testing and experimentation is integrated back into the process to build even better solutions. The design thinking cycle starts (to identify the needs of users) and ends (to test solutions to meet those needs with users) with empathy.

TECHNIQUES TO PRACTICE EMPATHY

Kouprie and Visser (2009) describe three main categories of techniques for developing empathy as part of the design thinking process: research, communication, and ideation. The first category is *research*. Empathy with users is acquired through the use of qualitative research techniques that include direct observation, one-on-one interviewing, group interviewing, shadowing, and self-documentation. Regardless of method, the emphasis is on field research to study the real lives of people in the settings where they live (Burgess, 1982; Johnstone, 2007). The field research takes an ethnographic tone, but we do not claim that the research we are purporting here is pure ethnography. The notion that field research is distinctly ethnographic is supported by Hammersley (1990), as discussed in Johnstone (2007). Field research is distinctly ethnographic because of the following:

- Behavior is studied in everyday contexts; there are no unnatural or experimental circumstances imposed by the researcher.
- Observation is the primary means of data collection, although various other techniques are also used.
- Data collection is flexible and unstructured to avoid pre-fixed arrangements that impose categories of what people say and do.
- The focus is normally on a single setting or group and is small-scale.
- The data is analyzed by attributing meanings to the human actions described and explained. (Johnstone, 2007, p. 98)

Table 3.1   Nine dimensions of observation

Dimension	Description
1 Space	The physical place or places
2 Actor	The people involved
3 Activity	A set of related acts people do
4 Object	The physical things that are present
5 Act	Single actions that people do
6 Event	A set of related activities that people carry out
7 Time	The sequencing that takes place over time
8 Goal	The things people are trying to accomplish
9 Feeling	The emotions felt and expressed

Source: Spradley (1980, p. 78).

Observation, as a research tool to develop empathy, has a central role in design thinking and is particularly useful in entrepreneurship education, where our students are too accustomed to "talking" to stakeholders. Observation is difficult and requires considerable practice, because it is through observations that the most interesting insights can be developed. Thus training students in observation techniques is an important first step, and "observation guidelines" can be quite helpful here. Table 3.1 borrows from cultural anthropology and offers nine dimensions of observations that students can use when in the field.

An alternative framework from the design world is called AEIOU (http://help.ethnohub.com/guide/aeiou-framework). It is similar to Table 3.1 but a little shorter and simpler, and students are encouraged to record observations or code field data based on five dimensions – activities, environments, interactions, objects, and users.

- **Activities** are goal-directed sets of actions – paths towards things people want to accomplish. What are the modes people work in, and the specific activities and processes they go through?
- **Environments** include the entire arena where activities take place. What are the character and function of the space overall, of each individual's spaces, and of shared spaces?
- **Interactions** are between a person and someone or something else; they are the building blocks of activities. What is the nature of routine and special interactions between people, between people and objects in their environment, and across distances?
- **Objects** are building blocks of the environment, key elements sometimes put to complex or unintended uses (thus changing their

function, meaning, and context). What are the objects and devices people have in their environments and how do they relate to their activities?

- **Users** are the people whose behaviors, preferences, and needs are being observed. Who is there? What are their roles and relationships? What are their values and prejudices?

(http://help.ethnohub.com/guide/aeiou-framework)

The second category of techniques is *communication*, where empathy with users is developed through the use and creation of data (Kouprie and Visser, 2009). For example, pictures or photographs can be used as a proxy for real time observation. Other techniques include "storytelling techniques" depicted through interactive or visual mediums such as role-playing, storyboarding, or persona creation. The uses of personas are particularly effective in helping students develop empathy. Personas are graphical representations of imaginary users, yet based on data collected through primary (interviews, observation, personal experience) or secondary means (Cooper, 1999). Storyboarding is another effective technique, where the student must visually depict a user in action in his or her environment. A recurring theme with communication techniques is that they are often visual and interactive – the researcher or student through the creation of the artifacts and interacting with the artifacts begins to develop empathy. When encouraging students to create imaginary users it is also important that students allow the characters to come alive. For example, students should answer the following questions of users represented as a persona or in a storyboard: What names do they have? Use names that describe their personality or suggest their character. Where do they live, what are their families like, where do they come from, what do they eat, how do they live their day, and what are their interests? What are their guiding beliefs? What makes them happy, sad, depressed, content, bored? What would they say?

The final category of techniques is *ideation* – "techniques for evoking the designer's own experiences in the domain relevant to the user" (Kouprie and Visser, 2009, p.439). In other words the designer "acts out" part of the user's life in order to feel what it is like to be a part of that life – often referred to as *experience prototyping* (Bucheneau and Fulton Suri, 2000). A fascinating example of experience prototyping comes from the Massachusetts Institute of Technology (MIT). Researchers at the MIT Agelab created a suit called AGNES (Age Gain Now Empathy System) that allows student researchers to develop empathy for a 75-year-old person. The suit and accessories are designed to simulate many problems faced by the elderly population: joint stiffness, slow pace, forward posture, lack of balance, poor hearing, and poor sight. This type of experience prototyping is designed to help designers create better shopping environments for our growing aging population.

There are various techniques that can be used to help students develop a more empathic nature. We would also like to suggest that instructors should consider practicing some of these techniques as well. Every day in every class we are designing for students. We design class sessions, courses, and assignments, but do we really know who we are designing for? The effectiveness of our own teaching, we posit, is directly correlated with our ability to develop empathy for our own students. Give it a try!

In summary, we return to why the practice of empathy is important to entrepreneurship education – the need for our students to develop skills that allow them to feel and understand others and to be able to act on that experience in order to connect with practicing entrepreneurs, attract and retain talented team members, connect with customers on a meaningful level, and continuously offer a desirable product or service. To bring some clarity to the burgeoning area, we offer seven integration points between design thinking (the tool), empathy (the practice), and entrepreneurship (the goal):

1. Design thinking can be learned in order to support the identification or creation of new opportunities.
2. Empathy is developed by being user-centered (customer-centered) and, therefore, begins with a desire to uncover needs and an awareness that supports the development of solutions to meet those needs.
3. Design thinking, based on empathy, can be a problem-solving tool that works best when you don't know where to begin.
4. Design thinking operates at the intersection of desirability (what do people need?), feasibility (can it be done?), and viability (can we make money doing it?), but it *starts* with desirability, and that requires empathy.
5. Empathy allows us to focus on finding customers and then creating something new rather than creating something new and having to find the customer.
6. Skills in empathy further enhance students' imagination, creativity, analysis, and synthesis.
7. Empathy is part of the overall entrepreneurial mindset and requires practice.

REFERENCES

Bhatta, S., Goel, A., and Prabhakar, S. 1994. Innovation in analogical design: A model-based approach. In J.S. Gero and F. Sudweeks (eds.), *Artificial Intelligence in Design '94* (pp. 57–74). January. Dordrecht: Springer.

Brown, T. 2008. Design thinking. *Harvard Business Review*, June, 84–92.

Brown, T., and Katz, B. 2009. *Change by Design: How Design Thinking Transforms Organization and Inspires Innovation*. New York: HarperCollins E-books.

Bucheneau, M., and Fulton Suri, J. 2000. Experience prototyping. In D. Boyarski and W.A. Kellogg (eds.), *Proceedings of the Conference on Designing Interactive Systems* (pp. 237–45). New York: ACM Press.

Burgess, R.G. 1982. *Field Research: A Sourcebook and Field Manual*. London: Allen & Unwin.

Carter, C.S., Harris, J., and Porges, S.W. 2009. Neural and evolutionary perspectives on empathy. In Jean Decety and William Ickes (eds.), *The Social Neuroscience of Empathy* (pp. 278–300). Cambridge, MA: MIT Press.

Church, R.M. 1959. Emotional reactions of rats to the pain of others. *Journal of Comparative and Physiological Psychology*, 52, 132–4.

Cooper, A. 1999. *The Inmates Are Running the Asylum*. Indianapolis, IN: Macmillan.

Decety, J., and Ickes, W. 2009. *The Social Neuroscience of Empathy*. Cambridge, MA: MIT Press.

Decety, J., and Jackson, P.L. 2004. The functional architecture of human empathy. *Behavioral and Cognitive Neuroscience Reviews*, 3, 71–100.

Dunne, D., and Martin, R. 2006. Design thinking and how it will change management education: An interview and discussion. *Academy of Management Learning and Education*, 5(4), 512–23.

Hammersley, M. 1990. *Reading Ethnographic Research*. London: Longman.

Ickes, W. 1997. *Empathic Accuracy*. New York: Guilford.

Johnstone, B.A. 2007. Ethnographic methods in entrepreneurship research. In H. Neergaard and J.P. Ulhoi (eds.), *Handbook of Qualitative Research Methods in Entrepreneurship* (pp. 97–121). Cheltenham, UK and Northampton, MA, USA: Edward Elgar Publishing.

Kline, S.J., and Rosenberg, N. 1986. An overview of innovation. In R. Landau and N. Rosenberg (eds.), *The Positive Sum Strategy: Harnessing Technology for Economic Growth* (pp. 275–306). Washington, DC: National Academies Press.

Kouprie, M., and Visser, F.S. 2009. A framework for empathy in design: Stepping into and out of the user's life. *Journal of Engineering Design*, 29(4), 437–48.

Krebs, D. 1970. Altruism: An examination of the concept and a review of the literature. *Psychological Bulletin*, 73, 258–302.

Lamb, S., and Zakhireh, B. 1997. Toddlers' attention to the distress of peers in a day care setting. *Early Education and Development*, 8(2), 105–18.

Leonard, D., and Rayport, J. 1997. Spark innovation through empathic design. *Harvard Business Review*, 75(6), 102–13.

Lipps, T. 1903. Einfühlung, innere Nachahmung, und Organempfindungen. *Archiv für die gesammte Psychologie*, 1, 185–204.

Masserman, J.H., Wechkin, S., and Terris, W. 1964. Altruistic behavior in rhesus monkeys. *American Journal of Psychiatry*, 121, 584–5.

McLaren, K. 2013. *The Art of Empathy*. Boulder, CO: Sounds True.

Noddings, N. 1984. *Caring: A Feminine Approach to Ethics and Moral Education.* Berkeley: University of California Press.

Norman, D.A. 1988. *The Design of Everyday Things.* New York: Basic Books.

Norman, D.A. 2002. *The Design of Everyday Things,* 3rd edn. New York: Basic Books.

O'Connell, S.M. 1995. Empathy in chimpanzees: Evidence for theory of mind? *Primates,* 36, 397–410.

Patnaik, D. 2009. *Wired to Care: How Companies Prosper When They Create Widespread Empathy,* Upper Saddle River, NJ: FT Press.

Preston, S.D., and Waal, F.B.M. de. 2002. Empathy: Its ultimate and proximate bases. *Behavioral and Brain Sciences,* 25, 1–72.

Reik, T. 1949. *Character Analysis.* New York: Farrar, Straus and Giroux.

Rice, G.E.J. 1964. Aiding behavior vs. fear in the albino rat. *Psychological Review,* 14, 165–70.

Sarasvathy, S.D. 2003. Entrepreneurship as a science of the artificial. *Journal of Economic Psychology,* 24, 203–20.

Sawyer, J. 1966. The altruism scale: A measure of co-operative, individualistic, and competitive interpersonal orientation. *American Journal of Sociology,* 71, 407–16.

Simon, H.A. 1996. *The Sciences of the Artificial,* 3rd edn. Cambridge, MA: MIT Press.

Spradley, J.P. 1980. *Participant Observation.* New York: Harcourt Brace.

Stinson, I., and Ickes, W. 1992. Empathic accuracy in the interactions of male friends versus male strangers. *Journal of Personality and Social Psychology,* 62, 787–97.

Titchener, E. 1909. *Lectures on the Experimental Psychology of the Thought Processes.* New York: Macmillan.

Waal, F.B.M. de. 1996. *Good: The Origin of Right and Wrong in Humans and Other Animals.* Cambridge, MA: Harvard University Press.

Wispé, L. 1987. History of the concept of empathy. In N. Eisenberg and J. Strayers (eds.), *Empathy and Its Development* (pp. 17–37). Cambridge, UK: Cambridge University Press.

Zahn-Waxler, C., Friedman, S.L., and Cummings, E.M. 1983. Children's emotions and behaviors in response to infants' cries. *Child Development,* 54, 1522–8.

4. The practice of creation

Creativity can be described as letting go of certainties. (Gail Sheehy)

In order to have any form of entrepreneurship, it is pretty much agreed that creation of something new of value is a core aspect. The process of creation requires some form of entrepreneurial action which leads to creating new products or processes, creating a new market, creating new ventures, and developing new channels of distribution or even personal initiatives (Schumpeter, 1934; Gartner, 1985). The approach to creation in the entrepreneurial context is most often characterized as a prescriptive, linear process. This process is inherent in our textbooks, our syllabi, and the way we generally teach entrepreneurship, which is often driven towards the writing of a business plan. A quick survey of business plan competitions shows that every year in the U.S. there are more than 230 business plan competitions. In any month, there are between 30 and 70 business plan events for the various phases, including submissions, presentations, final presentations, and awards (http://www.bizplancompetitions. com/competitions/).

This obsession with the business plan is rooted in what Neck and Greene (2011) refer to as a *process approach*, where entrepreneurship is taught in a linear fashion, by identifying an opportunity, developing the concept, assessing and acquiring resources, implementing the business, and exit (Morris, 1998). The predominant model is to approach teaching and pedagogy in entrepreneurship from a "planning" perspective, which generally involves identifying and evaluating an opportunity, determining the resources, and creating actions to exploit the opportunity (Neck and Greene, 2011). The assumption is that inputs are known and opportunities can be discovered and evaluated by following appropriate steps to precisely identify and quantify resources. This is an ends-driven model where execution is based on a plan.

Subsumed in the process approach is a predictive logic where if we know "x" then we can then calculate "y". It is not surprising that predictive logic (causation) underpins our approach to business planning, given the uncertainty in the entrepreneurial process (Stevenson and Jarillo, 1990; Shane and Venkataraman, 2000; McMullen and Shepherd, 2006). Building the analytical prowess of our students then becomes a solution to mitigating the uncertainty perceived in the entrepreneurial process (Drucker, 1998; Sarasvathy, 2001). This approach is rooted in the assumption that individuals are goal driven when pursuing opportunities and that managing and controlling resources will lead to a predetermined outcome (DeTienne and Chandler, 2010). The notion is that opportunities exist in the environment and are discovered, like a mountain waiting to be climbed, and entrepreneurs can discover an existing opportunity and exploit it to reap economic profit. If an entrepreneur is first to discover and exploit it, there is also hope for fame and success (Alvarez and Barney, 2007, p. 11).

In contrast to the process-based, predictive approach, there has been increased interest in a creative or effectual approach which, instead of being ends driven, is means driven. Sarasvathy (2001, p. 245) articulates this process as selecting between possible effects that can be created with a set of means. Effectual logic is rooted in what entrepreneurs have, who they know, and what they can afford to lose. The starting point is self-understanding: who you are, what you know, and your capabilities. Instead of having a bias towards a particular end or outcome, entrepreneurs create their environment through action, using the resources or means they have available, and bring along other stakeholders who can help (Dew et al., 2009). For instance, related work on bricolage (Baker and Nelson, 2005) and improvisation (Hmieleski and Corbett, 2006) suggests that entrepreneurship can be characterized by trial and error, serendipity, or other creative approaches. Creative actions, experimentation to clarify opportunities, and the discovery of new stakeholders are each embedded in a social context (Burt, 1992; Granovetter, 1992; Jack and Anderson, 2002). A creative approach to entrepreneurship is socially interactive, leveraging resources and relationships at hand and "within reach" – both in the founding process and as a course for venture development – versus fitting and acquiring resources from a pre-created plan (e.g. human resources, financial resources, physical resources). A creative approach implicitly recognizes that all entrepreneurial actors are embedded in, working in, and shaping idiosyncratic social structures. Hence, in this approach, entrepreneurial opportunities are not like mountains already there waiting to be climbed, but instead are created by the actions of entrepreneurs, and so the metaphor becomes "mountain building" (Alvarez and Barney, 2007, p. 11). Table 4.1 summarizes the creative and predictive approaches.

Following the notion of the creative approach, the creativity competencies of students play a significant role in the practice of creation. Creativity is generally thought of as an ability to produce something new through imaginative skill.[1] This can be a new solution to a problem, new

Table 4.1   Assumptions and examples of predictive and creative approaches

Predictive approach	Assumptions	Examples	vs.	Creative approach	Assumptions	Examples
Identify and evaluate the opportunity	Known inputs; opportunities can be discovered and evaluated	Mintzberg (1978); Ansoff (1988)		Self-understanding	Skills and capabilities of individuals; opportunities can be made or created	Fiet and Patel (2006)
Quantify the resources	Steps identified; precision approach	Robinson (1979); Timmons and Spinelli (2009)		Observation and reflection	Means driven	Neck and Greene (2011)
Create a plan	Predictive	Rich and Gumpert (1985); Morris (1998)		Bring along stakeholders	Interactive and social process	Sarasvathy (2001)
Execute	End driven	Timmons and Spinelli (2009)		Act and experiment	Creative and iterative	Sarasvathy (2001)
Measure results	Known outcomes			Build on results	Unknown outcomes	

Source: From Noyes and Brush (2012).

method or device, or new artistic form, artifact, or contribution. We think of creativity as arising out of a richness of ideas and some sort of original thought, where something novel (original and unexpected) is produced.[2] It is something we aspire to and believe is valuable for how we do business and live our lives.

However, most of us do not believe we are living up to our true creative potential. In fact, a global study showed only 25 percent of people feel they are living up to their potential to be creative.[3] Wide variations were reflected across countries – 52 percent of those in the U.S. described themselves as creative, while only 36 percent in France did so. Think about art created by Pablo Picasso or Georgia O'Keeffe, music created by Chopin or the Beatles, poetry by Elizabeth Barrett Browning, or movies created by Steven Spielberg. These manifestations of creativity seem unattainable to most of us. Further, in our daily lives, we devote most of our time to working, and often do not frame this work as "creative." This presents even bigger challenges when we try to unleash the creative abilities of our students.

So what holds students back? What are the barriers to helping students achieve their creative potential? At least six roadblocks are identified (Adams, 1986; Neck, 2010):

- fear;
- no appetite for chaos;
- a preference for judging over generating ideas;
- a dislike for incubating ideas;
- a perceived lack of challenge;
- an inability to distinguish reality from fantasy.

Fear is by far the most significant roadblock, because it stops us from creating new ideas (risk of making a mistake) and sharing our ideas with others (fear of social failure). As Neck (2010) notes, in the classroom setting especially, the fear factor influences "ideas in" (letting go, image, insecurity, self-doubt) and "ideas out" (failure, negative feedback, ridicule, imperfection, unoriginality). What happens when fear takes over? Students cannot move forward and explore their creative ideas. In fact, the fear of failure is a universal attitude that holds people back from starting a new business, even when the expected returns for starting are better than the next alternative. According to the Global Entrepreneurship Monitor, in those countries where the population has a lower fear of failure there is a higher rate of start-up (Xavier et al., 2013). Fear of failure is generally associated with level of country development, in that countries with lower rates of economic development have lower fear of failure rates (e.g. countries in Sub-Saharan Africa).

The importance of creativity cannot be overstated. In entrepreneurship, creativity assumes a central role, largely because, at its core, entrepreneurship is about introducing a "new" or "novel" product or service, means of distribution, market, ways of organizing, or means of production and supply (Schumpeter, 1934). Creativity is linked to the identification or creation of business opportunities, which generally starts with some sort of ideation, imagination, or creative process and results in doing things in a new and/or novel way (Timmons, 1989; Gundry and Kickul, 1996; Sarasvathy, 2001; DeTienne and Chandler, 2004). Innovative new products and processes lead to new technologies, re-combinations of value chains, and other elements leading to capital redistribution.

Fast Company Magazine created a list of the 100 most creative people, and guess what? They are entrepreneurs.[4] Tyler Perry is a moviemaker whose films have grossed $400 million worldwide, and he's been ranked the sixth highest-paid man in Hollywood. He has created TV shows, produced 20 films, and won an Oscar for a film called *Precious*. Then there is Jil Sander, a fashion designer and creative director for a Japanese retailer named Uniqlo. She created a new high-fashion collection, +J, which is sold worldwide, and is the first non-Japanese designer to win the prestigious Designer of the Year Award. There is also Dietrich Mateschitz, CEO and Founder of Red Bull, the energy drink. His company is the global market leader, serving 160 countries and grossing $4.7 billion a year. Not only are these examples of entrepreneurs who created a new opportunity and scaled their ideas, but their businesses help in the development of economies and societal growth.

But, despite the pervasiveness of creativity in business, art, and personal development, there remain popular myths about creativity. Here are a few:

- **Younger people are more creative than older people**: This belief is attractive, but there is no evidence that children produce more creative works than adults. Can you name more than one child composer, famous artist, or entrepreneur? Probably not. The reality is that creative instincts are often socialized out of us at an early age. Sir Ken Robinson[5] argues that our education system drums the creative thought out of us because of standards and norms. Research shows that there is little change in cognitive instincts over time, but approaches to teaching creativity may need to change across age groups (Alpaugh et al., 1976).
- **You can't teach creativity; you are born that way**: There is a perception that people are born with a special talent, like having blue eyes. The reality is creativity is learnable. A study by Teresa Amabile of

12 000 people from various occupations, levels of education, and ages finds that creativity depends on a number of things: your experience, knowledge, technical skills, and cognitive ability (Amabile and Kramer, 2011). Extensive attempts are made to identify particular traits associated with creativity, for instance independence, rebelliousness, playfulness, imagination, extroversion, and many others. But research shows that these traits can be conflicting and do not always exist in the same person; hence the linkage between creativity and particular traits is largely unsupported (Csikszentmihalyi, 1996).

- **To be creative, work must be wholly original and independently created**: There is a belief that creative people work by themselves, and create alone. This myth is often associated with artists or writers. But the reality is that creativity is frequently synthesized and collaborative, and can be an output of synthesis, collaboration, and incremental improvement (*Managing Creativity*, 2003). For example, some of the breakthrough technology developments, like the transistor created by scientists at Bell Labs, emerged through collaborative and synthesized efforts. The individual differences can produce creative friction and diversity of thought so that more and better ideas are produced (Amabile, 1985).
- **You have to wait for a creative inspiration to strike**: We have the cartoon image of the "light bulb going off" and a creative thought pouring forth. The reality is that inspiration (or creativity) more often comes from working on particular problems or ideas. Even Thomas Edison noted that inspiration was a very small portion of creativity. Most of his inventions came down to hard work. He stated that his inventions were not as a result of accident; rather they evolved after multiple trials – 1 percent inspiration, 99 percent perspiration.

The bottom line is that creativity can be learned. It is a set of skills and capabilities that individuals of any age can learn and practice. And creativity is not limited to the arts, but can be applied in a variety of settings.

A BRIEF HISTORY OF CREATIVITY RESEARCH

As a concept, *creativity* arises from the ancient Greek concept of art, *techne*, which is the root of "technique" and "technology," although there were not terms that corresponded to "create" or "creator" for artists or poets prevalent during that time. Over the centuries, the idea of creating something from nothing (in Latin, *creatio ex nihilo*) emerged and provided a basis for the Renaissance and rich contributions in painting, architecture, music, sculpture, philosophy, and poetry.[6]

Some suggest that the beginning of the scientific study of creativity emerged from J.P. Guilford's address to the American Psychological Association in 1950, where he challenged psychologists to pay attention to what he referred to as an important attribute, what he called *creativity* (Sternberg and Lubart, 1999). Between 1950 and 1994, research in psychology focusing on creativity grew slightly but remained comparatively under-researched, despite the importance to society. Early work focused on what is referred to as "mystical" approaches, where creativity was based on some sort of divine intervention directed by a "muse" or other source. For example, Plato argued that the poet created only what the muse dictated and, therefore, the poet was only the vessel through which the creativity flowed (Sternberg and Lubart, 1999).

Pragmatic approaches to studying creativity are rooted in the work of Edward de Bono (1985), who was concerned with practice over theory. Well known in business arenas is the tool known as the "thinking hats," where people brainstorm to solve problems using "metaphorical" colored hats representing different things (e.g. red hat for intuition, or white hat for data-based thinking). Following this approach, James Adams (1986) argued that beliefs can constrain creative functioning and that these hold us back in brainstorming and solving problems.

More recently, creativity is not only recognized as valuable for the artifacts and contributions resulting from this work, but studied empirically and theoretically. Psychodynamic studies examine the relationship between conscious reality and unconscious drives (Freud, [1910] 1964), while cognitive studies consider ways ordinary processes can yield novel new products (e.g. how many ways can a pen be used?) (Weisberg, 1993). Socio-personality studies examine traits and motivations (Amabile, 1983). In fact, recent categorization of theories shows ten different creativity theories, categorizing these based on whether they highlight the product, person, place, process, or persuasion (Kozbelt et al., 2010). When we think about helping students develop a practice of creation, not all theories apply. We argue that three main theories most relate to our view of a practice of creation. These are: cognitive theory; problem-solving and expertise-based theory; and problem-finding theory, also known as design thinking (see Table 4.2).

Table 4.2 Roots of creativity pedagogies

	Cognitive	Problem solving, expertise based	Problem finding, design thinking
Core assumptions	Ideational thought processes are foundational to creative persons and accomplishments.	Creative solutions to ill-defined problems result from a rational process which relies on general cognitive processes and domain expertise.	Creative people proactively engage in a subjective and exploratory process of identifying problems to be solved.
Key components	Remote association, divergent, convergent thinking, conceptual combination expansion, metaphorical thinking, imagery, metacognitive processes.	Ill-defined problems can be solved through a cognitive, computational approach. Expertise relative to the program can enhance problem representation and heuristics.	Subjective creativity processes, exploratory behaviors, online discovery.
Student actions	Focus on the student activities and the process, starting with everyday experiences, moving to big creative ideas.	Focus generally on person, process, and a product, whereby the student engages in creative cognition rooted in his or her self-understanding of competencies.	Focus on person, process, and potential, whereby the student engages in behaviors such as observing, manipulating objects, and exploring possibilities.
Instructor role	Ensures that students can suggest ideas openly without criticism or judgment.	Assist students in self-understanding of competencies, knowledge, and expertise. Provide tools for exploring appropriate channels of exploration relevant to individual students.	Provide students with background, sensitivity, and awareness of observation and interpretation. Facilitate synthesis of observations.
Outcomes	Generation of new concepts or ideas, improvements to existing products or services, business models, or initiatives.	Identification or discovery of opportunity spaces that can be possibilities for new ventures or initiatives.	Identification of user problems that can be the basis for new ventures or new initiatives.
References	Guilford (1968); Finke et al. (1992).	Simon (1981); Amabile (1983); Weisberg (1993); Ericsson (1999).	Runco (1994); Csikszentmihalyi (1996).

Source: Adapted from Kozbelt et al. (2010).

Cognitive Theory of Creativity

Cognitive theories of creativity are rooted in the assumption that people
can learn ideation thought processes in order to create new ideas. These
theories emphasize the creative process and the person, considering individual differences and the knowledge that each individual has acquired.
There is some variety across cognitive theories in terms of focus: Some
emphasize attention or memory, others emphasize divergent thinking
tasks, and still others center on problem-solving (Kozbelt et al., 2010).
The anchor is in divergent thinking, where ideas and associations move
in varied directions, as opposed to convergent thinking, which leads to
one correct or conventional answer, and is often the focus of our business school education (Guilford, 1989). Research shows that original
insights are more likely to emerge when disparate features are brought
together and connections between these are made (Estes and Ward in
Kozbelt et al., 2010). More practically, activities associated with cognitive creativity involve associations of ideas like brainstorming, word
associations, metaphorical thinking, combinations, minimizing, or maximizing. For instance, if you think of the word "laundry," what comes
to mind? The first associations might be "dirty," "quarters," "time,"
"soap," "noisy," "constant," and so on. Word associations can be used
as stimuli to identify new solutions and rethink approaches to how we
accomplish things.

Brainstorming is another popular technique used frequently in entrepreneurship to develop new venture ideas. Importantly, brainstorming
requires that there is no judgment, and is rooted in the notion that more
ideas produce better ideas. Rapid fire of ideas in a group setting creates
enthusiasm, and can help to stimulate new problem solutions or venture
ideas. A variation on this is to take an object and work on ways to maximize, minimize, or combine features (Adams, 1986). For instance, if you
take a "pen," what multiple uses could you come up with? Using it as a
hair ornament, changing the time on your radio, using it as a poker, and
so on? Alternatively, what are the ways you could combine features into a
pen? Make it a flashlight? Add a radio? Add a microchip?

A third variation on cognitive theory is the use of metacognitive processes. The idea is that creativity emerges from thinking backwards or
shifting perspective – by changing assumptions, students can come up with
new insights and ideas. In these types of exercises, students are engaged
collaboratively, and actually experience the exercise, while the faculty
member facilitates and encourages participation.

Problem-Solving and Expertise-Based Theory of Creativity

The problem-solving and expertise-based theory of creativity is rooted in the idea that creative solutions result from expert knowledge. It is assumed that domain experience provides the foundation for creative output (Amabile, 1983). Processes are structured and heuristics are used for searching through problem spaces where expertise can provide insights. In the entrepreneurial domain, James Fiet (2002) argues that a strong self-understanding and identification of capabilities based on past accomplishments can lead to information channels where your expertise will allow you to identify better, wealth-generating venture opportunities. In other words, expertise and domain knowledge bring some order to ill-defined problem spaces and allow students to have unique insights by identifying opportunities that fit their backgrounds. There is some evidence that, across domains, expertise influences creativity (Ericsson and Charness in Kozbelt et al., 2010).

In problem-solving and expertise-based approaches, creativity is viewed as more rational and empirical. Students are guided more narrowly to areas complementing their capabilities, while the instructor's role is to facilitate self-understanding and assist in structuring the creative investigation. Creativity in this form is more of a longer-term practice, because it involves deliberate search (Kozbelt et al., 2010).

Problem-Finding Theory and Design Thinking

Problem-finding theories assume that traditional problem-solving is not adequate to understand the existence of a problem in the first place. Instead, creators need to engage in a subjective and exploratory process to understand the problem (Csikszentmihalyi, 1996). There is no specified set of alternatives; rather, the problem must be discovered through observation in a particular setting. Problem-finding is more subjective than problem-solving, and it takes into account the open-endedness of the task. It might involve touching, listening, handling, experimenting, or asking questions (Csikszentmihalyi and Getzels, 1989).

In Chapter 3, we addressed the central role of empathy in design thinking. Building from this empathic foundation, there is a logical connection between empathy and problem-finding. A deep understanding of a space and the users in those spaces leads to insights and the identification of problems. As such problem finding is also an important aspect – even an outcome – of design thinking, which is a methodology for creative resolution of problems (Cross, 1982). Problem-finding using design thinking begins with observing users carrying out activities and empathetically considering the challenges or problems they may be experiencing. For instance, think about going to the airport and watching the check-in process. What activities do the ticket agents carry out? What are people in line doing? How long does it take? Is it noisy or quiet? All the things that could be going on might help us to understand problems that could benefit from creative solutions.

Students need to learn how to observe, listen, and carefully record their observations. The instructor facilitates by encouraging students to utilize all senses, without jumping to ideas too quickly. The solution is discovered with a range of information, rather than a narrow empirical search. (Chapter 3 discusses design thinking in greater depth.)

TEACHING CREATION AS A PRACTICE – EXAMPLES

Creating New Opportunities

We would like to briefly highlight some of our experiences in helping students develop a practice of creation. One example is a course at Babson, "Social Entrepreneurship by Design." This course integrates user-oriented collaborative design and entrepreneurship for the purpose of developing new products or services that contribute to the solution of a social problem. User-oriented collaborative design is a five-phase, iterative process designed to help students create products or services based on user needs; understanding the user is central to the design process. Students go out into the field and observe user groups, spending a great deal of time on observing and interpreting qualitative data. The user is only one of many stakeholders considered in the process. Students engage in an iterative process whereby they observe user groups, identify extreme users, and then converge on a product or service design that will yield both economic and social value for multiple stakeholder groups. Because the focus of the course is "social," students need to consider ways of addressing these social problems through collaboration, partnerships, alliances, and even special funding. The course is taught in a studio setting whereby students do "design reviews" every two weeks to present their progress. The chief aim of the course is to understand and apply a design process with far-reaching implications for social activists and social entrepreneurs. While the problems of the world are large, the course forces students to focus on challenges that are narrowly defined and potentially solvable. Because the course is experiential, students are expected to engage with multiple stakeholders to motivate their entrepreneurial approaches and solutions.

Creating Career Pathways

We most often think about our career pathway as somewhat linear, whereby each job or endeavor logically leads to the next one and we continually develop new skills and capabilities, acquire bigger titles, and earn more money. But, more often than not, careers cannot be "planned" and are often more "created." Drawing again on the idea of predictive and creative logic presented earlier in this chapter, an exercise illustrating both approaches to careers involves students doing pre-work by assessing and recording the accomplishments they have had in each job in a time line. Then, using the Nash and Stevenson (2004) dimensions of success, happiness, achievement, success, and legacy, they evaluate the extent to which their previous jobs have met these success objectives. Then in class they are asked to identify a career objective, and to brainstorm around this career objective doing a word association exercise, following the Mind Dumping for Ideation exercise format (see Chapter 9). From this they develop themes which they then consider relative to the success criteria. In this exercise, students almost always develop new insights about what things are important to them and start to think about creating their career in a different way.

ROLE OF INSTRUCTOR

When teaching creation as a practice, instructors need to consider three things: *pedagogy*, *environment* and *instructor behavior* (Lin, 2011). The *pedagogy* has to do with consideration of a variety of approaches that stimulate multiple learning styles (e.g. those that learn from reading, hearing, writing, or seeing) and achieve higher-level learning goals. For example, Bloom's typology (Bloom and Krathwohl, 1956) suggests that lower-level learning goals would be to have someone describe or repeat, and these would be achieved by lecturing or assigning a reading. Higher-level goals would be to have students apply and synthesize, which are achieved by interacting, experiencing, and discovering. The instructor's role is to facilitate engagement in creative processes and skills.

The *environment* for teaching creativity includes the climate or atmosphere in the classroom, as well as the physical classroom environment. The climate has to do with the social norms set by the instructor. Are ideas accepted and encouraged or is the atmosphere constrained and ideas ignored (de Souza Fleith, 2000)? When creative ideas and thinking are encouraged, students are more likely to gain self-confidence and trust their own judgment. The physical environment also makes a difference. While most schools are constrained by existing structures and space, aspects such as moveable furniture, views of the natural environment, and natural materials and lighting make a difference in enhancing creative thinking (McCoy and Evans, 2002).

Instructor behavior has to do with the actual role that the instructor assumes in the process. Instead of exerting control and commanding a teacher-centric posture, it is more effective to stand back, encourage learner agency, and create time and space for students to engage (Lin, 2011). Students are encouraged to explore out of curiosity, rather than told to learn by authority (Torrance, 1963). This also means that sometimes the instructor will need to go off script and engage in playfulness, collaboration, and supportive behaviors (Kangas, 2010; Oral in Lin, 2011).

NOTES

1. "Creativity: the ability to make new things or think of new ideas. The quality of being creative. The ability to create" (*Merriam-Webster's Dictionary*).
2. Sternberg and Lubart (1999).
3. Adobe Corporation, State of create study: A global benchmark study on attitudes and beliefs about creativity at work, school and home (2012). This study surveyed 5000 adults, 1000 per country in the U.S., the U.K., Germany, France, and Japan.
4. http://www.fastcompany.com/1651696/most-creative-entrepreneurs-business
5. http://www.ted.com/talks/ken_robinson_says_schools_kill_creativity.html
6. History – concept of creativity, Wikipedia.org.

REFERENCES

Adams, J. 1986. *Conceptual Blockbusting: A Guide to Better Ideas*, 3rd edn. Reading, MA: Perseus Books.

Alpaugh, P., Renner, J., and Birren, J. 1976. Age and creativity: Implications for education and teachers. *Educational Gerontology*, 1(1), 17–40.

Alvarez, S., and Barney, S. 2007. Discovery and creation: Alternative theories of entrepreneurial action. *Strategic Entrepreneurship Journal*, 1(1–2), 11–26.

Amabile, T. 1983. *The Social Psychology of Creativity*. New York: Springer-Verlag.

Amabile, T.M. 1985. Motivation and creativity: Effects of motivational orientation on creative writers. *Journal of Personality and Social Psychology*, 48(2), 393–9.

Amabile, T., and Kramer, S. 2011. *The Progress Principle: Using Small Wins to Ignite Joy, Engagement and Creativity at Work*. Boston, MA: Harvard Business School Press.

Ansoff, I. 1988. *The New Corporate Strategy*. New York: Wiley.

Baker, T., and Nelson, R. 2005. Creating something from nothing: Resource construction through entrepreneurial bricolage. *Administrative Sciences Quarterly*, 50(3), 329–66.

Bloom, B., and Krathwohl, D.R. 1956. *Taxonomy of Educational Objectives: The Classification of Educational Goals by a Committee of College and University Examiners*, Handbook 1: *Cognitive Domain*. New York: Longman.

Bono, E. de. 1985. *Six Thinking Hats*. New York: Little, Brown & Company.

Burt, R.S. 1992. *Structural Holes*. Cambridge, MA: Harvard University Press.

Cross, N. 1982. Designerly ways of knowing. *Design Studies*, 3(4), 221–7.

Csikszentmihalyi, M. 1996. *Creativity Flow and the Psychology of Discovery and Invention*. New York: HarperCollins.

Csikszentmihalyi, M., and Getzels, J.W. 1989. Creativity and problem finding. In F.H. Farley and R.W. Neperud (eds.), *The Foundations of Aesthetics* (pp. 91–116). New York: Praeger.

DeTienne, D., and Chandler, G. 2004. Opportunity identification and its role in the entrepreneurial classroom: A pedagogical approach and empirical test. *Academy of Management Learning and Education*, 3(3), 242–57.

DeTienne, D., and Chandler, G. 2010. The impact of motivation and causation and effectuation approaches on exit strategies. *Frontiers of Entrepreneurship Research*, 30(1), 1–113.

Dew, N., Read, S., Sarasvathy, S.D., and Wiltbank, R. 2009. Effectual versus predictive logics in entrepreneurial decision-making: Differences between experts and novices. *Journal of Business Venturing*, 24(4), 287–309.

Drucker, P. 1998. The discipline of innovation. *Harvard Business Review*, November–December. *HBR* reprint 98604.

Ericsson, K.A. 1999. Creative expertise as superior reproducible performance: Innovative and flexible aspects of expert performance. *Psychological Inquiry*, 10, 329–33.

Fiet, J.O. 2002. *The Systematic Search for Entrepreneurial Discoveries*. Westport, CT: Quorum.

Fiet, J., and Patel, P.C. 2006. Entrepreneurial discovery as constrained systematic search. *Small Business Economics*, 30, 215–29.

Finke, R., Ward, T., and Smith, S. 1992. *Creative Cognition: Theory, Research and Applications*. Cambridge, MA: MIT Press.

Freud, S. [1910] 1964. *Leonardo da Vinci and a Memory of His Childhood*. New York: Norton.

Gartner, W.B. 1985. A conceptual framework for describing the phenomenon of new venture creation. *Academy of Management Review*, 10(4), 696–706.

Granovetter, M. 1992. Economic institutions as social constructions: A framework for analysis. *Acta Sociologica*, 35, 3–11.

Guilford, J.P. 1989. *Creativity, Intelligence and Their Educational Implications*. San Diego, CA: Knapp Publishing.

Gundry, L.K., and Kickul, J.R. 1996. Flights of imagination: Fostering creativity through experiential learning. *Simulation and Gaming*, 33, 94–108.

Hmieleski, K.M., and Corbett, A.C. 2006. Proclivity for improvisation as a predictor of entrepreneurial intentions. *Journal of Small Business Management*, 44(1), 45–63.

Jack, S.L., and Anderson, A.R. 2002. The effects of embeddedness on the entrepreneurial process. *Journal of Business Venturing*, 17, 467–87.

Kangas, M. 2010. Creative and playful learning: Learning through game co-creation and games in a playful learning environment. *Thinking Skills and Creativity*, 5(1), 1–15.

Kozbelt, A., Beghetto, R., and Runco, M. 2010. Theories of creativity. In

68   *Teaching entrepreneurship*

J. Kaufman and R. Sternberg (eds.), *Cambridge Handbook of Creativity*. New York: Cambridge University Press.

Lin, Y.S. 2011. Fostering creativity through education: A conceptual framework for creative pedagogy. *Creative Education*, 2(3), 149–55.

Managing Creativity and Innovation. 2003. Boston, MA: Harvard Business School Publishing.

McCoy, J.M., and Evans, G.W. 2002. The potential role of the physical environment in fostering creativity. *Creative Research Journal*, 14(3–4), 409–26.

McMullen, J.F., and Shepherd, D.A. 2006. Entrepreneurial action and the role of uncertainty in the theory of the entrepreneur. *Academy of Management Review*, 31(1), 132–52.

Mintzberg, H. 1978. Patterns of strategy formation. *Management Science*, 24(9), 934–48.

Morris, M.H. 1998. *Entrepreneurial Intensity: Sustainable Advantages for Individuals, Organizations and Societies*. Westport, CT: Quorum.

Nash, L., and Stevenson, H. 2004. Success that lasts. *Harvard Business Review*, February.

Neck, H.M. 2010. Idea generation. In B. Bygrave and A. Zacharakis (eds.), *Portable MBA in Entrepreneurship* (pp. 27–52). Hoboken, NJ: Wiley.

Neck, H., and Greene, P.G. 2011. Entrepreneurship education: Known worlds and new frontiers. *Journal of Small Business Management*, 49(1), 55–70.

Noyes, E., and Brush, C. 2012. Teaching entrepreneurial action: Application of creative logic. In A.C. Corbett and J.A. Katz (eds.), *Advances in Entrepreneurship, Firm Emergence and Growth*, Vol. 14: *Entrepreneurial Action* (pp. 253–80). Bingley, UK: Emerald Group Publishing.

Rich, S.R., and Gumpert, D.E. 1985. How to write a winning business plan. *Harvard Business Review*, 3, 3–8.

Robinson, R. 1979. Forecasting and small business: A study of the strategic planning process. *Journal of Small Business Management*, 17, 19–27.

Runco, M.A. 1994. *Problem Finding, Problem Solving and Creativity*. Norwood, NJ: Ablex Publishing.

Sarasvathy, S. 2001. Causation and effectuation: Toward a theoretical shift from economic inevitability to entrepreneurial contingency. *Academy of Management Review*, 26(2), 243–63.

Schumpeter, J. 1934. *The Theory of Economic Development*. New York: Oxford University Press.

Shane, S., and Venkataraman, S. 2000. The promise of entrepreneurship as a field of research. *Academy of Management Review*, 25, 217–26.

Simon, H. 1981. *The Sciences of the Artificial*, 2nd edn. Cambridge, MA: MIT Press.

Souza Fleith, D. de. 2000. Teacher and student perceptions of creativity in the classroom environment. *Roeper Review*, 22(3), 148–53.

Sternberg, R.J., and Lubart, T. 1999. Concept of creativity: Prospects and paradigms. In R.J. Sternberg (ed.), *Handbook of Creativity*. New York: Cambridge University Press.

Stevenson, H., and Jarillo, J. 1990. A paradigm of entrepreneurship: Entrepreneurial management. *Strategic Management Journal*, 11, 17–27.

Timmons, J. 1989. *The Entrepreneurial Mind*. Andover, MA: Brick House Publishing.

Timmons, J.A., and Spinelli, S. 2009. *New Venture Creation: Entrepreneurship for the 21st Century*, 6th edn. New York: McGraw-Hill Irwin.

Torrance, E.P. 1963. *Education and Creative Potential.* Minneapolis: University of Minnesota Press.

Weisberg, R. 1993. *Creativity: Beyond the Myth of Genius.* New York: Freeman.

Xavier, S.R., Kelley, D., Kew, J., Herrington, M., and Vorderwülbecke, A. 2013. *The Global Entrepreneurship Monitor: 2012 Global Report.* Wellesley, MA: Babson College.

5. The practice of experimentation

All life is an experiment. The more experiments you make the better. (Ralph Waldo Emerson)

If you double the number of experiments you do per year you're going to double your inventiveness. (Jeff Bezos)

Entrepreneurship is about experimenting – trying something, seeing what the results are, learning from the results, and then trying it again. Jeff Bezos, founder of Amazon.com, identifies experimentation as one of the core principles of the company. Other entrepreneurs will tell you that experimentation is imperative for their ventures, because this is how new innovations, initiatives, ideas, and opportunities are discovered or created. A new technology company would have a concept prototype, while a new organic food venture would experiment with recipes and flavors. Fashion ventures experiment with designs, fabrics, distributions, and brands, while drug companies experiment with trials and tests. Automotive companies have concept cars; food companies experiment with new foods and flavors. Tech companies often have "labs" like Google Labs; and many high-performing companies, like Google, allow their employees to experiment. Even sports teams experiment with new plays and/or players. Experimentation is everywhere and is always happening.

Experimentation is, by definition, a scientific process. *Merriam-Webster's Dictionary* defines experiment as "a test or trial," "a tentative procedure or policy," and "an operation or procedure carried out under controlled conditions in order to discover an unknown effect or law, to test or establish a hypothesis, or to illustrate a known law."[1] While true experimental testing is commonly associated with the hard sciences whereby testing is carried out in controlled laboratories (e.g. biology, medicine, chemistry, and physics), social scientists often use experiments outside of the lab setting to test propositions for organization or business decisions (e.g. sociology, marketing, accounting, finance, and psychology). The process of experimentation usually involves forming a hypothesis, designing a study and collecting data, analyzing the data and reaching conclusions, and then sharing the results. Technically, experiments should be replicable and have the ability to be validated under other conditions before they can be theoretically interpreted with confidence (Campbell and Stanley, 1963). Of course, colleges and universities have been teaching hard science for years and have labs, facilities, and mechanisms to teach students how to develop these experiments. In the social sciences and business arena, the theory and practices behind rigorous experimental and quasi-experimental design in social science research are well articulated, but when it comes to the context of entrepreneurship, and entrepreneurship education particularly, the rigorous scientific objectives are perceived as less practical.

Why is this the case? Most often entrepreneurship is taught in a classroom environment or physical facility that is office based. Even though many schools, NGOs, colleges, and universities have designated accelerator or incubator space, the opportunity to experiment and learn from experiments that allow students to practice entrepreneurship is usually constrained by space, technology, resources, and time. At the same time, the concept of experimentation has great value when we think about how students can gain knowledge of entrepreneurship experientially. Furthermore, the role of the instructor changes – it becomes one of learning process facilitator where the instructor is a guide. Following the socially situated view of constructivist pedagogy, the instructor pays attention to each individual student's background and beliefs, facilitates dialogue in a way that is purposeful, provides opportunities for students to test, challenge, and change beliefs, and helps students to develop a meta-awareness of their own understanding and learning processes (Richardson, 2003). In other words, the instructor migrates from teaching content to teaching students how to learn. Of course, it takes a lot of work, but the outcomes for the student are priceless.

The practice of experimentation in entrepreneurship is to "acquire knowledge germane to entrepreneurship" by actively experimenting in hands-on projects, and learning by doing (Curran and Stanworth, 1989; Block and Stumpf, 1992; Garavan and O'Cinneide, 1994; Alberti et al., 2004). In other words, experimentation in entrepreneurship is about acquiring knowledge of the concepts and techniques that can be applied in entrepreneurial situations, which we would define as identifying or creating an opportunity, acquiring the resources, and providing the leadership to create something of social or economic value. However, unlike the traditional approach of scientific experimentation, in entrepreneurship this process almost always occurs under conditions of uncertainty (relational, resource, or other), or even complete unpredictability whereby subjectivity is involved (Aldrich, 1999; Sarasvathy, 2001; Alvarez and Barney, 2005; McMullen and Shepherd, 2006; Neck and Greene, 2011).

Entrepreneurs engage in small action experiments to test a concept, initiative, market, or product idea, or to innovate so that they can take further action and decrease the uncertainty as they move forward (Mitchell et al., 2012). The practice is iterative, and with each set of experimental actions entrepreneurs can increase their competency and reduce uncertainty. Learning by doing reduces personal uncertainty, because if a person feels more competent there is less uncertainty (Frese, 2009). Hence, the learning by doing and experimentation in entrepreneurship involves feelings, attitudes, and values alongside information, and utilizing multidisciplinary resources (Gibb, 1993).

We argue that experimentation can be taught as a "practice." This practice of experimentation should be creatively grounded so that students are exposed to problem-solving and taught strategies to deal with ambiguous and complex situations (McMullan and Long, 1987; Hills, 1988; Stumpf et al., 1991). Experimentation is not simply trial and error. The essence of experimentation as a practice is rooted in the scientific principles of developing hypotheses, testing, measuring, and building on results. The testable hypotheses are anchored in potential action paths – what might work? Because trial and error is less often purposeful, or goal directed, it often leads to lower learning (Frese, 2009). We draw from the concept of deliberate practice, which consists of individualized, self-regulated, and effortful activities that are designed to help students improve performance and can be predictive of entrepreneurial success (Unger et al., 2009). Moreover, deliberate practice involves activities specifically designed to improve performance within a particular domain (Ericsson et al., 1993). Experimentation as a practice of entrepreneurship involves a set of activities, with instruction and feedback at a deliberate pace. Further, as noted in Chapter 1, experimentation as a practice in entrepreneurship education assumes that it is meaningful performance, involves human agency and interaction, becomes a foundation for culture formation, and results in shared meaning.

THEORETICAL BACKGROUND – EXPERIMENTATION AS A PEDAGOGICAL PRACTICE

Experimentation as a practice follows the constructionist view of teaching, which assumes that humans interact in their environment to gain knowledge by applying, discovering, and extending it (Zahorik, 1995). It is a descriptive theory of learning (how people actually learn) rather than prescriptive (how people should learn) (Richardson, 1997). It is theorized that individuals create their own understanding based on what they already know and believe, and the knowledge and ideas with which they come in contact. Learning occurs through social interaction, dialogue, exchanges, and interaction with others (Fletcher, 2009). While there are different views, one from psychology focusing on the individual and the other from sociology emphasizing social interactions, in the entrepreneurship domain we follow the socially situated view (Richardson, 1997). Learning is usually socially situated, and the instructor's role is to create experiences that provide learning experiences without just "telling" the students. We

Table 5.1   Theoretical foundations of experimentation

	Problem-based learning	Evidence-based learning	Sensemaking
Core assumptions	Subject is learned through experiences.	Use of most appropriate information to make complex decisions.	Learning is enacted reality, part of social construction.
Key components	Cognitive conflict, puzzlement.	Acceptance of fallibility and incomplete information.	Organizing activities are discovered through talking and thinking.
Student actions	Communication, problem solving, collaboration.	Interpret, critique, and synthesize evidence.	Design, and explain perceptions, grapple with simultaneity, debate.
Instructor role	Facilitator, tutor.	Guide.	Encouraging dialogue, sensitivity to roles.
Outcomes	Learning through social negotiation and evaluation of understanding.	Cumulative interactive learning.	Storytelling, scenarios, metaphors.
References	Dewey ([1938] 1991); Barrows (1985); von Glaserfeld (1989); Gassner (2011).	Howard et al. (2003); Bilsker and Goldner (2004).	Duffy (1995); Weick (1995); Dehler et al. (2001); Holliway (2009).

draw from three different theoretical approaches: problem-based learning, evidence-based learning, and sensemaking (see Table 5.1).

Problem-Based Learning

Problem-based learning begins with the assumption that students can learn about a subject through experience. The pedagogy is student-centered where students learn both thinking strategies and domain knowledge. Students work in groups to identify what they already know or what they think they know, what they need to know, and where to access new information that may lead to resolution of the problem. Because content and information are often a commodity, the role of the instructor is more crucial. The instructor is the facilitator (known as the *tutor* in problem-based learning) supporting, guiding, and monitoring the learning process. The facilitator's role is to build student confidence to take on the problem and encourage students while stretching understanding. Pioneered by Howard Barrows in the medical school program at McMaster University in Hamilton, Ontario, in the late 1960s, the approach was developed to stimulate learners, assist them, and help them to see the relevance of learning to their future roles (Barrows, 1985). Since its initial introduction, the approach has been used in health science, math, law, education, economics, social studies, and engineering (Gassner, 2011).

Problem-based learning fosters the development of communication, problem-solving, critical thinking, collaboration, and self-directed learning skills. This follows the constructivist learning approach, which is rooted in the pragmatic philosophy of Richard Rorty (1991). There are three fundamental concepts:

1. Understanding, or learning, is gained by our interactions with the environment (von Glaserfeld, 1989).
2. Cognitive conflict, or puzzlement, is the stimulus for learning (Dewey, [1938] 1991).
3. Knowledge evolves through social negotiation and through the evaluation of viability and understandings. This usually occurs through collaborative groups who work together to solve the problem (von Glaserfeld, 1989).

In the entrepreneurship education context, an example might be where students are given a dilemma, such as how to price a new pro-biotic beverage for a venture that does not yet exist. They might start with what they know of prices for similar products (existing knowledge), and then think about possible pricing strategies (cost-based, perceived value, competitive pricing). In discussions they would debate the merits of different pricing strategies, think about where they would find more, and design an experiment to test the price in some way. This process would require negotiation, communication, and scenario building among group members, with the instructor facilitating. The experiment might be to take samples of the beverage into different settings (student lunch room, sidewalk, student center) and sell it at different prices based on the scenarios built by the group.

Evidence-Based Learning

Evidence-based learning is based on the premise that a learner will use the most appropriate information to make complex and conscientious decisions. Widely used in health care and clinical medical practices, evidence-based practice argues that, where possible, it should be grounded on prior findings that are likely to produce predictable, beneficial, and effective results, where scientific information is integrated with informed professional judgment (Howard et al., 2003). In the social work context, social workers examine a situation, consider the evidence from possible effective interventions, and then apply the intervention using a combination of judgment and evidence.

Evidence-based practice requires the acceptance of fallibility and imperfections in diagnoses and treatment. As a result, there is less emphasis on number crunching and data-based results and, instead, a recognition of the humanistic approach to the practice (Bilsker and Goldner, 2004). Skills required for evidence-based learning include the ability: to search for empirical evidence; to critique, interpret, and synthesize the findings; and, finally, to decide how the literature (evidence) supports or not the particular intervention. In practice, evidence-based learning is self-directed, iterative, and cumulative.

If we apply the evidence-based experimentation approach to our new venture making the pro-biotic beverage, in this case students would start with existing data and studies of pricing of new beverages. Some information would be acquired that reflects industry average prices and the results of pricing strategies used by other new ventures. Because it is not possible to fully access all the empirical evidence, some judgments, best guesses, and interpreting the existing evidence of pricing strategies would be central to the discussion. The design of the experiment would be rooted in the evidence and discussion and synthesis of other experiments. This experiment would be to take samples of the beverage into different settings (student lunch room, sidewalk, student center) and sell it at different prices based on previous examples gleaned from the synthesis of the evidence.

Sensemaking

Sensemaking is derived from the concept of an enacted environment, whereby reality is a product of social construction (Weick, 1995). An enacted environment is the output of organizing activities and is discovered through talking and thinking. Weick (1995) lists the questions that reflect an approach to sensemaking as a learning pedagogy: "How they [i.e. active agents] construct what they construct, why, and with what effects, are the central questions for people interested in sensemaking" (p. 4). Sensemaking research asks people not just to generate answers or responses to questions that researchers pose, but also to articulate the questions that they must pose to themselves in order to answer the researcher's questions. When sensemaking is applied to the activities of teaching and learning, it emphasizes cultural aspects of education and acknowledges that, when people do show up in the classroom, they influence that cultural inscription just as surely as they are influenced by it (Duffy, 1995). Such a perspective is implicitly reflexive. The distinctions between self and other, teacher and learner, culture and individual become blurred. Sensemaking follows the constructionist approach whereby the emphasis is on how entrepreneurial activities are constructed and coordinated between people in conversations and actions in relation to their culture, context, or environment (Fletcher, 2009).

Sensemaking is often utilized in math, information technology, languages, and other disciplines, where students are learning to solve problems and understand patterns. For example, in languages, students learn to pronounce, define, and use new words from a new language in the context of the country. Through writing, speaking, and thinking critically, they identify patterns and make sense of the new language (Holliway, 2009). In management learning, paradoxical thinking may be applied to understanding women in management or power relationships in organizations (Dehler et al., 2001). The process requires recognition of the simultaneous appearance of contradictions, which are inherently perceptual. Students are encouraged to design and explain polarized perceptions, juxtapose and contradict perspectives, debate and grapple with simultaneity, and then recognize biases and limits. Reflexive dialogue is another sensemaking pedagogy, often used in online courses, management education, or consulting. In this approach, there is a deliberate consciousness of an individual's role as well as sensitivity to other roles, which can be done through storytelling, metaphors, myths, or scenario-building (Abma, 2001). Through public discussion and reflection, sensemaking occurs.

If we apply the sensemaking experimentation approach to our new venture making the pro-biotic beverage, students might set up an experiment whereby they compare and contrast possible prices for the same beverage. The conversation with potential customers would involve probing why, when, and how for pro-biotic beverage pricing. Students would interact, weigh, discuss, and construct new possible price points based on the new input from customers.

In all three of the pedagogies (problem-based learning, evidence-based learning, and sensemaking), the process is interactive and iterative. Learning is rooted in student experience and faculty interaction around a problem. Students evaluate evidence, critically assess perspectives, and look for patterns that can be understood. In general, the practice of experimentation is iterative and collaborative, involving personal perspectives. Next we consider how experimentation applies in the entrepreneurial context.

PRACTICING EXPERIMENTATION IN THE ENTREPRENEURIAL CONTEXT

The focus of this book is on the practices of entrepreneurship, and we share a set of exercises in Part II that can be used in the classroom to help the students with their practice. But we would be remiss not to address some of the experimentation built into our program at the co-curricular level. At Babson College, we use a start-up experimentation methodology in our venture accelerator. Outside the classroom, students live entrepreneurship through the comprehensive John E. and Alice L. Butler Venture Accelerator Program, which is the result of faculty and staff working together to define a framework that provides access to resources for student and alumni entrepreneurs to move their business ideas forward (see Figure 5.1).

The program is open to every student at Babson from first-year undergraduates to all MBA students and an increasing number of alumni as resources permit. Entry is initiated by the participant completing the Accelerator assessment questionnaire consisting of about 15 questions. Responses are evaluated to determine the level at which participants enter the program:

- **Explore**: In this phase students are generating and exploring ideas, conducting research, and validating market opportunities. These activities involve industry and market analysis to determine the feasibility of an opportunity and an articulation of the problem or social and/or economic need. A feasibility study must be completed before moving to the next phase.

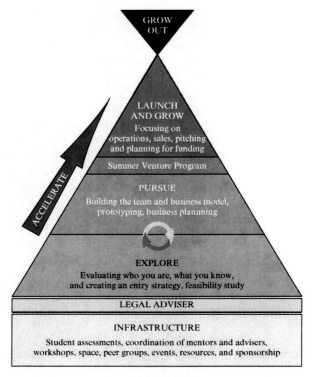

Figure 5.1   John E. and Alice L. Butler Venture Accelerator framework

- **Pursue**: This phase involves shaping the opportunity and planning for business execution, with an emphasis on taking action and making progress through the test-and-learn approach. This process involves talking to customers, building prototypes, proving technologies, and building leadership teams. The goal is to create a minimal viable product or service.
- **Launch and grow**: In this phase ventures are launched and executed, and students "live" the experience, creating a revenue stream, finding investors, and marketing their products and services.

The Accelerator is designed based on three key assumptions:

- **Action**: Resources, space, and mentoring are earned through proven action and efforts put forth by students. By taking action and demonstrating progress, they can move forward to a new level, and earn access to different levels of resources, space, and mentoring.

Resources become more individualized and customized as students progress through the program. Students earn more resources as they achieve specific milestones. For example, the explore level has group advising and peer mentoring. The launch and grow level has individual advising and mentoring. A workshop at the explore level may focus on "trends and opportunities in entrepreneurship." A workshop at the pursue level is "division of equity among partners." Students at the pursue level work in the co-working space on the ground floor of the Blank Center; students in the launch and grow level can apply for dedicated office space in the Babson Hatcheries. These are just a few examples of how the program is organized, and how students access resources.

- **Practice**: Student learning of entrepreneurial skills needs to be practiced, and through practice students develop competencies and confidence in their entrepreneurial abilities. To this end, assessment is based on student confidence in entrepreneurial skills. A technique referred to as "the hot seat" requires that students pitch their business idea on a weekly basis, receiving active feedback from peers and faculty. In this process, students learn to accept the feedback, asking only clarifying questions, but cannot respond or defend. Each week that a student presents in the hot seat, learning and changes to the business concept or model are discussed.

- **Participation**: Another key component for the Accelerator is that participation is open to any student or alumnus, whether or not they intend to start a business. Because the focus is on developing entrepreneurial thought and action capabilities, all pathways into situations where they can practice entrepreneurial thought and action are open. For instance, students interested in family businesses, corporate entrepreneurship, franchising, buying a business, non-profits, or social initiatives are welcome to participate. Further, they don't even have to be the "key" entrepreneur; rather they can desire to be part of a team or even be a funder or service provider to a new, growing, or entrepreneurial concern. This diversity of perspectives, roles, and experience leads to broad experimental student learning.

In the 2012–13 academic year, the Butler Venture Accelerator Program provided resources to 416 students working on 327 concepts or businesses, with 54 percent of the participants at the explore level, 33 percent at the pursue level, and 13 percent at the launch and grow level. This tiered approach to business acceleration has dramatically increased the number of student entrepreneurs who have access to co-curricular programming and has enriched the entrepreneurial ecosystem at Babson College.

Concept Testing

Concepts are ideas, and concept tests measure consumers' reactions to the ideas. Early-stage product development requires testing of ideas to determine whether or not they should be pursued further. Concept or product tests can measure reactions to statements and prototypes, as well as user satisfaction, desirability, and feasibility of exploring the idea further (Moore, 1982). In the early phases tests are focused and hypothesis driven, and, because they are early in the product or service development stage, usually conducted with minimal resources. Output from the testing leads to information to refine the product or service features, position it to a particular segment, determine economics of development, and other key decisions.

In the product development arena, concept generation, testing, and selection processes of new product development are designed to provide information for allocating resources, adapting the product, and moving forward during the "fuzzy front end" of the development phase (Wheelwright and Clark, 1992). Concept tests help to reduce uncertainty by quantifying the importance of various attributes, price sensitivity, and other dimensions that allow designers to optimize attribute level trade-offs (Dahan and Mendelson, 2001). In practice, the purpose is to estimate consumer reactions to a product idea before committing substantial funds to it.

Similar approaches have been manifested recently in the entrepreneurship education world. The notion of the lean start-up and business model canvas applies the ideas of experimentation to the new venture start-up process (Osterwalder and Pigneur, 2010; Reis, 2011; Blank and Dorf, 2012; Blank, 2013). In this framing, entrepreneurs follow a build–measure–learn approach whereby the vision of the entrepreneur is tested in small steps, iteratively, so that the business concept and ultimately business model can be validated. Two basic hypotheses are tested: first, the value hypothesis, which tests whether or not the product or service really delivers value to customers once they are using it; and, second, the growth hypothesis, which tests how new customers will discover a product or service. Osterwalder and Pigneur (2010) provide an elaborate methodology for validating the hypotheses of the business model to find a repeatable and scalable model. A key component is in prototyping and field-testing customer acceptance and feasibility.

In the lean start-up language, the build–measure–learn loop is completed quickly by fast prototyping of small batches: this facilitates learning and allows for the testing of hypotheses so that changes can be made or the business model can be pivoted. More specifically, the example of an X-ray field system scheduled the project time accordingly: one day to build the virtual prototype, three days to assemble the hard prototype, five days for design iteration, and 15 days for initial assembly (Reis, 2011, pp. 195–7). The purpose of the experimental approach is to obtain important customer information quickly.

The practice of experimentation is designed to help entrepreneurship students manage uncertainty and make sense of chaotic or extremely uncertain situations. When you do not really know what to do, the only choice is to take action, and learn from the action in order to make sense of the world. This is akin to meaning making, how people make sense out of their experience in the world (Weick, 1995).

NOTE

1. http://www.merriam-webster.com/dictionary/experiment

REFERENCES

Abma, T.A. 2001. Reflexive dialogues: A story about the development of injury prevention in two performing-arts schools. *Evaluation*, 7, 238–52.

Alberti, F., Sciascia, S., and Poli, A. 2004. Entrepreneurial education: Notes on an ongoing debate. Proceedings of the 14th Annual International Entrepreneurship Conference, University of Napoli Federico II, Italy.

Aldrich, H.E. 1999. *Organizations Evolving*. Thousand Oaks, CA: Sage Publications.

Alvarez, S.A., and Barney, J.B. 2005. How do entrepreneurs organize firms under conditions of uncertainty? *Journal of Management*, 31(5), 776–93.

Barrows, H. 1985. A taxonomy of problem based learning methods. *Medical Education*, 20, 481–6.

Bilsker, D., and Goldner, E. 2004. Teaching evidence based practice: Overcoming barriers. *Brief Treatment and Crisis Intervention*, 4(3), 271–5.

Blank, S. 2013. *The Four Steps to Epiphany: Successful Strategies for Products That Win*, 2nd edn. K&S Ranch.

Blank, S., and Dorf, B. 2012. *The Startup Owner's Manual: The Step-by-Step Guide for Building a Great Company*. K&S Ranch.

Block, Z., and Stumpf, S.A. 1992. Entrepreneurship education research: Experience and challenge. In D.L. Sexton and J.D. Kasarda (eds.), *The State of the Art of Entrepreneurship*. Boston, MA: PWS-Kent Publishing.

Campbell, D.T., and Stanley, J.C. 1963. *Experimental and Quasi-Experimental Designs for Research*. Boston, MA: Houghton, Mifflin Company.

Curran, J., and Stanworth, J. 1989. Education and training for enterprise: Some problems of classification, evaluation, policy and research. *International Small Business Journal*, 7(2), 11–22.

Dahan, E., and Mendelson, H. 2001. An extreme-value model of concept testing. *Management Science*, 47(1), 102–16.

Dehler, G.E., Welsh, M.A., and Lewis, M.W. 2001. Critical pedagogy in the "new paradigm." *Management Learning*, 32(4), 493–511.
Dewey, J. [1938] 1991. Logic: The theory of inquiry. In *John Dewey: The Later Works, 1925–1953*, Vol. 14: *1939–1941*, ed. J.A. Boydston (pp. 3–90). Carbondale: Southern Illinois University Press.
Duffy, M. 1995. Sensemaking: A collaborative inquiry approach to doing learning. *The Qualitative Report*, 2(2), October, http://www.nova.edu/ssss/QR/QR2-2/duffy.html.
Ericsson, K.A., Krampe, R.T., and Tesch-Römer, C. 1993. The role of deliberate practice in the acquisition of expert performance. *Psychological Review*, 100, 363–406.
Fletcher, J.D. 2009. From behaviorism to constructivism. In S. Tobias and T.M. Duffy (eds.), *Constructivist Theory Applied to Instructions: Success or Failure?* (pp. 242–63). New York: Taylor & Francis.
Frese, M. 2009. Toward a psychology of entrepreneurship: An action theory perspective. *Foundations and Trends in Entrepreneurship* (NOW Publishers), 5(6), 435–94.
Garavan, T.N., and O'Cinneide, B. 1994. Entrepreneurship education and training programmes: A review and evaluation – part 1. *Journal of European Industrial Training*, 18(8), 3–12.
Gassner, K.W. 2011. Five ideas for 21st century math classrooms. *American Secondary Education*, 39(3), 108–16.
Gibb, A.A. 1993. The enterprise culture and education: Understanding enterprise education and its links with small business, entrepreneurship and wider educational goals. *International Small Business Journal*, 11(3), 11–34.
Glaserfeld, E. von. 1989. Cognition, construction of knowledge and teaching. *Synthese*, 80, 121–40.
Hills, G.E. 1988. Variations in university entrepreneurship education: An empirical study of an evolving field. *Journal of Business Venturing*, 3, 109–22.
Holliway, D. 2009. Towards a sense-making pedagogy: Writing activities in an undergraduate learning theories course. *International Journal of Teaching and Learning in Higher Education*, 20(3), 447–61.
Howard, M.O., McMillen, C.J., and Pollio, D.E. 2003. Teaching evidence-based practice: Toward a new paradigm for social work education. *Research on Social Work Practice*, 1(2), 234–59.
McMullen, W.E., and Long, W.A. 1987. Entrepreneurship education in the nineties. *Journal of Business Venturing*, 2, 261–75.
McMullen, J.S., and Shepherd, D.S. 2006. Entrepreneurial action and the role of uncertainty in the theory of the entrepreneur. *Academy of Management Review*, 31(1), 132–52.
Mitchell, J.R., Mitchell, R.K., Mitchell, B.T., and Alvarez, S.A. 2012. Opportunity creation, underlying conditions and economic exchange. In A.C. Corbett and J.A. Katz (eds.), *Advances in Entrepreneurship, Firm Emergence and Growth*, Vol. 14: *Entrepreneurial Action* (pp. 89–123). Bingley, UK: Emerald Group Publishing.
Moore, W.L. 1982. Concept testing. *Journal of Business Research*, 10(3), 279–94.
Neck, H.M., and Greene, P.G. 2011. Entrepreneurship education: Known worlds and new frontiers. *Journal of Small Business Management*, 49(1), 55–70.
Osterwalder, A., and Pigneur, Y. 2010. *Business Model Generation*. Hoboken, NJ: Wiley.

Reis, E. 2011. *The Lean Start-Up*. London: Penguin.

Richardson, V. 1997. Constructivist teaching and teacher education: Theory and practice. In V. Richardson (ed.), *Constructivist Teacher Education: Building a World of New Understandings* (pp. 3–15). London: Routledge.

Richardson, V. 2003. Constructivist pedagogy. *Teachers College Record*, 105(9), 1623–40.

Rorty, R. 1991. *Objectivity, Relativism and Truth*. Cambridge, UK: Cambridge University Press.

Sarasvathy, S. 2001. Causation and effectuation: Toward a theoretical shift from economic inevitability to entrepreneurial contingency. *Academy of Management Review*, 26(2), 243–63.

Stumpf, S.S., Dunbar, R.L., and Mullen, T.P. 1991. Simulations in entrepreneurial education: Oxymoron or untapped opportunity? *Frontiers of Entrepreneurship Research* (pp. 681–94). Wellesley, MA: Babson College.

Unger, J.M., Keith, N., Hilling, C., Gielnik, M., and Frese, M. 2009. Deliberate practice among South African small business owners with education, cognitive ability, knowledge and success. *Journal of Occupational and Organizational Psychology*, 82(1), 21–44.

Weick, K.E. 1995. *Sensemaking in Organizations*. Thousand Oaks, CA: Sage Publications.

Wheelwright, S.C., and Clark, K.B. 1992. *Revolutionizing Product Development*. New York: Free Press.

Zahorik, J.A. 1995. *Constructivist Teaching*. Bloomington, IN: ERIC Clearinghouse.

6. The practice of reflection

For it is not enough to have a good mind: one must use it well. (Descartes)

This entire book is based on the proposition of approaching the teaching of entrepreneurship as a method: one which goes beyond understanding, knowing, and talking to focus on specific sets of practices, namely those of creation, reflection, experimentation, play, and empathy. As we shared in Chapter 1, each of our designated elements of practices is characterized by a shared set of criteria. Each involves a heavy emphasis on doing along with a recognition of the importance of intentional iteration. We found it most intriguing to think through the idea of reflection as a practice, particularly around the area of "doing." In other words, thinking is a form of doing.

The practice of reflection actually is supported, at least to some degree, by each of the other practices. Reflection is required in play, empathy, creation, and experimentation. Because of this we believe that reflection is the pathway to our notion of synthesis discussed in Chapter 1 – a synthesis of theory and practice, a synthesis of thinking and acting, a synthesis of learning and doing. The practice of reflection is arguably the most important of all the practices for entrepreneurship education. As we have illustrated throughout the previous chapters, entrepreneurship coursework based on a method of practice requires continuous doing. An environment is created where students are taking action in order to learn. Such an environment creates an accelerated pace of student activity and can often be perceived as having "little time to think." But reflection is a form of "doing" and is the primary way for students to codify their action-based learning.

Reflection has been called one of the greatest innovations in education (Procee, 2006), but the importance of reflection in entrepreneurship education is merely anecdotal. Indeed, we find that very little has been written by entrepreneurship educators on *how* students reflect. Intuitively we know reflection is good, but reflecting is not intuitive for our students. They need guidance in order to become disciplined reflectors. In general, reflection in entrepreneurship is seen as a journaling assignment. It is almost always done individually and is not at the top of a student's to-do list. The typical scenario is that the assignment given to the student is to reflect at the end of the day or at some specified designated times through-out the week or even the course. Sometimes it is explicitly equated to journaling. Sometimes the notes are handed in, sometimes not. Sometimes the instructor provides feedback. We'd suggest that this is more often not the case. And, when feedback is provided, it is more likely that both the reflective assignment and the instructor's feedback are what we like to call "James Joycean" in nature, stream-of-consciousness reactions instead of being guided and organized by any particular framework for responses. The question then becomes: to what end is the journaling – or the responding?

While we have no significant quantitative data, we would propose that anecdotal evidence through observation strongly suggests that faculty using this type of assignment have rarely themselves reflected on the actual nature of and opportunities inherent in this type of reflec-tion and the potential richness in the outcomes for our students. After all, we can accept that the higher the level at which we teach, the less actual training we have had in that teaching, and who among us, espe-cially business educators, has been trained to reflect and/or respond to reflections? As the field of entrepreneurship has matured, it is now a good time for each of us to reflect on our own teaching. Therefore, in this chapter we are going to review the theoretical foundations of reflec-tion and present a framework that is a suggested guide for pedagogical reflection – while stressing that it is important to consider developing your own framework that fits your students, your learning objectives, and your teaching philosophy.

THE ROLE OF THEORY AND PRACTICE IN REFLECTION

Earlier in this book we addressed the relevance of the theory/practice debate for our approach to teaching through the practices of entrepre-neurship. This debate is particularly relevant for the practice of reflection. As we mentioned, while the dominance of the importance of theory is strongly supported by the early philosophers (Socrates, Plato, and even Descartes), the critical importance of practice in education has emerged more strongly over the last half-century. Exemplars of advocates of this change in the educational approach are John Dewey and Alfred North Whitehead.

John Dewey was an American educational reformer in the early part of the twentieth century and is considered the founder of the practice of using reflection in education (Koole et al., 2011). Dewey's overriding concern

was that formal education would become too isolated from practical concerns. "There is the standing danger that the material of formal instruction
will be merely the subject matter of the schools, isolated from the subject
matter of life-experience" (Dewey, 1916, p. 9). In fact, Dewey claimed
that "It would be impossible to state adequately the evil results which
have flowed from this dualism of mind and body, much less to exaggerate
them" (Dewey, 1916, p. 152). His concern was how to have the appropriate balance between the formal and the informal, and between theory and
practice. For Dewey, the informal means of approaching practice was
social learning by direct sharing. He promoted learning as a social activity
rooted in participation in life. He also reviewed and passed judgment on
what he saw as the basic assumptions for the general function of education: direction, control, and guidance:

> Of these three words, direction, control, and guidance, the last best conveys the
> idea of assisting through cooperation the natural capacities of the individuals
> guided; control conveys rather the notion of an energy brought to bear from
> without and meeting some resistance from the one controlled; direction is a
> more neutral term and suggests the fact that the active tendencies of those
> directed are led in a certain continuous course, instead of dispersing aimlessly.
> Direction expresses the basic function, which tends at one extreme to become a
> guiding assistance and at another, a regulation or ruling. (Dewey, 1916, p. 27)

Dewey's approach brings us firmly back to our goal of synthesis and
of needing both theory and practice and the use of reflection to connect
the two by presenting reflection as a pathway to direction, control, and
most importantly guidance. His desire was that education should focus
not only on things, but on the relations and connections between things.
Dewey also connects us back to the need for using reflection as a practice
in teaching. Dewey explicitly deconstructed the concept of learning from
experience into the activity itself, and the consequences of that activity.
His example is of a child sticking his hand into a flame. The learning
does not come from the activity of touching the fire; the learning actually
comes from the consequences of that activity. It hurts, and it hurts badly
enough for learning to take place. "To 'learn from experience' is to make a
backward and forward connection between what we do to things and what
we enjoy and suffer from things in consequence" (Dewey, 1916, p. 152).
In Dewey's words, "Thought or reflection . . . is the discernment of the
relation between what we try to do and what happens in consequence."
Perhaps most importantly for our argument on reflection, Dewey positions thinking as a form of doing: Thus, reflection is a *practice* of entrepreneurship education.
    Dewey believed that (subject) matter and (delivery) method must be

connected. He positioned his approach as a reflective practice of deciding how content should be delivered in the most powerful way as to
really make a lasting impression upon the minds of students. And lasting
impression implies that students are actually able to put the subject
matter or content into practice. Dewey's further consideration of reflection, however, was also focused on the what (input) for the reflection, the
source of the data, rather than the how. He posited that the "essentials of
learning are identical with the essentials of reflection." Bringing all of this
together, we end up with a proposed method for a virtuous circle of continuous learning – with a crucial and defining element of reflection firmly
ensconced in the middle.

Alfred North Whitehead, a British mathematician and philosopher,
also contributed to the debate over the role of theory and practice and,
ultimately, thinking and reflection. One of his lines of thought focused
upon how to think about what is important. Not surprisingly given his
mathematical background, Whitehead strongly supported the idea of
systems and using frameworks for thought; however, he stressed that
before systems must come "assemblage." He strongly valued the importance of the idea while stressing the need to experience things in order to
better think about them, thus the assemblage. In a most entrepreneurial
vein, Whitehead wrote:

> Again there is the introduction of novelty of feeling by the entertainment of
> unexpressed possibilities. This second side is the enlargement of the conceptual
> experience of mankind. The characterization of this conceptual feeling is the
> sense of what might be and of what might have been. It is the entertainment of
> the alternative. In its highest development, this becomes the entertainment of
> the idea. (Whitehead, [1938] 1966, p. 26)

Overall, as educators, and aligned with Dewey and Whitehead, we
want our students to learn, really learn, and not just on the surface, but in
a deep, sustained, and meaningful manner (Marton, 1975). Our concern
is that surface learning is what we see in traditional approaches to education. At the same time we see it as more passive, largely consisting of
learning, absorbing, and regurgitating. By contrast, our goal of deep
learning is considered to be actively acquired through not only obtaining
the information, but synthesizing for the long term.

From a very basic perspective we can start from the idea of looking at
a mirror, considering what you see, and recognizing what you see looking
back at you in that mirror (Onions in Keevers and Treleaven, 2011). The
mirroring metaphor generally includes both a sense of distance from the
outside and the concept of detachment: each of these based on an objective reality as grounds for consideration of what is being viewed (Cunliffe

and Jun in Keevers and Treleaven, 2011). The major issue in moving from what Keevers and Treleaven (2011) describe as the "optical metaphor" is actually to transition ourselves from the noun to the verb. Reflection then can be seen as a thoughtful exercise in which one reviews what happened, considers it deeply, and evaluates the experience (Boud et al., 1985).

From a theoretical perspective, we can approach it as a foundation for metacognition: thinking about thinking – the ability to reflect upon, understand, and control one's learning (Schraw and Dennison, 1994). While the general approach to reflection is more about the "observe and understand" part, the "controlling one's learning" also becomes a desired outcome of reflection. In essence, reflection is an important process by which knowledge is developed from experience. When reflecting, one considers an experience that has happened and tries to understand or explain it, which often leads to insight and deep learning – or ideas to test on new experiences. Reflection is particularly important for perplexing experiences, working under conditions of high uncertainty, and problem solving. As a result, it should not be a surprise that reflection is an integral component of entrepreneurship education.

THE NATURE OF REFLECTIVE LEARNING

The idea of reflecting as a part of learning is not new from either an individual or an organizational perspective, and there are quite a few reviews, explorations, and applications that inform the discussion (Vince, 2002; Cope, 2003; Korthagen, 2005; Yanow and Tsoukas, 2009; Jordan, 2010). Brockbank and McGill (2007, p. 36), in their excellent work on reflective learning in higher education, shared a number of definitions that we now suggest illustrate an evolution of usage over the last few decades (see Table 6.1).

There are four points across these definitions that we found particularly intriguing. First, two of these (Boud et al. and Brookfield) include a seemingly positive outcome in their definition. For these authors, reflective learning leads to new understanding and appreciation (Boud et al., 1985) and, in an even more instrumental approach, Brookfield's (1987) definition leads us to increased productivity and enhancing political literacy.

Second is the question of whether or when reflective learning is an individual or group activity. For most of the definitions, the assumption either seems to be around the individual engaging in the activity or, at best, is ambiguous on this topic. Brockbank and McGill (2007) explicitly move reflective learning into the social sphere. While an important approach, for the purposes of this chapter we will focus on individual reflection.

Table 6.1   Evolution of reflective learning

Definition	Author(s)
"The process of internally examining and exploring an issue of concern, triggered by an experience, which creates and clarifies meaning in terms of self, and which results in a changed conceptual perspective."	Boyd and Fales (1983, p. 100)
"A generic term for those intellectual and affective activities in which individuals engage to explore their experiences in order to lead to new understandings and appreciation."	Boud et al. (1985, p. 3)
"The outcome of these activities is a change in assumptions about oneself and the world requiring a corresponding change in one's behavior and relationships."	Schlossberg (1981, p. 5)
"A lived activity, not an abstract academic pastime [*sic*] and crucial to understanding our personal relationships, envisioning alternative and more productive ways of organizing the workplace, and becoming politically literate."	Brookfield (1987, p. 14)
Reflection-on-practice (do–learn–think as a process). Reflection-in-practice (do–learn–think as a behavior).	Schön (1983, 1987)
"We define reflective learning as an intentional social process, where context and experience are acknowledged, in which learners are active individuals, wholly present, engaging with others, open to challenge, and the outcomes involve transformation as well as improvement for both individuals and their environment."	Brockbank and McGill (2007, p. 36)

Third, the nature of the reflective activity comes into question. For Boud et al. (1985), reflective learning is a set of "intellectual and affective activities," while Brookfield's (1987) approach seems to have a quite different orientation, specifically and perhaps rather defensively saying that reflective learning is "not an abstract academic pastime."

And, fourth, Donald Schön (1983, 1987) essentially changed how we view reflection. He coined the term *reflective practice* while studying applied university programs such as medicine, law, and architectural design. He argued that the knowledge acquired through coursework, what he called *propositional knowledge*, was limited in its impact because it did not take into consideration the reality of practice. Yet he discovered that professionals graduating from applied programs were still effective despite how they were taught. Schön learned that professionals enhanced their practice through engagement and developed "practice experience" (Brockbank and McGill, 2007).

Schön distinguished "reflection-on-practice" (do–learn–think as a process) from "reflection–in–practice" (do–learn–think as a behavior). Both are important and represent a continuous cycle of learning.

> Schön found the teachers and students engaged in *reflection* on emergent practice that was to underpin their learning and therefore enhance their practice. Putting it more simply, students learned by listening, watching, doing and by being coached in their doing. Not only did they apply what they had heard and learned from lectures, books, and demonstrations but when they did an action that was part of their future profession, for example using a scalpel, they also learned by reflecting themselves and with their [teachers], how the action went. They *reflected* on their practice. In addition, they would "take with them" that reflection on their previous actions as a piece of "knowledge" or learning when they went into the action the next time. Thus in the next action they would be bringing all their previously acquired understanding and practice and be able to *reflect* in the action as they did it, particularly if a new circumstance came up. (Brockbank and McGill, 2007, p. 87)

Given the nature of entrepreneurship as a continuous cycle of acting, creating, and building, reflection-on-practice and reflection-in-practice must play a paramount role in entrepreneurial development.

REFLECTION FRAMEWORKS

We now offer frameworks that can help guide the practice of reflection. Types of reflective frameworks have been approached in several different ways. For example, Koole et al. (2011), while exploring the topic in the context of medical education, provide an overview of the concept to which we add some additional thoughts. (See Table 6.2.)

The final addition, of Brockbank and McGill (2007), has been delineated in more detail by Stevens, and we offer an additional type of reflection as well. (See Table 6.3.) It is this framework that we now adapt even more to serve as the tool for guiding reflection exercises in entrepreneurship education. While adding emotional reflection to the Brockback and McGill chart as broken down by Stevens (Table 6.3), we began to see other types of questions emerge in order to meet an additional desired purpose. The narrative begins by telling the story, the basic who, what, where, and when. We suggest that some consideration of what came before the experience being reflected upon is also important. What kind of prepara-

Table 6.2   Theories and models of reflection

Author	Theory, model or finding	Summary
Atkins and Murphy (1993)	Reflective processes (model)	Three key stages of the reflective process: 1) awareness of uncomfortable feelings; 2) critical analysis of feelings and knowledge; 3) new perspectives: associated skills – self-awareness, description, critical analysis, synthesis, and evaluation.
Keevers and Treleaven (2011)	*Reflective practices (model)*	*Four categories of reflective practices: 1) anticipatory; 2) deliberative; 3) organizing; and 4) critically reflective.*
Boud et al. (1985)	Promoting reflection in learning (model)	Reflection process consists of three interrelated stages: 1) returning to the experience; 2) attending to feelings; 3) re-evaluating experience, triggered by experiences and leading to outcome.
Korthagen (2005)	ALACT model	Reflection is a cyclic process of Action, Looking back on action, Awareness of essential aspects, Creating alternative methods of action, and Trial.
Mamede and Schmidt (2004)	The structure of reflective practice in medicine (finding)	Reflective practice consists of a five-factor model: deliberate induction; deliberate deduction; testing and synthesizing; openness for reflection; and meta-reasoning.
Mezirow and Associates (2000)	Transformative learning theory	Reflection leads to changed assumptions and frames of references which ground transformative learning.
Moon (1999)	Input–outcome model	Reflection is a mental process that is based on input (theories, constructed knowledge, or feelings) that has an outcome or purpose (self-development, learning, decisions, resolutions of uncertainty, etc.).
Schön (1983, 1987)	The reflective practitioner (theory)	Reflection is a key factor for professionals to deal with complex situations and for professional development. He identified reflection-in-action and reflection-on-action.

Table 6.2 (continued)

Author	Theory, model or finding	Summary
Stockhausen (2000)	Clinical learning spiral (model)	Reflective practice is related to professional growth. Clinical learning consists of preparative phase, constructive phase, reflective practice, and reconstructive phase.
Brockbank and McGill (2007)	*Reflective practice framework (model)*	*Steps in reflective practice: 1) narrative – return to an event and describe what happened; 2) percipient – think about the perceptions and reactions involved; 3) analytical – think about the situation analytically (e.g. what steps were involved, what skills were employed, and does it relate to previous experience?); 4) evaluative – evaluate the experience (what went well, what criteria are being applied); 5) critical – consider implications for the future (why did you do what you did, what else might you have done, and does the experience tell you anything about yourself?).*

Source: Adapted from Koole et al. (2011, p. 3). Italicized notes are added by the authors.

Table 6.3 Types of reflection

Reflection type	Questions to answer	Desired purpose	Criteria for evaluation (examples)
1 Narrative reflection Return to an event and describe what happened	What took place? When and where? Who was involved? What was done/said? What background information is relevant? *What preparation did you do for the teaching task?*	Recall observations. Select and communicate. Consider the overall context.	Make purposeful observations and communicate them effectively. Identify relevant context(s).
2 *Emotional reflection*	*What were you feeling and why? What prompted the emotions? How did you manage the emotions?*	*Be aware of emotional cues. Be aware of the impact of feelings.*	*Appreciate the effect of feelings on the experience.*
3 Percipient reflection Think about the perceptions and reactions involved	What were your responses? What were you thinking and why? How did others respond? Can you identify different viewpoints, needs, or preferences? *Is your reflection more subjective or objective?* How do these affect the situation?	Be aware of your perceptions and habits. Be aware of others (their needs and characteristics). Be aware of the impact of preferences or prejudices. Be aware of the interpretive nature of experience.	Demonstrate self-awareness. Appreciate the effect of preferences and prejudices on a situation. Identify and respond to different viewpoints, needs, and contributions. Understand the interpretive nature of experience.

Table 6.3 (continued)

Reflection type	Questions to answer	Desired purpose	Criteria for evaluation (examples)
4 Analytical reflection Think about the situation analytically	What stages, processes, or roles were involved? What skills and knowledge did you and others employ or develop? Does the experience relate to what you have read, seen, or heard about, or learned before? How? Is the experience relevant to other areas of your practice or your everyday experience?	Explain the process by which something is achieved. Identify and relate significant elements or components of practice. Relate diverse experiences and knowledge. Synthesize theory and practice, scholarly and personal.	Identify and explain the process. Relate (or integrate) ideas, knowledge, and experience (theory and practice). Investigate, apply, and/or deeply develop theory and/or practice.
5 Evaluative reflection Evaluate the experience	What seemed to go well and what seemed to go badly? What criteria are you applying and what evidence have you considered? What were the outcomes (anticipated or unanticipated)? Was the experience positive or negative, useful or helpful?	Assess the experience Identify and apply criteria. Recognize value(s). Identify outcomes (anticipated and unanticipated). Make judgments.	Formulate and/or apply criteria Collect and evaluate evidence. Judge evidence against criteria.

| 6 Critical reflection Consider implications for the future | Why did you do what you did? What else might you have done? *How might you have prepared differently?* Does the experience tell you anything about yourself? Your practice? Your values? What questions or new knowledge do you now have? What do you need to consider or do as a result? | Examine assumptions and methods. Seek out contradictions and alternatives. Identify abilities and weaknesses, learning and learning needs. | Identify and investigate the basis of practice. Demonstrate learning. Monitor progress. Develop plans for active experimentation. |

Source: Adapted from Jayne Stevens, "The Performance Reflective Project De Montfort University," published in Brockbank and McGill (2007, pp. 126–7). Italicized notes are added by the authors.

tion was made? This approach helps to tie the time line together, while allowing the reflector (person doing the reflection) to consider the flow of events.

We do suggest continuing to separate the emotive from the percipient phases of reflection. Distilling (the separation piece) our emotions allows us to consider more carefully how our feelings had their own, potential critical impact on the experience. Thinking about what remains, our perceptions, helps us think through the focal question of how objective we can really be in any situation. As earlier mentioned, the metaphor for reflection is gazing into the mirror. The questions now are about how objectively we actually receive that reflection, and how important is the distinction. From the theoretical perspective, the question is critical, with Bourdieu claiming that, "Of all the oppositions that artificially divide social science, the most fundamental, and the most ruinous, is the one that is set up between subjectivism and objectivism" (Bourdieu, [1980] 1990, p. 25). From another expert point of view, the Grimm Brothers' fairy tale of Snow White allows us to consider the idea of an objective reflection. "Mirror, mirror, on the wall, who is the fairest of them all?" After all, the evil queen was shocked when the mirror told her she was no longer the fairest. To her eyes, she still reigned in that department.

In the original framework, the authors touch on the emotional; however, our version goes more broadly. As considered by these authors, it begins with prompting for what the respondent is "thinking and feeling"; however, we believe the focal point of this dimension is more on getting to the point of recognizing the viewpoint of others, and ultimately their needs. It is more about recognizing the potential impact of your feelings as they relate to how others might see the situation than a deep reflection on what your emotions mean for the respondent. Overall, it is the relative perspective that is being probed here, not the emotions per se. For this reason it seems helpful to add the emotional dimension as one on its own (Neck and Greene, 2011).

Are the dimensions actually linear? While the types do seem to increase in cognitive complexity, some are more linear than others. The narrative reflection is the most basic dimension, as it is completely descriptive. It simply captures what has actually taken place. However, already the percipient (when used, as we suggest, to focus on the perspectives of others) is less so and would seem to be of use as an integrated part of each of the other dimensions. For instance, an analytical reflection is a useful next step after the description from the narrative reflection. It is in this step that theory and practice come together, potentially in the use of frameworks to guide the analysis. However, in the analytical dimension the reflector is still not questioning the experience being reflected upon, but is digging deeper into the results of the narrative reflection in order to break down the experience into more finite chunks in order to be able to more carefully think about the relationship of those chunks.

The evaluative reflection dimension is the point at which the reflector really begins to think about assessment, and how the experience being reflected upon worked. While Stevens suggests the first step as assessing the experience and the second as identifying and applying criteria, it seems more logical to first decide upon the criteria in order to have the necessary framework to make such an assessment. This dimension already seems a good place to bring back the percipient reflection to consider whether others would select the same criteria and evaluate the experience in the same way.

All in all, the emotional type of reflection is a sideboard of each of the other types, asking the reflector to intentionally consider any emotions raised (or lack thereof) in the actual experience being reflected upon, and then also to consider the emotions raised (or, again, lack thereof) during the reflection practice. What is most important to consider is the full person, including the intellectual, emotional, and spiritual, as sources of learning (Ramsey and Fitzgibbons, 2005), with each of these aspects contributing to the whole (Palmer, 1998, p. 4).

REFLECTION IN ENTREPRENEURSHIP EDUCATION

This type of reflective cycle is highly relevant for entrepreneurship education, and absolutely also relevant for the practice of entrepreneurship. One example is to consider the different uses of courses in which students are asked (in one fashion or another) to start a business. In many, if not most, schools, this is a capstone experience. Any reflection on the process would draw from both acquired theory and practice gained throughout the educational experience to date, as well as from accumulated life experiences. At Babson, our long-standing approach to introducing entrepreneurship to every undergraduate student is to have them work in teams to start a business in their very first year. This experience then grounds their learning for the rest of their time at Babson and ideally gives them a foundation for a type of learning approach for the rest of their lives.

How the "think" part of the equation works is our point of concern. In earlier work (Neck and Greene, 2011) we proposed three worlds of teaching entrepreneurship: the entrepreneur world (characteristics of an entrepreneur), the process world (the steps of new venture creation), and the cognition world (how do entrepreneurs think). While reflection as a teaching exercise or assignment has certainly been used in each of these worlds, also known as approaches, it would seem to have the strongest base in the world of cognition. The foundation of the research in this particular world can be traced through works looking at how "entrepreneurs" think in order to understand the *why* of the *what* that they do (Sarasvathy, 2008). The development of this line of reasoning can be seen in studies about biases and heuristics in strategic decision making (Bird, 1992) and perceptions of feasibility and desirability, along with planned behavior and self-efficacy (Krueger, 1993), cognitive-based constructs (Mitchell, 1994; Corbett, 2007), risk taking (Palich and Bagby, 1995), the relationship of this approach to pedagogy (Mitchell and Chesteen, 1995), entrepreneurial cognition (Busenitz and Lau, 1996), cognitive mechanisms including counterfactual thinking, attributional style, planning fallacies, and self-justification (Baron, 1998), cognitive errors such as overconfidence and the illusion of control (McGrath and MacMillan, 2000; Simon et al., 2000), heuristic-based logic (Alvarez and Busenitz, 2001), and the cross-culture impact of cognitive constructs (Mitchell, Busenitz et al., 2002; Mitchell, Smith et al., 2002).

This line of research on the cognitive approach is well thought out and well studied. However, the glaring question starts where the research starts: How do entrepreneurs think? This, of course, is where we part paths with some of this research, for our approach to teaching entrepreneurship is focused on the goal of teaching people to be entrepreneurial and to have the mindset and skillset to support entrepreneurial behaviors and activities. Reflection provides a pathway to increased self-awareness and understanding and is essential in achieving this goal – a goal which has the potential to change the nature of individual organizations, communities, economies, and societies.

Therefore, when we incorporate cognitive-based approaches, we consider the practice of reflection from the perspective of how people think – most relevantly, how people think entrepreneurially. This distinction is particularly important given the necessity of starting from a point of definition: What are we teaching? The world of the entrepreneur and the process world are largely based on the idea of entrepreneurship as starting a business, generally relegated to starting a small business. This approach diminishes the potential of entrepreneurship. Babson uses a broader definition. For one example, in designing the Goldman Sachs 10000 Small Businesses curriculum we definitely were inspired by Babson and used a model of entrepreneurship as a mindset and a skillset that can be used in all types of contexts.

REFLECTION ON AND IN PRACTICE

Our final framework is quite comprehensive and, in fact, which components are used and how they are used depend on the learning objectives and the students (Brockbank and McGill, 2007). Starting with a framework is just that, a start from which any instructor can combine as needed, depending on his or her goals. For example, if a learning objective is to "assess," then the analytical or evaluative categories may be useful. And so on.

The actual reflective assignments can also vary a great deal, by both subject matter and method, and several examples are presented in the teaching notes later in this book (Chapter 11). In general, the subject matter may be on an exercise or a longer (or shorter) experience. Methods may include:

- a reflection journal handed in to the instructor at specified times;
- a reflection "outtake" – asking the students to share a specific selection of their reflections (the choice may be at the discretion of the instructor or the student);
- assigning one of the framework categories to be reflected upon each day: Monday is narrative, Tuesday is emotion, and so on;
- using a mobile app to allow for in-the-moment reflection;
- developing a Twitter reflection assignment (on one hand, the 140-character restriction puts severe bounds on the reflection, but, on the other hand, the size limitation may be used to drive to the heart of any matter).

CONCLUSION

Reflection is one of the hardest things we ask our students to do. In entrepreneurship we know that we are trying to impart that mindset and skillset that they can use in any context for the rest of their lives. Taking the time to think about all of this is a critical component of entrepreneurship education – in balance with all the "doing."

One of the hardest things we have seen people struggle with in preparing to teach in new ways (as opposed to stand and deliver) is to let go of the power, in essence giving the student more responsibility for the learning (Ramsey and Fitzgibbons, 2005, p. 338). We do like to be seen as the experts, and yet, as with theory, sometimes the more invisible we are, the stronger the lesson. There is no doubt that teaching entrepreneurship as a method requires deep content knowledge as well as expert facilitation skills. Frameworks such as those presented in this chapter help students identify what is important and how the pieces fit together. That is critical learning.

Reflection also helps us keep entrepreneurship personal. After all, we teach people and they act entrepreneurially, in most cases starting and growing businesses. Dewey described the value of reflection as:

> a personal sharing in what is going on and the fact that the value of the reflection lies upon keeping one's self out of the data . . . Only gradually and with a widening of the area of vision through a growth of social sympathies does thinking develop to include what lies beyond our direct interests; a fact of great significance for education. (Dewey, 1916, p. 160)

REFERENCES

Alvarez, S., and Busenitz, L. 2001. The entrepreneurship of resource-based theory. *Journal of Management*, 27, 755–75.

Atkins, S., and Murphy, K. 1993. Reflection: A review of the literature. *Journal of Advanced Nursing*, 18(8), 1188–92.

Baron, R.A. 1998. Cognitive mechanisms in entrepreneurship: Why and when entrepreneurs think differently than other people. *Journal of Business Venturing*, 13(4), 275–94.

Bird, B.J. 1992. The operations in time: The emergence of the new venture. *Entrepreneurship: Theory and Practice*, 17(1), 11–20.

Boud, D., Keogh, R., and Walker, D. 1985. *Reflection: Turning Experience into Learning*. London: Kogan Page.

Bourdieu, P. [1980] 1990. *The Logic of Practice*. Stanford, CA: Stanford University Press. (Original work published in French.)

Boyd, E.M., and Fales, A.W. 1983. Reflective learning key to learning from experience. *Journal of Humanistic Psychology*, 23(2), 99–117.

Brockbank, A., and McGill, I. 2007. *Facilitating Reflective Learning in Higher Education*, 2nd edn. New York: McGraw-Hill and Open University Press.

Brookfield, S.D. 1987. *Developing Critical Thinkers: Challenging Adults to Explore Alternative Ways of Thinking and Acting*. San Francisco: Jossey-Bass.

Busenitz, L., and Lau, C. 1996. A cross-cultural cognitive model of new venture creation. *Entrepreneurship Theory and Practice*, 20(4), 25–39.

Cope, J. 2003. Entrepreneurial learning and critical reflection: Discontinuous events as triggers for "higher-level" learning. *Management Learning*, 34(4): 429–50.

Corbett, A.C. 2007. Learning asymmetries and the discovery of entrepreneurial opportunities. *Journal of Business Venturing*, 22(1), 97–118.

Dewey, J. 1916. *Democracy and Education: An Introduction to the Philosophy of Education*. A public domain book. Kindle.

Jordan, S. 2010. Learning to be surprised: How to foster reflective practice in a high-reliability context. *Management Learning*, 41(4), 391–413.

Keevers, L., and Treleaven, L. 2011. Organizing practices of reflection: A practice-based study. *Management Learning*, 42(5), 505–20.

Koole, S., Dornan, T., Aper, L., Scherpbier, A., Valcke, M., Cohen-Schotanus, J., and Derese, A. 2011. Factors confounding the assessment of reflection: A critical review. *BMC Medical Education*, 11(1), 104.

Korthagen, F.A.J. 2005. The organization in balance: Reflection and intuition as complementary processes. *Management Learning*, 36(3), 371–87.

Krueger, N. 1993. The impact of prior entrepreneurial exposure on perceptions of new venture feasibility and desirability. *Entrepreneurship: Theory and Practice*, 18(1), 5–21.

Mamede, S., and Schmidt, H.G. 2004. The structure of reflective practice in medicine. *Medical Education*, 38(12), 1302–08.

Marton, F. 1975. What does it take to learn? In N.J. Entwistle (ed.), *Strategies for Research and Development in Higher Education*. Amsterdam: Swets & Zeitlinger.

McGrath, R.G., and MacMillan, I. 2000. *The Entrepreneurial Mindset*. Boston, MA: Harvard Business School Press.

Mezirow, J., and Associates. 2000. *Learning as Transformation: Critical Perspectives on a Theory in Progress*. San Francisco: Jossey-Bass.

Mitchell, R.K. 1994. The composition, classification, and creation of new venture formation expertise. Dissertation, University of Utah, Salt Lake City.

Mitchell, R.K., and Chesteen, S.A. 1995. Enhancing entrepreneurial expertise: Experiential pedagogy and the entrepreneurial expert script. *Simulation and Gaming*, 26(3), 288–306.

Mitchell, R.K., Busenitz, L., and Lant, T. 2002. Toward a theory of entrepreneurial cognition: Rethinking the people side of entrepreneurship research. *Entrepreneurship Theory and Practice*, 27(2), 93–104.

Mitchell, R.K., Smith, J.B., Morse, E.A., Seawright, K.W., Peredo, A.M., and McKenzie, B. 2002. Are entrepreneurial cognitions universal? Assessing entrepreneurial cognitions across cultures. *Entrepreneurship Theory and Practice*, 26(4), 9–32.

Moon, J.A. 1999. *Reflection in Learning and Professional Development: Theory and Practice*. London: Kogan Page.

Neck, H. 2010. *Price-Babson SEE Reflective Practice Guide*. Wellesley, MA: Babson College.

Neck, H.M., and Greene, P.G. 2011. Entrepreneurship education: Known worlds and new frontiers. *Journal of Small Business Management*, 49(1), 55–70.

Palich, L.E., and Bagby, D.R. 1995. Using cognitive theory to explain entrepreneurial risk-taking: Challenging conventional wisdom. *Journal of Business Venturing*, 10(6), 425–38.

Palmer, P. 1998. *The Courage to Teach: Exploring the Inner Landscape of a Teacher's Life*. San Francisco: Jossey-Bass.

Procee, H. 2006. Reflection in education: A Kantian epistemology. *Educational Theory*, 56(3), 237–53.

Ramsey, V.J., and Fitzgibbons, D.E. 2005. Being in the classroom. *Journal of Management Education*, 29(2), 333–56.

Sarasvathy, S. 2008. *Effectuation: Elements of Entrepreneurial Expertise*. Cheltenham, UK and Northampton, MA, USA: Edward Elgar Publishing.

Schlossberg, N.K. 1981. A model of analyzing human adaption to transition. *Counseling Psychologist*, 9(2), 2–18.

Schön, D. 1983. *The Reflective Practitioner*. New York: Basic Books.
Schön, D. 1987. *Educating the Reflective Practitioner*. London: Jossey-Bass.
Schraw, G., and Dennison, R.S. 1994. Assessing metacognitive awareness. *Contemporary Educational Psychology*, 19(4), 460–75.
Simon, M., Houghton, S.M., and Aquino, K. 2000. Cognitive biases, risk perception, and venture formation: How individuals decide to start companies. *Journal of Business Venturing*, 15(2), 113–34.
Stockhausen, L. 2000. Teaching and learning the practice of nursing: Perspectives of registered nurse and undergraduate students of nursing. Unpublished Ph.D. thesis, University of Queensland, Brisbane, Australia.
Vince, R. 2002. Organizing reflection. *Management Learning*, 33(1), 63–78.
Whitehead, Alfred North. [1938] 1966. *Modes of Thought*. New York: Free Press.
Yanow, D., and Tsoukas, H. 2009. What is reflection-in-action? A phenomenological account. *Journal of Management Studies*, 46(8), 1339–64.

PART II

The practices of entrepreneurship education: the application

Part I detailed the theory behind the five practices of entrepreneurship. What follows in Chapters 7 through 11 is a series of classroom-based exercises that can be used to help students "practice the practices." The exercises range from simple to complex, original to borrowed, creative to analytical, playful to thoughtful, and short to long. Even though the exercises are organized by practice (play, empathy, creation, experimentation, and reflections), we also provide a table starting on page 314 that lists the various content areas each exercise relates to.

The teaching notes for the exercises were written by us and our colleagues at Babson College. Special thanks to our contributors: Matt Allen, Lakshmi Balachandra, Craig Benson, Dennis Ceru, Les Charm, Andrew Corbett, Caroline Daniels, Anne Donnellon, Elaine Eisenman, Sebastian Fixson, Mary Gale, Bradley George, Donna Kelley, Julian Lange, Edward Marram, Erik Noyes, Angelo Santinelli, Phyllis Schlesinger, Rosa Slegers, Yasuhiro Yamakawa, and Andrew Zacharakis.

7. Exercises to practice play

EXERCISE: PUZZLES AND QUILTS

AUTHORS: HEIDI NECK AND PATRICIA GREENE

Description

This exercise is an interactive challenge designed to help raise student awareness of the difference between managerial and entrepreneurial thinking. It also is a strong illustration of how to gain a better understanding of the impact of increasing degrees of uncertainty on the entrepreneurial process. Given the unprecedented level of uncertainty in business and entrepreneurship, students must learn how to navigate effectively in an increasingly uncertain world.

The exercise consists of students starting in one room with the task of completing a jigsaw puzzle. Students are systematically moved to another room, where they are asked to create a quilt from a selection of fabric pieces. The debrief explores jigsaw puzzles as managerial thinking and quilt making as entrepreneurial thinking. There is an optional debrief that includes leadership.

Usage Suggestions

This exercise works for all audiences, undergraduate, graduate, or practitioner. Ideally the exercise should be done on day one of a general entrepreneurship course as a way to set up how entrepreneurs think and the difference between entrepreneurial and managerial thinking.

Learning Objectives

- Experience the difference between managerial and entrepreneurial thinking.
- Engage with conditions of uncertainty and ambiguity.
- Illustrate how entrepreneurs think.

Materials List

- Jigsaw puzzles (one per group, 300 pieces).
- Fabric remnants (approximately six pieces per person).
- Two rooms (one with tables equal to number of groups and one empty).

Pre-Work Required by Students

None.

Theoretical Foundations

Neck, H.M. 2011. Cognitive ambidexterity: The underlying mental model of the entrepreneurial leader. In D. Greenberg, K. McKone-Sweet, and H.J. Wilson (eds.), *The New Entrepreneurial Leader: Developing Leaders Who Will Shape Social and Economic Opportunities* (pp. 24–42). San Francisco: Berrett-Koehler.

Sarasvathy, S. 2008. *Effectuation: Elements of Entrepreneurial Expertise.* Cheltenham, UK and Northampton, MA, USA: Edward Elgar Publishing.

Schlesinger, L., and Kieffer, C. 2012. *Just Start.* Cambridge, MA: Harvard Business School Press.

Time Plan (60–80 minutes)

The exercise begins in a room with tables for each team. Students are asked to clear their table in preparation. The second room required is a large empty space. A table (fairly long) is placed in front of this room or space, and fabric pieces are piled on the table. The piles should be messy, with all the fabrics mixed up (not sorted by size, color, or any other dimension).

Puzzle time   0:00–0:05 (5 minutes)

Divide students into groups of five to seven and give them the following directions: "Your task is quite easy but you don't have a lot of time. Your goal is to put together the puzzle that is sitting on the table as fast as you possibly can. It's only 300 pieces! You can do it. Get started. You are being timed. Don't worry; there are no cameras in the room!"

Random pull-out to quilting room   0:05–0:30 (25 minutes)

Pull students at random from the puzzle room, one at a time, asking for one volunteer from each group. The individual volunteered or selected from each group is taken to the empty room with the table of fabric.

At the fabric table the first group is told: "Your new task is quite easy but you don't have a lot of time. You are now designated quilt leaders. Your goal is to construct a design for a quilt. Choose six pieces of fabric from the table – no more and no less. Select an area in the room and begin to construct a quilt. You may not come back to the table for more or different fabric. No sewing is required. Simply place your fabric on the ground as if you were going to sew patches of fabric together to create the quilt. The goal is to build the best quilt you possibly can. Others will join you a bit later. Have fun!"

Note: Each quilt leader should choose six pieces of fabric, and each will begin his or her own quilt in different areas of the room.

Subsequent "volunteers" are taken out of the puzzle rooms at two- to three-minute intervals and instructed to take six pieces of fabric and join any quilt in progress that interests them. "Your new task is quite easy but you don't have a lot of time. Join one of the groups in the room. You do *not* have to stay with the team members from your puzzle group. Your goal is to construct a design for a quilt. Choose six pieces of fabric from the table – no more and no less. Next, join a group to help them build the best quilt you can. You may not exchange fabric once you choose. No sewing is required. Simply place your fabric on the ground as if you were going to sew patches of fabric together to create the quilt. Have fun!"

When all individuals are out of the puzzle room and in the quilt room, allow two more minutes to complete the quilts.

Debrief 0:30–1:00 (30 minutes)
The debrief may take place inside the quilt room or back in the classroom depending on group size. If debriefing inside the quilt room, have each quilt leader describe how the design of the quilt emerged. If debriefing outside the quilt room, give students time to walk through the quilt room to study all of the quilt designs before leaving the room.

Begin with questions:

● How many preferred the puzzle? Why?
● How many preferred the quilt? Why?

Focus on quilts:

● Ask the leaders about how the design came to be.
● Ask team members why they joined one team versus another.
● How did it feel moving from puzzle to quilts?
● What type of thinking was required for each part of the exercise?

Summary   At this time, it's important to introduce the concepts of puzzle as managerial thinking and quilts as entrepreneurial thinking.

Puzzle as managerial thinking:

- The goal is well defined (the puzzle picture is typically on the outside of the box).
- Determine resources to achieve the goal (puzzle pieces).
- Create a plan (put pieces in piles by color, and start with the edges).
- Execute the plan (edges first).
- Measure progress along the way.
- Goal achieved – the puzzle looks just like the picture on the front of the box! Well done!

Quilt as entrepreneurial thinking:

- Entrepreneurs start with what they have rather than what they need (fabric pieces).
- When entrepreneurs are not sure what to do their only choice is to act (pick a group and get to work).
- The design of the quilt emerges over time because it's difficult to plan (the quilt keeps changing every time a new person enters the group and the environment and resources change).
- You never really know when it's quite finished.
- Creating something new requires iteration rather than linear problem solving.

Optional leadership debrief   1:00–1:20 (20 minutes)
- What is leadership? (Ask them to write down their definition.)
- How did you "see" leadership around you? (Call on several different quilt groups.)
- How did you "see" followership?
- Who were the assigned leaders?
- Did the rest of you know there were assigned leaders?
- Pick an assigned leader and ask that person to describe his or her experience.
- When and how do you decide whether to lead or follow?
- What is the difference between leadership, management, and entrepreneurship?
- What is entrepreneurial leadership?

Key Takeaways

- Under conditions of extreme uncertainty the only choice is action.
- One form of thinking (entrepreneurial or managerial) is not necessarily better than the other, yet it is important to understand the environmental context. If the skills for completing a jigsaw puzzle (managerial thinking) are used to solve a complicated problem in an uncertain environment, students are likely to run into one roadblock after another. However, if students can get more comfortable with quilt making (entrepreneurial thinking), then they may be able to navigate the terrain of entrepreneurship with greater aptitude.
- Action trumps planning in uncertain environments.

Teaching Tips

It is preferable *not* to refer to the exercise as the "quilt exercise" prior to conducting the exercise, as it rather gives away the punch line. Pacing is very important. As soon as the quilt leaders have placed their fabric on the ground, volunteers should be pulled out of the puzzle room approximately every three minutes. Fast pace is much better than a slow pace.

Attribution

The exercise is adapted from Saras Sarasvathy's crazy quilt principle within her work on effectual entrepreneurship.

EXERCISE: BUILDING THE CULTURE OF YOUR BUSINESS WITH *THE SIMS*

AUTHOR: PATRICIA GREENE

Description

By the time most enterprise founders start thinking about ensuring a healthy culture in their business, it is usually too late. The culture has already emerged and is not always the most conducive to the health of the founder and employees, or even the enterprise itself. The culture of the enterprise emerges from the mind, values, and practices of the founder(s) while the business is being created, a time when the founder generally places more priority on the creation of economic value than the creation of culture. This exercise is based on a combination of organization and entrepreneurship theory and uses an off-the-shelf computer game, *The Sims: Open for Business*™, to investigate the core values, assumptions, interpretations, and approaches that combine to define the culture of a new venture. The students are assigned to play the game for a minimum of two hours outside of class, with no introduction given around the concept of culture. The heart of the exercise is the in-class debrief (including viewing the game), which reveals the culture that was created, what it means for all stakeholders, and what actions could be taken to adjust that culture.

Usage Suggestions

This content of the exercise works for all audiences, undergraduate, graduate, executive, or practitioner. The delivery requires that the students have access to the game and are able to play it before the discussion. The exercise lends itself well to online courses, as the debrief and illustration can also be done online, preferably in a synchronous mode, although asynchronous will work too. The exercise works best when each student is able to log on to his or her game for the debrief. This exercise is positioned in the course when emphasis is on resources. Culture is presented as a resource that can either add to or detract from the value of the company.

Learning Objectives

- Use and explain the critical interdisciplinary definitions related to organizational culture and entrepreneurship.
- Describe the relationship between organizational culture, structure, and leadership.

- Evaluate personal approaches to a professional worklife.
- Design and assess an emerging organizational culture.
- Critically evaluate the approaches to the intentional creation of organizational culture.

Materials List

Video game: *The Sims* and the expansion packet *The Sims: Open for Business*™.

Pre-Work Required by Students

Play *The Sims: Open for Business*™ for a minimum of two hours.

Suggested assigned reading:

Schein, Edgar H. 2010. *Organizational Culture and Leadership*, Vol. 2, Chapters 1 and 11. Wiley.com.

Theoretical Foundations

Barney, J.B. 1986. Organizational culture: Can it be a source of sustainable competitive advantage? *Academy of Management Review*, 11, 656–65.
Brush, C.G., Greene, P.G., and Hart, M.M. 2001. From initial idea to unique advantage: The entrepreneurial challenge of constructing a resource base. *Academy of Management Executive*, 15(1), 64–78.
Cameron, K.S., and Quinn, R.R. 1999. *Diagnosing and Changing Organizational Culture: Based on the Competing Values Framework*, Chapters 2 and 3 only. Reading, MA: Addison-Wesley.
Schein, E. 1983. The role of the founder in the creation of organizational culture.
Stinchcombe, A.L. 1965. Social structure and organizations. In J.G. March (ed.), *Handbook of Organizations* (pp. 142–93). Chicago: Rand-McNally.

Time Plan (90 minutes)

This 90-minute exercise can be adapted to fit various time schedules, including an entire class. Prior to the exercise the students would have been told to play the game for two hours. No other instructions are given. In this way, playing the game provides a shared experience and serves as the live case for the discussion.

Step 1 (Introduction)   0:00–0:10 (10 minutes)
Ask the students to open their laptops and log on to their games. Each game should open at the point at which the student left the game. The opening or warm-up questions should be about just playing the game:

- How many of you had played some version of *The Sims* before? Anyone played this particular expansion version?
- How was it? Did you enjoy it? If so, why? If not, why?
- Were there any particular challenges?
- Where there any particular surprises?
- How long did you actually play? (Probe for who played the longest and why.)

Step 2   0:10–0:40 (30 minutes)
Divide students into groups of five to six and give them the following directions: "Please select a scribe and a reporter to first capture the themes of your work and then be ready to report out to the full class on your work. First, individually, each write down the answer to this question: What is the culture of the business you created – and how can you tell? You have five minutes for this individual work. After five minutes, and I'll tell you when the time is up, we'll switch to working with your team.

1. First, each student please share with your group the business you created.
2. Second, as a group create your list of criteria that create an organizational culture.
3. Third, please describe the impact of how people will carry out work given the culture you have created.

Step 3 (First report out and discussion)   0:40–1:10 (30 minutes)
Start with the first table and have the reporter share their top two criteria, along with an explanation and illustration of each. Then ask each table to add two criteria to the ones already listed. If desired, you can take a hand count at the end to establish what was considered as most important, and so on. The board map should match the theoretical criteria of your choice. For the purposes of this teaching note the primary source is Schein (1983) and focuses on the basic underlying assumptions around which cultural paradigms form. Examples include:

- The organization's relationship to its environment: Is recycling important?
- The nature of reality and truth: How important is time?

- The nature of human nature: how employees (insiders) are treated and how customers (outsiders) are treated.
- The nature of human activity: the physical design of the employee break room.
- The nature of human relationships: Is the focus on competition or cooperation?

Summary and close 1:10–1:30 (20 minutes)

Ask the students to again work individually and list the three things they would keep about their culture and the three things they would change, along with how they would implement that change. Lead the closing discussion in such a way that the students discover:

1. What types of cultural approaches are common across most businesses?
2. What is the role of fit between the founder, the company, and the environment in creating culture?
3. How does culture become a positive resource for your business?

Key Takeaways

- The importance of intentionally creating organizational culture during firm emergence.
- Organizational culture can be a positive or negative firm resource.
- Organizational culture needs to be a fit between the founder, the firm, and the environment.

Teaching Tips

The game generally has to be ordered online, so you need to allow students time to order and receive it. The ideal experience is for the classroom to have wireless internet access and for each student to have a laptop. However, if teaching students with no access to computers or ability to buy the game, the instructor can lead the class in playing the game as a group, with one computer and the screen projected on the wall.

EXERCISE: RAINMAKERS

AUTHOR: HEIDI NECK

Description

How do you make rain inside a room? This is the opening question for a playful, kinesthetic exercise that can help students begin to think more creatively and collaborate as a group. In a round circle of 15 or more, participants work together to create the sound of light rain that then escalates to a powerful storm and back to light rain.

Usage Suggestions

This exercise works for all audiences, undergraduate, graduate, and executive. The exercise is best positioned at the start of a session or a class as a non-traditional opener.

Learning Objectives

- Break the ice and build energy in a classroom setting.
- Encourage students to think more creatively when problem-solving.
- Feel how movement can be an active component of the learning process.

Materials List

None.

Pre-Work Required by Students

None.

Theoretical Foundations

Gardner, H. 2011. *Frames of Mind: The Theory of Multiple Intelligences*. New York: Basic Books.

Time Plan (15 minutes)

Exercise   0:00–0:08 (8 minutes)
The instructor should begin with the following challenge: "If we wanted to
make it rain in this classroom right now, how could this be accomplished?"
Students will offer the more obvious solutions such as: light a fire so the
sprinkler system will go off; bring in a bucket of water and throw it up in
the air; shake a closed bottle of carbonated water and then open it. Note
that many of these solutions are individual based, and they are neither
realistic nor innovative.

When there are no more ideas, ask the students to form a circle (shoulder to shoulder) in the room and announce the following: "We are going
to make rain together as a group. Only do what the person to your right
is doing and don't start until the person on your right starts." The "rain"
is made during a series of seven rounds. The instructor begins each round,
and then the person to the left will do exactly as the instructor does. The
rounds flow into one another; there is never a break in the flow of making
the rain.

- Round 1: rubbing hands together. The instructor begins by
  rubbing his or her hands together palm to palm. The person on the
  immediate left should immediately follow. Eventually the entire
  group will be rubbing their hands together. When hand rubbing
  reaches the person to the immediate right of the instructor, it's time
  for round 2.
- Round 2: snaps. While everyone is still rubbing their hands together
  the instructor then begins snapping his or her fingers of both hands.
  The person on the left should immediately follow. Eventually the
  entire group will move from rubbing hands to snapping fingers.
  When the snapping of fingers reaches the person to the immediate
  right of the instructor, it's time for round 3.
- Round 3: slapping hands on thighs. Repeat the format of the previous rounds. Transition to round 4 when thigh slapping reaches the
  person to the instructor's immediate right.
- Round 4: stomping feet while slapping hands on thighs. The storm is
  at its peak during this round. Repeat the format of previous rounds.
- Round 5: return to slapping hands on thighs. Repeat the format of
  the previous rounds.
- Round 6: snaps return, and the storm begins to subside. Repeat the
  format of the previous rounds.
- Round 7: rub hands together so the light rain returns, and then end.
  Repeat the format of the previous rounds.

Congratulate the students for making rain and creating a storm and initiate a round of applause.

Debrief   0:08–0:15 (7 minutes)
The following questions are suggested for debriefing:

- When I asked the question about creating rain, why did your answers not consider "sound" or other ways to create rain?
- What does this mean for how you think about creating opportunities? Problem solving?
- What was your reaction when I asked you to get into a circle?
- How did you feel before, during, and after the exercise?

Key Takeaways

- Our frames of reference are the starting point for problem solving and creating, yet these frames are limiting.
- There is usually uncertainty associated with asking students to get into a circle, but through collaboration this uncertainty is diminished and something completely unexpected is created.
- Entrepreneurship requires action. Simply moving your body can have an immediate impact on emotions, motivation, and confidence to continue.

Teaching Tips

Here are a few tips to ensure a true rainmaking experience:

- Every round must flow into the next without stopping.
- The instructor sets the tone for each round because he or she is the first to go. For example, it's important to slap hands on thighs rather hard to get the sound needed. The same can be said for stomping.
- Students have a tendency to want to all start rubbing their hands together when the first person starts. It's important that each person waits to start (or change) until the person to his or her right starts or changes. The instructor may have to start, stop, and restart in the first round to make the point regarding who does what activity when.

The following YouTube video illustrates the power of the exercise: http://www.youtube.com/watch?v=LKDGCgXtETc.

Attribution

This exercise has been used by teachers of all levels, though it's not clear who created the exercise. See http://www.teampedia.net/wiki/index.php?title=Make_it_Rain.

EXERCISE: IMPROVISATION FOR CREATIVITY

AUTHOR: LAKSHMI BALACHANDRA

Description

This series of three short improvisational exercises offers students the opportunity to identify personal limitations to idea generation and reflect on situations where creativity may have been stifled. Students will consider their personal abilities and reactions to their improvisational abilities, as well as approaches to incorporate improvisational thinking in entrepreneurial endeavors. The overall goal is to demonstrate how students can develop an entrepreneurial mindset through improvisation. Such exercises are routinely used for developing improvisational actors as well as for pre-show warm-ups for the actors. This methodology was created in the 1960s and remains the standard by which individuals learn to improvise. Improvisation is an important component of the entrepreneurship method because idea generation and the ability to incorporate relevant, timely information are critical skills for developing new ventures that will not only survive but thrive.

Usage Suggestions

These exercises work for all audiences, undergraduate, graduate, or practitioner. It is particularly relevant for new venture creation courses, entrepreneurial creativity and/or leadership courses, entrepreneurship bootcamps, and workshops.

Learning Objectives

- Cultivate an entrepreneurial mindset.
- Recognize limitations of entrepreneurial thinking (what holds one back).
- Practice improvisation for idea generation and creativity.

Materials List

None.

Pre-Work Required by Students

The optional readings below may be used for pre-work or post-work, depending on the audience.

Theoretical Foundations

Spolin, V. 1959. *Improvisation for the Theater: A Handbook of Teaching and Directing Techniques.* Evanston, IL: Northwestern University Press.

Johnstone, K. 1999. *Impro for Storytellers.* New York: Routledge/Theatre Arts Books.

Hmieleski, K.M., and Corbett, A.C. 2008. The contrasting interaction effects of improvisational behavior with entrepreneurial self-efficacy on new venture performance and entrepreneur work satisfaction. *Journal of Business Venturing,* 23(4), 482–96.

Neck, H.M. 2010. Idea generation. In B. Bygrave and A. Zacharakis (eds.), *Portable MBA in Entrepreneurship* (pp. 27–52). Hoboken, NJ: Wiley.

Balachandra, L., and Wheeler, M. 2006. What negotiators can learn from improv comedy. *Negotiation,* 9, 1–3.

Time Plan (1 hour)

This exercise can be extended to longer sessions so that students can begin brainstorming entrepreneurial ventures. For the purposes of an initial introduction to improvisation, this teaching note has been written so that the exercise requires at least 60 minutes.

Introduction 0:00–0:05 (5 minutes)

Begin the exercise by introducing the concept of improvisation: Ask students generally if they know what improvisation means. Opening questions for the discussion can include:

- What does improvisation mean to you?
- Where have you seen improvisation?
- Has anyone performed improvisation? Seen it performed?

Overview 0:05–0:15 (10 minutes)

Explain how the students will learn the basics of improvisation and see how they could apply it to entrepreneurship, in particular idea generation and creating new ventures. The instructor can show examples of comedy improvisation performance (either live or through video clips from YouTube. Some good short examples include scenes from the ABC show *Whose Line Is It Anyway?* An example clip can be found at http://www.youtube.com/watch?v=Qd8bvNW9_h4). After sharing an example, discuss how performing improvisation can be learned: there are lessons offered for comedy improvisation and improvisational acting performance in improv theaters worldwide. An established framework exists to learn how to improvise. For this class, improvisation equals thinking on your feet. They will now be "in" an improv classroom, and every improvisation theater class begins with warm-ups. In order to think on their feet, they have to get up on their feet.

Warm-up 1   0:15–0:20 (5 minutes)

- Tell them to begin walking around the classroom and to observe every single object in the room.
- Then tell them to point at objects as they walk past them.
- As they point at each object they are to say what it is out loud – only they cannot call it what it actually is. They are to label it something it is *not*. And they are to do it quickly. Provide a quick example by pointing to an object in the room like the board and then say out loud "dog," and then point at another object like the desk and call it "potato" or whatever comes to mind.

After one to two minutes of them walking and pointing and labeling out loud, ask them to stop and be silent wherever they are for a group discussion.

When they stop, have them discuss how the experience of labeling objects was for them. Try to push them to explain what they were feeling. Some of the following questions can be used for this debrief:

- How was this experience?
- Did you find this exercise difficult to do? Why?

Summary of warm-up 1 Students should experience and be able to articulate:

- how difficult it is to break away from known "answers";
- how frequently they can get stuck in known patterns of thinking;
- the ease with which they start creating patterns with a known grouping (e.g. eggplant, cucumber, tomato, lettuce), which is a way to make the experience easier (get the "right" answer) as opposed to pushing and fostering creativity;
- the need for students to want to be in control, rather than searching for newness or playing;
- feeling the sense of awkwardness in saying the "wrong" label out

loud, but having others around doing a similar activity makes the exercise less awkward;

• how easy it can be just to listen to others and follow their answers rather than coming up with their own new idea.

Warm-up 2   0:20–0:25 (5 minutes)

• Tell them to begin walking around the classroom again.
• When they come up to another student, they are to point at another student and name an animal, any animal that comes to mind, e.g. two students face each other and one points at the other and says "horse."
• Then tell them that the student who has been pointed at and labeled with a type of animal has to make the sound of the animal. If they do not know what sound the animal makes, they are to make it up and make some sort of sound.
• Then they switch, and the student who just produced the animal sound – in this example, the horse sounds – points at the first student and names an animal, e.g. "cat." This student then makes the sounds of whatever animal he or she was given.
• Once the interaction is completed, and both students in the pair have completed their animal sounds, they are to find new partners and repeat the warm-up exercise with two or three other students.

After two to three minutes of animal sounds, ask them to stop and be silent wherever they are for a group discussion.

Have them discuss how the experience of making animal sounds was for them. Try to push them again to explain what they were feeling. Some of the following questions can be used for this debrief:

• How was this experience?
• Did you find this exercise difficult to do? Why?

Summary of warm-up 2 Students should experience and be able to articulate:

• feeling a great sense of awkwardness – they are doing something they would normally be comfortable doing with children, but typically have never done in a classroom of adults or peers;
• not knowing the right "answer" or sound a particular animal makes, they would feel very frustrated, and then forget the instruction they were given to just make it up;

- once again, the ease with which they follow patterns – patterns offer a way to make the exercise "easier," as they offer a means to come up with an answer or a label quickly rather than pushing creativity;
- how difficult it is for them to have no control as to what they have to do, rather than stepping back, enjoying the ambiguity, and searching for newness or playing;
- the fear they have of being "foolish" in a professional setting, how they do not want to be embarrassed by acting silly in front of others, and, in addition, the fear of feeling guilty, foolish, or rude for labeling others as certain types of animals with distinct connotations;
- this fear leads to self-judging and/or editing before they label their peer with an animal or before making the corresponding animal sound.

Warm-up 3   0:25–0:35 (10 minutes)

- Tell them to form groups of four wherever they are in the room.
- Then instruct them to play a game of word association, where anyone can go first, say a word, whatever word comes to mind.
- The person to the left listens to the word and then says a word that comes to mind based on the word he or she just heard.
- They continue in this way until you stop them, and they are to go as fast as they can (tell them to listen for further instruction).
- Once they get started, let them go for a minute or so, and then very loudly instruct them to "Switch directions!"

After another one to two minutes of word association, ask them to stop and be silent. You can have them return to their seats at this point or have them stay where they are for the final group discussion.

Now have them discuss how the word association experience was for them. Most will say this was easier to do, as they were in a group setting. So push them to explain what was happening rather than what they were feeling. Some of the following questions can be used for this debrief:

- How was this experience? If this was easier than the last two warm-ups, why?
- If you found this exercise more difficult than the last two, why?
- What happened when you were told to change directions? Why did this happen?

Summary of warm-up 3 Students should experience and be able to articulate:

- the ease again they experienced of getting into routines or patterns – how much they wanted to "control" the situation and outcomes;
- how much they were trying to be clever, or funny, rather than just coming up with any word that came to mind and following the exercise;
- typically they do not enjoy the ambiguity and opportunity to play and explore newness;
- self-judging occurs again, they feel limited in the direction for the exercise, and what words they allow themselves to say owing to their need to feel included or pressure to continue established patterns rather than pushing creativity and undefined randomness;
- students typically are *not* listening to the last word they just heard, and instead they focus on the words that people two ahead of them in the exercise are saying, as this way they can plan their response (this is highlighted with the change directions instruction).

Discussion   0:35–1:00 (25 minutes)
Once the students return to their seats, have them form groups of three to four and discuss what might be preventing their idea generation efforts related to initial new venture concepts. They should explore what holds them back when considering what they might do. Have them discuss the specific difficulties they experienced personally during the improvisation exercises and how they might get past these limitations to develop a more entrepreneurial mindset. Have a member of each group report out one recommendation for fostering creativity through improvisation. A closing discussion should include how to incorporate improvisation in their idea generation practices.

Key Takeaways

- How to incorporate improvisation to develop an entrepreneurial mindset: being quick on your feet and adapting or reacting rather than planning and pre-judging.
- Identifying and recognizing personal limitations to entrepreneurial thinking (why students are held back from creativity in idea generation, what their personal pitfalls are).
- How to develop an entrepreneurial mindset by incorporating tenets of fast and free thinking through improvisation for idea generation and creativity.

Teaching Tips

It is important to keep the warm-up exercises moving fast. It might be helpful to tell the students before they begin the exercises that they will feel really uncomfortable, but feeling uncomfortable is the point of the exercise. In the debrief discussions, some students will genuinely enjoy the exercises and will say they found nothing in them difficult. Asking for a show of hands of those who found the exercise difficult to do first is often a better way to begin the debrief, before asking about how they found the experience (in case the students who enjoyed the exercises stifle the discussion). In warm-up 3 it is very helpful to move around the room encouraging groups to speed up their words so that there are no long pauses. It is important for them to think quickly and see how to come up with new ideas rather than thinking or planning and judging their ideas before they see where the new ideas can take them.

Attribution

These exercises are based on foundational exercises used in improvisational training, widely taught in improvisational theater courses worldwide.

EXERCISE: MARSHMALLOW TOWER

AUTHOR: BRADLEY GEORGE

Description

Groups of students compete to see who can build the tallest freestanding structure supporting a marshmallow on top out of 20 pieces of spaghetti, three feet of tape and three feet of string. This exercise is used to illustrate that under conditions of uncertainty, entrepreneurs rely on experimentation and iterative learning as a means to discover information about their environment. Students are often taught and are familiar with traditional methods of planning and analysis, which work well in stable environments where the future is likely to be similar to the present. In these cases the future is fairly well known and understood. While some uncertainty exists, it can be categorized as risk. However, if the future is unknowable, the only way to learn what may work is through experimentation. Typically many of the students spend a large portion of their time designing and planning the structure and only start to build it at the end to find out at the last moment that it cannot support the weight of the marshmallow, and they then go into "crisis" mode. The teams that perform the best are usually those that just start experimenting, learning what works and then modifying their tower based on what they learn. If you are using lean start-up concepts it is also a good way to illustrate the value of market tests.

Usage Suggestions

This exercise works for all audiences, undergraduate, graduate, executive, or practitioner. It is appropriate for new venture creation courses, entrepreneurship bootcamps, or workshops. The session is best positioned early in the course for discussions around planning versus action.

Learning Objectives

- Practice and learn the concepts of effectual versus causal logic.
- Illustrate when planning is appropriate versus action.
- Employ experimentation techniques.

Materials List

- Create a kit for each team (about four people per team), with each kit containing 20 sticks of spaghetti, one yard of masking tape, one yard of string, and one marshmallow. These ingredients should be placed into a paper lunch bag or manila envelope (excluding the masking tape), which simplifies distribution and hides the contents, maximizing the element of surprise. The masking tape should be hung on the desks or on the wall for distribution, as putting it in the bags generally causes problems.
- Ensure that you use uncooked spaghetti. Avoid spaghettini, as it is too thin and breaks easily. Fettuccine is too thick.
- Include string that can be easily broken by hand. If the string is thick, include scissors in your kit.
- Use standard-size marshmallows that measure about 1.5 inches across. Avoid mini or jumbo marshmallows. Also avoid stale marshmallows – you want squishy marshmallows that give the impression of lightness.
- You will also need a measuring tape and a stopwatch or countdown application.
- Having a countdown application projected on the screen where they can see the time counting down is preferred (use an online stopwatch on your computer if convenient).

Pre-Work Required by Students

None.

Theoretical Foundations

Kiefer, C.F., and Schlesinger, L.A. 2010. *Action Trumps Everything: Creating What You Want in an Uncertain World.* Duxbury, MA: Black Ink Press.

Ries, E. 2011. *The Lean Startup: How Today's Entrepreneurs Use Continuous Innovation to Create Radically Successful Businesses.* New York: Crown Business.

Sarasvathy, S.D. 2001. Causation and effectuation: Towards a theoretical shift from economic inevitability to entrepreneurial contingency. *Academy of Management Review,* 26(2), 243–88.

Time Plan (45 minutes)

Step 1   0:00–0:05 (5 minutes)
Hand out the kits to each of the teams. Introduce the challenge. Be clear about the goals and rules of the Marshmallow Challenge. It is

also helpful to tell them that this has been done by tens of thousands of people around the world from children to CEOs. The rules and goals are as follows.

Goal Build the tallest *freestanding* structure: The winning team is the one that has the tallest structure measured from the table top surface to the top of the marshmallow. That means the structure cannot be suspended from a higher structure, like a chair, ceiling, or chandelier.

Rules

- The *entire* marshmallow must be on top: The entire marshmallow needs to be on the top of the structure. Cutting or eating part of the marshmallow disqualifies the team.
- Use as much or as little of the kit as you choose: The team can use as many or as few of the 20 spaghetti sticks, and as much or as little of the string or tape, as they choose. The team cannot use the paper bag as part of their structure.
- Break up the spaghetti, string, or tape if you choose: Teams are free to break the spaghetti or cut up the tape and string to create new structures.
- The challenge lasts 18 minutes: Teams cannot hold on to the structure when the time runs out. Those touching or supporting the structure at the end of the exercise will be disqualified.

Ensure everyone understands the rules: Don't worry about repeating the rules too many times. Repeat them at least three times. Ask if anyone has any questions before starting; a good idea is to provide a handout with the instructions in the kit.

Step 2   0:05–0:25 (20 minutes)
Begin the challenge by starting the clock.

- Walk around the room and note the process that different teams are using.
- Remind the teams of the time: Increase the reminders as time gets shorter (for example, you might remind them at 9 minutes, 5 minutes, 3 minutes, 2 minutes, 1 minute, 30 seconds and then a 10-second countdown.
- Call out how the teams are doing: Let the entire group know how teams are progressing. Build a friendly rivalry and encourage people to look around.

- Remind the teams that holders will be disqualified: Several teams will have the powerful desire to hold on to their structure at the end, usually because the marshmallow, which they just placed on to their structure moments before, is causing the structure to buckle. The winning structure needs to be stable.

Step 3   0:25–0:30 (5 minutes)
After the clock runs out, ask everyone in the room to sit down so everyone can see the structures. Usually only about half the teams will have a standing structure.

- Measure the structures: From the shortest standing structure to the tallest, measure and call out the heights. If you're documenting the challenge, have someone record the heights.
- Identify the winning team: Ensure they get a standing ovation and a prize (if you've offered one).

Step 4   0:30–0:45 (15 minutes)
Start by asking some of the teams about the process they used to go about building their structures. You can choose based on what you observed during the challenge. You will generally notice as you go around the room that teams that spend most of their time planning will fail to have a standing structure in the end. Those who experiment and learn through trial and error tend to do much better. It is usually best to start with some of the teams whose structures collapsed.

- What process did you use in building your structure?
    - Focus on whether they spent a lot of time planning and drawing their structure or trial and error.
- What went wrong?
    - This often highlights issues around unknown factors such as how much weight the spaghetti could support or how much the marshmallow weighed relative to the structure.
- How did you deal with that?
    - This will often point out the fact that extensive planning leaves little time for adjusting and learning from experience and results in a "crisis."

Repeat this with one or more of the more successful groups and try to capture differences and commonalities between them.

You can draw comparisons to various other groups who have done this challenge. The creator of the challenge, Tom Wujec, has performed this challenge numerous times with a variety of different groups and has found the following:

- The best performers tend to be engineers (good thing). They understand structures and stresses, so this is a more certain environment for them.
- The worst performers tend to be recent business school graduates. They are in a very uncertain environment given limited knowledge about structures. However, they have typically been taught to plan, plan, plan. They spend most of their time planning and then try to build the structure at the last minute. When they put the marshmallow on top it weighs much more than they anticipated and the structure collapses, creating a crisis.
- After engineers, the best performers are recent kindergarten graduates. They are also in an uncertain environment, but they tend to experiment to see what works, learn from that, and build off it to create much more interesting structures.

Emphasize the importance of market tests and experimentation when entering a new, unknown environment. If your students are already working on business ideas, this can be a good place to have them try to think about low-cost ways they could experiment with their concept before making large investments.

As an alternative debrief, you can show the TED talk by the creator of this exercise by going to www.marshmallowchallenge.com.

Key Takeaways

- In an unknown environment, it is better to take action than to plan.
- Learning from small experiments and trials can produce more unique solutions – particularly if the future cannot be predicted.
- Failure can provide important insights to improving products or services.

Teaching Tips

Be very clear about the goals and rules of the challenge. Generally, you'll want to repeat them three times and reinforce them visually. In almost every challenge, there is at least one team who will want to cheat or bend the rules in their favor. The clearer you are about the rules the better the results.

Attribution

This exercise was originally developed by Tom Wujec for teaching collaborative design. His website containing the instructions, a TED talk about the exercise, and other supporting material can be found at http://marshmallowchallenge.com.

EXERCISE: AIRPLANE CONTEST

AUTHOR: BRADLEY GEORGE

Description

Rocket pitches or elevator pitches are often the first opportunity for an entrepreneur to convince potential investors that they have an idea that represents a profitable opportunity. These are often only one- to five-minute presentations, but they can have a significant impact on the entrepreneur's ability to attract investors as well as other potential stakeholders. This can be particularly true in the early stages of a venture before the entrepreneur has a viable product, and he or she has to quickly convince potential stakeholders of his or her vision and the potential of the idea. Entrepreneurs often think that their idea is the most important aspect of the pitch, but studies have shown that U.S. venture capitalists consider personal characteristics such as the entrepreneur's ability to articulate his or her venture to be critical in determining whether or not they will reject an entrepreneur's plan.

In this exercise, students design a paper airplane that must be capable of carrying a predetermined amount of currency in the form of coins. The airplanes will compete in two categories – time that the plane can stay aloft and the distance it can travel. However, students pitch their design to their classmates (the investors) in an effort to convince them their design is the best before the contest takes place. The exercise has worked well for illustrating the importance of a good pitch and helps students to better understand what constitutes a good pitch from an investor's perspective.

Usage Suggestions

This exercise works with both undergraduate and graduate students. It is appropriate for new venture creation courses, entrepreneurship boot-camps, or workshops. The session is best positioned after students have identified a venture concept, project, or family or corporate initiative to pursue and are preparing for an elevator speech or rocket pitch type presentation. Technology entrepreneurship or innovation classes are also appropriate.

Learning Objectives

- Practice pitching new concepts.
- Critique pitches for new concepts.

- Understand the importance of pitch versus idea.
- Simulate prototype development and feasibility testing.

Materials List

Provide students with paper for their airplanes in order to maintain a
standard paper type and weight. Alternatively, you can leave this open
to interpretation as a means of encouraging greater creativity among
the teams. You will need a tape measure and a stopwatch for the actual
competition.

Pre-Work Required by Students

Students are to be given the following instructions in the class period prior
to running the exercise: "You are to design and create a new paper airplane capable of keeping one U.S. dollar of coins aloft for as long (time)
as possible while simultaneously transporting the coins as far (distance) as
possible. The assignment is as follows:

1. You may work individually or in a group of up to four students; the
   only group-related implication is that your airplane design must use
   the same number of standard size sheets as the number of people in the
   group (for example, a group of four must create an airplane that uses
   four sheets of paper in its design).
2. Your plane must be designed to transport one U.S. dollar of coinage
   (or other local currency). You may choose the number and denomi-
   nations of coins used; your only constraint is that their total value be
   exactly one dollar.
3. You may not simply crumple the paper into a ball, as this would constitute a projectile rather than an aerodynamically sensitive aircraft-
   based design.

You will be required to pitch your design to your classmates. You will have
two minutes to convince your classmates that your design will perform the
best. Performance on the exercise will be based on a combination of actual
performance of your airplane and the number of votes your design gets
from your classmates in each category (time and distance)."

Theoretical Foundations

MacMillan, I.C., Siegel, R., and Subba Narisimha, P.N. 1985. Criteria used by venture capitalists to evaluate new venture proposals. *Journal of Business Venturing*, 1, 119–28.
Ries, E. 2011. *The Lean Startup: How Today's Entrepreneurs Use Continuous Innovation to Create Radically Successful Businesses.* New York: Crown Publishing.

Time Plan (80 minutes)

Because each team will pitch their idea, the time required for the exercise will vary with class and team size. The timing outlined here is based on a class size of 30 students and ten teams.

Step 1   0:00–0:02 (2 minutes)
Begin the exercise by explaining the voting rules to the students. Students are allowed to vote for only one team (excluding their own) in each of the two categories (distance and time). They are not required to vote for the same design in each category. It helps to provide a sheet for each of the students to record their votes, or, if your students have computers and internet access, you can use an online voting system (this will require you to set it up before the class).

Step 2   0:02–0:27 (25 minutes)
Next, have each team pitch their idea to their classmates. Teams should be strictly limited to two minutes each.

Step 3   0:27–0:32 (5 minutes)
Have the students record their votes for the design they think will perform best in each category. Remind them that they cannot vote for their own design.

Step 4   0:32–0:52 (20 minutes)
Take the class to an open area in which to conduct the actual flights. An indoor area such as a gymnasium works best, but you can run it outdoors as well (which can introduce additional uncertainty into the performance for the students).

Each team gets one throw. You should have a line that they cannot cross for throwing, and you should record the time that their plane stays aloft. After the plane has landed, measure and record the distance. It helps if you assign this task to one or more of the students.

Step 5   0:52–1:00 (8 minutes)
Return to the classroom. Record the votes and the actual performance for
each team on the board.

Step 6 (exercise debrief)   1:00–1:20 (20 minutes)
If time allows, you can have a short discussion about their process with
regard to creating their design. This can help to illustrate how an entrepreneur can take a constraint and turn it into an opportunity. Additionally,
this can highlight the importance of prototyping and learning from failure,
and many of the teams that perform well often trial several different
designs. Some possible questions include:

- How did they view the issue of the coins?
  - Did they see it as a negative constraint? Why?
  - Did they see it as an opportunity to incorporate it into the
    design and improve its performance?
- How did they try to differentiate their design?
- Did they try to optimize for time or distance or try both?
- Did they prototype and test designs?

Next, discuss the aspect of effective pitching. The idea here is to get them
to appreciate the importance of the entrepreneur and his or her pitch to
investors. Owing to the uncertainty inherent in many early-stage entrepreneurial ventures, investors will typically put more emphasis on the entrepreneur and his or her ability to "sell" the idea, as well as their confidence
in the entrepreneur's ability to execute on his or her pitch – one has to be
careful not to oversell the concept.

- How did it feel to try to "sell" your classmates on your design?
  - What were the biggest challenges?
- How did you decide to invest?
  - How important was the way in which they presented the
    concept?
  - Confidence?
  - What was compelling about the pitch or the entrepreneur?
- Why do you think people did or did not vote for your design?
  - What would you do to improve your pitch?

Wrap the discussion up with a summary of the importance of clearly articulating your idea and convincing the audience of your ability to execute
on your idea.

Post-Work

Have the students read the following articles (this can be done beforehand if you prefer):

Elsbach, K.D. 2003. How to pitch a brilliant idea. *Harvard Business Review*, 81(9), 117–23.
Santinelli, A., and Brush, C. 2013. *Designing and Delivering the Perfect Pitch.* Wellesley, MA: Babson College Case Collection.

Teaching Tips

Students will often try to game the system (depending on how much freedom you give them). For example, they may choose to use different weights of paper or design a flying disc as opposed to a traditional airplane. You can decide how vague you want to be. If you want to have more discussion on the creative process and pushing the boundaries, then being more vague in the instructions can lead to a good discussion on how entrepreneurs try to push the rules and boundaries. Some students will feel "cheated," but this can still provide a good learning point.

Key Takeaways

- Ability to quickly and clearly articulate an idea is often more important than the idea itself.
- Investors often focus on their belief in the entrepreneur's ability to execute on the idea rather than the idea itself – particularly under conditions of uncertainty.
- Prototyping can be an effective way to deal with an unknown environment and develop your product or service.

Attribution

Reginald A. Litz, Dell McStay, Sergio Janczak, and Carolyn Birmingham, "Kitty hawk in the classroom: A simulation exercise for facilitating creative and entrepreneurial behavior," United States Association for Small Business and Entrepreneurship (USASBE) 2011 conference – Entrepreneurship: Changing the Present, Creating the Future, South Carolina, United States, January 2011.

EXERCISE: BUSINESS MODEL CANVAS GAME

AUTHOR: HEIDI NECK

Description

The Business Model Canvas (http://www.businessmodelgeneration.com/ canvas) has become a popular teaching tool in entrepreneurship classrooms. It is not my intention here to introduce the canvas or illustrate how it works. Osterwalder and Pigneur (2010) do a magnificent job explaining the canvas, articulating the theory behind the canvas, and offering many ways to use the canvas. This exercise is a quick game to help students reflect on the nature and ordering of the nine business model components found on the canvas as proposed by Osterwalder and Pigneur.

Usage Suggestions

This exercise works well for both undergraduate and graduate audiences. The exercise is best used in a course or class session where the Business Model Canvas is first being introduced.

Learning Objectives

- Reflect on the meaning and importance of the nine business model components.
- Demonstrate how the ordering on the canvas categorizes components as generating value or creating efficiency to deliver value.
- Discuss and debate the ordering proposed by Osterwalder and Pigneur (2010).

Materials List

Instructors will need to create decks of "business model component cards." One deck is needed per team in the class. Each deck is comprised of nine index cards. On each card should be one of the nine business model components: customer segments, value propositions, channels, customer relationships, revenue streams, key resources, key activities, key partners, cost structure. Given that this is the actual order recommended by Osterwalder & Pigneur, it is important that the cards in the deck are not in this order. You may also want to have copies of the Business Model Canvas to distribute as well, but after the game. A copy of the canvas can be obtained at http://www.businessmodelgeneration.com/canvas.

Pre-Work Required by Students

None.

Theoretical Foundations

Osterwalder, A., and Pigneur, Y. 2010. *Business Model Generation*. Hoboken, NJ: John Wiley & Sons.

Time Plan (30 minutes)

The Game Setup   0:00–0:05 (5 minutes)
Before introducing the canvas, simply introduce that there are nine components of a business model. I typically show a PowerPoint slide with the nine components listed in random order. Tell the students that there is a particular order to the components, but they need to figure out what the order is. In other words, they need to determine which of the components should be considered first, second, and so on. What's most important to start with and what's least important? Separate students into teams of five (maximum).

The Game   0:05–0:15 (10 minutes)
Give each team a deck of cards and ask them to place them in order from one to nine (10 minutes). After 10 minutes, give each team a long piece of masking tape and have them tape the order of their cards to the wall or board, so everyone can see the differences across the team.

The Discussion   0:15–0:30 (15 minutes)
Now it is time to introduce the ordering that Osterwalder and Pigneur use. Their book (see Theoretical Foundations) is quite helpful if you are not familiar with the canvas. I typically give out a copy of the Business Model Canvas to each student prior to disclosing the order.

The ordering of the components is: 1) customer segments, 2) value propositions, 3) channels, 4) customer relationships, 5) revenue streams, 6) key resources, 7) key activities, 8) key partners, 9) cost structure. Usually student teams will have either customer segments or value propositions first and this creates a wonderful debate in the class. Introduce the order of the components one by one while also explaining what each component is.

After walking through the components and discussing the differences in order created by each team I end the exercise with a brief discussion summarizing the order. At the end of the day, the ordering really does not matter because the canvas is meant to be an iterative, working document that will continuously change as you learn new information from every action taken or experiment conducted. What is most interesting about the design of the canvas and its ordering is found when you fold the canvas in half (left to right). According to Osterwalder and Pigneur, the right side of the canvas is concerned with creating and generating value. The left side of the canvas is concerned with generating efficiencies to deliver that value. As such, an entrepreneur needs to first determine or create the value and then develop the approach to deliver that value. Innovation, novelty, creativity, and competitive advantage are most often found in the value creation. So, start on the right!

Key Takeaways

- It is important to think about the ordering of the components but not be wedded to one particular ordering.
- A business model is about value creation, delivery, and capture – but start with creation and think about cost last.
- Focusing too soon on cost structure and resources can diminish the innovativeness of new ideas. This can happen when we start on the left side of the canvas.

Teaching Tips

The most important reason that I do this exercise is to get the students thinking about each component on their own in teams rather than just "telling" them about each component. Expect raging debates about customer segments versus value propositions as being first in the order. It is always a great conversation to have.

8.   Exercises to practice empathy

EXERCISE: THE POWER OF OBSERVATION

AUTHOR: SEBASTIAN FIXSON

Description

This exercise is a powerful mechanism to have students experience the challenges and benefits of direct observation. The exercise includes two types of observations: observing an inanimate object, and observing several people conducting a specific task. Both exercises are best assigned as individual homework assignments, and are subsequently discussed in class. The handout at the end of this exercise provides detailed instructions for the students, and the time plan section provides some discussion questions for the instructor.

For the first exercise, the students are asked to reserve an hour of their time and spend this hour observing a known inanimate object, for example a fruit. The students are asked to write down two types of observations during the exercise. One type of observation the students are asked to record is about the observed object itself. The second type of observation the students should note is about themselves in the observation process.

The second exercise also requires students to individually observe a known entity, but this time it is a process executed by someone else. A good example setting is an ATM machine. Students will be asked to observe a couple of ATM customers while they arrive at the ATM, operate it, and leave. Once the students have observed several ATM users, they typically notice something that they cannot immediately explain. At this point, the students are asked to approach a subject after he or she has used the ATM and try to find out the underlying explanation of the observed but unexplained behavior through interviewing.

There is a long-standing tradition in social science fields such as anthropology of employing observation as a data-gathering technique. As background literature for the instructor we recommend classics in this field such as the works of Donald Schön (1982) and Michael Agar ([1980] 1996). More recently, the growing interest in teaching and learning about innovation has renewed the importance of developing a deep understanding of the needs and wants of users and stakeholders (Beckman and Barry, 2007). In this context, the methods from design, sometimes packaged under the headline of *design thinking*, have proven particularly helpful. Example settings from higher education are design-related courses (Fixson, 2009; Fixson and Rao, 2011; Fixson and Read, 2012). Recent research demonstrates the power of deep user needs understanding even when novices apply these methods such as direct observation for the first time (Seidel and Fixson, 2013).

Usage Suggestions

The exercise fits in all creative and entrepreneurial courses in which direct observation (of users, customers, clients, etc.) is of value, for example courses on product development, problem solving, or opportunity development. The exercise should be conducted early in the course to prepare students for the challenging task of primary data collection. The exercise itself consists of two parts: individual student work (best assigned as pre-class homework) and in-class discussion.

Learning Objectives

- Recognize the power (and challenges) of direct observation.
- Assess how the self is involved while observing other humans and objects.
- Experience one's own emotions and their effect on the observation outcome.

Materials List

See "Handout: Observation Exercise Instruction" at the end of this exercise.

Pre-Work Required by Students

The actual exercise is the pre-work. It will require at least 2 hours' time from each student. In addition, the instructor should reserve some time in a class session preceding this exercise to discuss the basics of ethical behavior when conducting research with human subjects. Particularly for the second part of the exercise, which involves observing other human beings, it is helpful for the students to have a frame of reference and some rules for ethical behavior in conducting observational research.

Theoretical Foundations

Agar, M.H. [1980] 1996. *The Professional Stranger: An Informal Introduction to Ethnography*, 2nd edn. San Diego: Academic Press.

Beckman, S., and Barry, M. 2007. Innovation as a learning process: Embedded design thinking. *California Management Review*, 50(1), 25–56.

Fixson, S.K. 2009. Teaching innovation through interdisciplinary courses and programmes in product design and development: An analysis at sixteen U.S. schools. *Creativity and Innovation Management*, 18(3), 199–208, doi:10.1111/j.1467-8691.2009.00523.x.

Fixson, S.K., and Rao, J. 2011. Creation logic in innovation: From action learning to expertise. In D. Greenberg, K. McKone-Sweet, and H.J. Wilson (eds.), *The New Entrepreneurial Leader: Developing Leaders Who Shape Social and Economic Opportunity* (pp.43–61). San Francisco: Berrett-Koehler.

Fixson, S.K., and Read, J.M. 2012. Creating innovation leaders: Why we need to blend business and design education. *Design Management Review*, 23(4), 4–12.

Mayfield, M. 2007. *Thinking for Yourself: Developing Critical Thinking Skills through Reading and Writing*, 7th edn. Boston, MA: Wadsworth Publishing Company.

Schön, D.A. 1982. *The Reflective Practitioner*. New York: Basic Books.

Seidel, V.P., and Fixson, S.K. 2013. Adopting "design thinking" in novice multidisciplinary teams: The application and limits of design methods and reflexive practices. *Journal of Product Innovation Management*, 30(supplement), 19–33.

Time Plan (2 hours outside of class, 30–60 minutes inside class)

In class
Introduction to ethics in human subject research   0:00–0:15 (15 minutes)

Outside of class (homework)
Each student can schedule this time independently.

Exercise 1	0:00–1:00 (60 minutes)
Exercise 2	0:00–1:00 (60 minutes)

In class

Discussion	0:00–0:30 (30 minutes)

The following debrief questions are suggested for exercise 1:

- What details did you observe at your everyday object (fruit, vegetable) that you had never noticed before? Why do you think you noticed them this time? What does this experience tell you about how to find new insights?
- How did you feel during the observation period? How do you think

your emotions affected your observation outcome? How would you describe the link between the two?
- How could you improve the observation process? What would that do?

The following debrief questions are suggested for exercise 2:

- What details did you notice watching someone else perform a process (e.g. using an ATM) that you have performed many times yourself? How do you think your own experience colored your observation? How can you work against these biases?
- How did your observation subject react when you approached him or her with additional questions? How did that make you feel?
- How could you improve this process? What would that do?

In-class debriefing can take anywhere between 30 and 60 minutes, depending on the class size.

Post-Work

None directly. However, you may want to consider assigning a reflection write-up.

Key Takeaways

- Recognize the power (and challenges) of direct observation.
  - Careful observation sometimes allows the revealing of insights and understanding that subjects could not even articulate.
  - Careful observation requires paying close attention over time, and thus can feel exhausting.
- Assess how the self is involved while observing other humans and objects.
  - One of the consequences is that different people will see different things while observing the same object or process. This provides advantages for teamwork (e.g. diversity of input) and challenges (e.g. agreeing on an interpretation of the observation data).
- Experience one's own emotions and their effect on the observation outcome.
  - Going through this exercise provides a sense of accomplishment for many students. Witnessing the power of one's own emotion also helps to increase the mindfulness.

Teaching Tips

Both exercises are quite challenging for most students. Consequently, how they experienced, dealt with, and overcame this challenge becomes most often the core of the debriefing discussion, in addition to the actual (often very diverse) observation results. These emotional experiences and how the students reacted to them represent a good vehicle to discuss the power, and limitations, of observations as a data-gathering technique, as well as how to interpret the results. The instructor should provide sufficient time for students to share, and compare, their experiences.

Both exercises are great lead-ins to present tips and advice for data gathering via observation or interviews. Many of the experiences can be used to introduce more structured frameworks to record observations such as AEIOU (actions, environment, interactions, objects, users) or to conduct interviews (interview etiquette, subject selection, preparation of interview guides, including probing prompts and scenario questions, data-recording methods, data analysis techniques, etc.).

Attribution

The first exercise, the observation of a fruit or vegetable, was published by Marlys Mayfield (2007) in her book *Thinking for Yourself*. The second exercise, the observation of ATM users, has been developed by Sara Beckman of UC Berkeley, and Michael Barry of the d.school at Stanford.

Handout: Observation Exercise Instruction

The two exercises described below are meant to be conducted individually, that is, by each student alone. Each exercise requires one hour of uninterrupted time. Please schedule accordingly.

1. Observation of a familiar inanimate object (Mayfield, 2007)

- Before you begin: This will be a difficult assignment for some of you. The exercise aims to provide you an initiation experience to the process of observation. If you commit to the task as laid out in the instructions, it can provide some surprising rewards. But it may test your ability to "hang in there" despite cycles of discomfort. The only necessary prerequisite is a willingness to stretch your limits by spending at least one hour in the process of observing and recording. So start by setting up a place (and time) when you will not be distracted or interrupted.

- Prepare note-taking sheets as follows: Separate the space on your sheets into two halves by drawing a vertical line down the center to create two columns, using the following headlines:
  - Physical details: Use this column to note what you observe and discover about the object.
  - Inner process details: Use this column to note what you observe and discover is happening with you as you work: your moods, reactions, associations, and thoughts.
- Select as your object a vegetable or fruit. Choose one that you have seen and handled many times before. Whatever you can find in your neighborhood grocery store or your refrigerator will do. Your selection will be your specimen for this observation study.
- Set up your workplace for the observation. You may want to have a knife and cutting board handy, as well as some drawing paper for sketching.
- Begin by really taking your time to explore this object. Let yourself become absorbed in the task like either a curious child or a dedicated scientist. As your mind slows down, your sensations will tell you more, and you will make more and more discoveries.
  - Remember to notice not only parts but also wholes, not only see, but also touch, hear, smell, and taste.
  - Whenever you become aware of a characteristic that you can articulate, write that down in the left column under "Physical details."
- Use the right column for noting your personal reactions as you work.
  - At what points did you become bored? Excited? Angry? Impatient? Lost in daydreams? Acknowledge these distractions by writing them down as you bring your attention back to the task of observing your object.
  - See how many times you need to renew your commitment to keep observing. Note all the stages of interest and concentration that you pass through: the plateaus, valleys, and peaks.
- When you know for certain that you have finished, assemble your notes and prepare to write up a complete description of your fruit or vegetable. Your final description may take one of two forms:
  - a report that describes the object completely, with the addition of a final paragraph describing your own inner personal process;
  - a narrative – or story of your observing process – that describes your object, the stages you went through, and the progression of your discoveries, insights, and reactions.

- Type up your final draft as a double-spaced paper. Suggested length is at least two pages. Bring this to class to share and then turn in. If you created additional sketches, bring those to class too.

2. **Observation of a human being conducting a specific task (Beckman and Barry, 2007)**

- Spend one hour doing the following observation and interview exercise; include about 30 minutes of observation and about 30 minutes capturing the results.
- Find a local ATM machine.
  - Start by observing what's happening as customers approach and use the machine.
  - As you observe, look for interesting behaviors that you don't entirely understand. Use the skills you learned in the fruit or vegetable observation exercise. You may find yourself moving through the same cycles of interest in what you are seeing.
  - Once you've seen an interesting behavior, formulate a question around your observation – a question to which you don't know the answer. The question in your mind could take the form of a hypothesis you create to explain that behavior. (Be careful not to assume that the people you are watching are thinking the way that you do about ATM transactions!)
- Approach a user of the ATM and ask your question – learn what you can to help you better understand your observation or resolve your curiosity as to why you observed the behaviors you did. In short, test your hypothesis.
  - *Note*: Make sure that you do not misrepresent your intentions.
- Once you have completed your 30-minute observation, write a short (one-page) summary of both what you learned about ATM use and what you learned about observation and interviewing.
- Bring your work to class with you to share and then turn in.

EXERCISE: NEGOTIATION FOR RESOURCE ACQUISITION

AUTHOR: LAKSHMI BALACHANDRA

Description

This exercise provides exposure to the practice of negotiation, in particular how to use the principles of integrative negotiation. This type of negotiation skill is particularly relevant for entrepreneurs in the early stages, when they may feel disadvantaged by being in weaker bargaining positions. Students learn to look past merely financial outcomes or common distributive bargaining traps for their negotiations. Instead, they learn to incorporate creative options and solutions to obtain non-financial resources that are critical but not obvious to many would-be and early-stage entrepreneurs. This exercise is one of the most popular negotiation simulations in negotiation courses worldwide. It is based on the seven elements of negotiation, a theory developed by Roger Fisher and Bill Ury in the 1970s. Introducing the framework for integrative bargaining provides a foundation for the exercise and a basic lesson in negotiation theory relevant for entrepreneurs.

Usage Suggestions

This exercise works for all audiences, undergraduate, graduate, executive, or practitioner. It is particularly relevant for new venture creation courses, entrepreneurship bootcamps, and workshops. The session is best positioned after a discussion of entrepreneurial resources and capital requirements, as it incorporates new ways to approach obtaining valuable start-up assets and new ways to consider potential "resource" providers.

Learning Objectives

- Practice negotiation with an entrepreneurship focus.
- Learn a framework for integrative negotiation and entrepreneurial value creation.
- Identify non-financial resources that could be acquired through negotiation.

Materials List

- Sally Soprano case (ordered from Program on Negotiation Clearinghouse); order equal number of roles in order to have one-on-one negotiation simulations (pairs of students).
- Program on Negotiation offers an excellent teaching note for a more detailed debrief related to general negotiation lessons related to integrative negotiations.

Pre-Work Required by Students

Read an assigned confidential role (assign roles and pairings ahead of time to allocate roles appropriately). The best scenario is to have the students read their roles as homework before class. It is possible to hand out the roles and have them read them in class, and, if this is done, add 15 minutes to the overall timing of the session.

Theoretical Foundations

Fisher, R., Ury, W., and Patton, B. 2011. *Getting to Yes*. New York: Penguin.

Time Plan (1.5–2 hours)

This exercise can be extended into a longer session to have students spend time together preparing to negotiate. For the purposes of an initial negotiation session, this teaching note has been written so that the exercise requires at least 1.5 hours.

Introduction   0:00–0:10 (10 minutes)

Begin class by discussing the overall perception of negotiation. Ask students how they define negotiation. Opening questions could include:

- What does negotiation mean to you?
- What is the role of negotiation in entrepreneurship?

Explain how negotiation is everywhere – pervasive in life and in entrepreneurship, as you try to gain resources you need to launch a new venture. Explain how negotiations often fail and deals are not made, because most people do not have a systematic framework for preparing, conducting, and analyzing negotiations. Also, negotiations are often viewed as win-or-lose outcomes. This session is designed to introduce students to a simple, systematic way to measure success in negotiation and find ways to create value and resources critical to entrepreneurs. Typical ways of defining success include: reaching agreement, not fighting, fairness, winning, or breaking their bottom line. The seven-elements framework offers a method to prepare to negotiate as well as evaluate outcomes for success.

Overview   0:10–0:30 (20 minutes)
Define and explain the seven elements of negotiation (Fisher and Ury, 1981), which is the theoretical framework for this session. In a lecture, show how negotiators should use the framework to identify for themselves (their perspective in the negotiation), as well as for the other party, the seven elements:

- alternatives (walk-away possibilities);
- interests (needs, concerns, goals, desires, etc. of the parties);
- options (possibilities or outcomes on which parties could agree);
- legitimacy (standards used to measure options, possible agreements);
- communication (method and means of communicating with the other party);
- relationship (connection to the other party);
- commitment (what is agreed to in the negotiation).

PowerPoint slides to define each element are useful, but examples are more useful to illustrate how the concepts can be identified to any setting. The most relevant illustration for students is a new job opportunity. For example, when looking for a job, an individual's alternatives are the other job offers the person has or staying in his or her current job. If there are no other offers, then the alternatives are not very good. That may happen in any deal, in particular for entrepreneurs, where there are more established companies that can be used. Interests focus on the "why" of the negotiation: what you really want out of the deal. For the job possibility, the individual may not care about having a higher salary, as the job may be with a company in an industry in which the individual wants to work or perhaps the company is located much closer to the individual's home. Thus, there are many interests for an individual for a new job. Interests should be identified and then ranked in order of importance. Options refer to the ways the potential job opportunity being negotiated can be constructed: salary, days of vacation, benefits, shares, a parking spot, childcare, and so on. Legitimacy can be used when identifying what other companies are paying for the same type of position. Communication is how the individual will negotiate with the company – face to face or email, and so on. Relationship refers in this case to the relationship the individual has with the other; perhaps they knew each other beforehand, or perhaps it is a new introduction to the HR representative. Finally, commitment is whether there is an offer on the table, whether the individual agrees to the job, and whether the other party has the authority to approve the job offer. These are all the considerations for the individual to consider from his or her perspective, but this analysis should also be done from the company's perspective: What are the alternatives to hiring the individual for the company? What are the company's interests, and so on?

Explain how this analysis differs from traditional bargaining, and that analyzing the negotiation in this way offers a means to expand the "pie" and create new value that can be then divided up.

Preparation   0:30–0:45 (15 minutes)

- Have the groups separate by role (Sally Soprano's agent or Lyric Opera's agent).
- Each group discusses the components of the seven elements and decides what the appropriate "answers" are for each side – given what they know from their confidential instructions.
- Given the short time to prepare, tell students to focus on the first three elements (alternatives, interests, and options).

Negotiation   0:45–1:00 (15 minutes)

After the preparation phase, they meet with their negotiation counterpart and negotiate the case. They are to negotiate as if they were actually in the roles they were given, and their goal is to get the best possible outcome for their side. They do not have to arrive at a deal. After they finish their agreement, if before the time limit, they are not to discuss the information of the case. Make sure to tell them to be prompt to arrive at the debrief, as it's important to have everyone together before discussing the case.

Debrief   1:00–1:30 (30 minutes)

Once the students return (and they may need prodding, as some will inevitably want to negotiate longer than 15 minutes, but 15 minutes is enough time to negotiate), discuss the case using the following questions as possible discussion starters:

- How many agreements? (List a few agreements on the board, especially if there are some creative solutions.)
- Ask the students who came up with creative solutions how they arrived at these outcomes. For the ones who only came up with a financial solution, ask them why they focused only on money rather than on non-monetary options.

- Ask students in Sally Soprano's agent role what sorts of resources would be of value to Sally. Why?
- Ask students in Lyric Opera's manager role what sorts of resources would be of value to the Lyric Opera. Why?

These questions should all enable the instructor to open up a discussion of how and why entrepreneurs need to be aware of how to negotiate with regard to gaining resources of all kinds – and how these are often more valuable to entrepreneurs in the early stages of the venture. This is very similar to Sally Soprano in this case, as she would be willing to work for free, which is what many start-ups do. They offer their services for free in exchange for marketing, references, and future contract potential.

Key Takeaways

- Incorporating value creation negotiation principles for the entrepreneurial process: learning how a win–win negotiation approach can enable entrepreneurs to garner valuable start-up resources.
- Showcasing the role of gaining customers for start-ups rather than solely focusing on raising cash from investors.
- Using the negotiation framework to foster entrepreneurial thinking by identifying outcomes with resource providers and prospective partners such that both sides create and add value.
- Encouraging creativity for the entrepreneurial mindset to acquire creative resources that are highly beneficial to the entrepreneur, like marketing, that may not "cost" much.

Post-Work

After the simulation, students can meet up with their negotiation partner to provide feedback on negotiation styles – what each person did well, what they might have brought up during the negotiation to change the discussion, and what they might practice for future negotiations.

Teaching Tips

It is not necessary to provide too much time to negotiate, as agreements may be made quickly and the desire to share confidential information will be high. This will lead to a less rich debrief discussion. While the zero salary possibility is a stretch for some students, this can lead into a strong discussion of how entrepreneurs often will offer services for free to potential clients in the start-up phase just to have credibility and references, especially for brand-name client referrals and marketing potential. Such marketing potential provides a high-value resource for entrepreneurs, much greater than any salary that they could have negotiated.

Attribution

Norbert Jacker, *Sally Soprano*. Cambridge, MA: Clearinghouse of the Program on Negotiation, Harvard Law School, 1979.

EXERCISE: MONKEY BUSINESS

AUTHOR: ROSA SLEGERS

Description

In this exercise, students reenact an experiment originally devised by biologists studying monkeys to trace the evolutionary roots of our sense of fairness in order to get a better understanding of what we mean when we cry: "That's not fair!" The exercise is designed to raise questions about our notion of fairness in entrepreneurship and help students think about the world of business they help create. Where does our sense of fairness come from, and what are the hidden assumptions behind our use of the term? Is it natural or necessary for us to feel outraged at unfairness? Do we have a responsibility to think about fairness in the realm of entrepreneurship?

Monkeys are closely related to human beings from an evolutionary perspective. This suggests that, if we observe similar behavior in both species, those behaviors likely spring from the same evolutionary principles. If this is true (and biological research shows that it is), what should we do with the scientific insight that it is natural for us to feel outraged when we are unfairly treated, while our inclination to feel outraged at being unfairly privileged is not anywhere near as strong (or at least not as deeply ingrained in our evolutionary history)? What are the implications for entrepreneurship?

Usage Suggestions

This exercise can be part of any introduction to entrepreneurial thinking. Being entrepreneurial is about more than starting a business for financial rewards. It brings the opportunity to impact the way business is done. Depending on the goals of the class and the time available, this exercise can lead into a discussion of fairness in business systems around the world. It works for any audience, youth, family enterprises, adults, or undergraduate or graduate students.

Learning Objectives

- Critically evaluate the use and application of the concept "fairness."
- Explore questions of inequality in a non-intimidating manner, starting with monkey behavior instead of loaded issues related to race, class, gender, and so on. The instructor may of course choose to engage with these very important topics, but can do so at his or her own comfort level.

- Discover that some moral responses are at least in part "pre-rational," stemming from a deeply ingrained evolutionary principle rather than from reasoned debate.

Materials List

Two identical pens (pieces of chalk will do as well, as long as both objects are the same), 30 identical pieces of paper with the picture of a cucumber (or just the word "cucumber"), and 15 identical pieces of paper with a picture of a grape (or just the word "grape").

Pre-Work Required by Students

None.

Theoretical Foundations

Aldrich, H.E., and Ruef, M. 2006. *Organizations Evolving*. London: SAGE Publications.

Waal, F. de. 2005. *Our Inner Ape*. New York: Riverhead Books.

Waal, F. de. 2006. *Primates and Philosophers: How Morality Evolved*. Princeton, NJ: Princeton University Press.

Time Plan (60 minutes)

Step 1   0:00–0:05 (5 minutes)
Ask students to volunteer for the following roles:

- capuchin monkeys (two);
- research biologist (one).

The remaining students are research assistants.

Step 2   0:05–0:15 (10 minutes)
For this exercise, it is important that the two students volunteering to be monkeys and the student playing the part of the research biologist are all in on the purpose of the exercise, while the rest of the students (the "research assistants") are left in the dark. Take the three volunteering students to a separate location and explain their roles to them. Note that the researcher and the monkeys should not speak once the exercise is underway – though monkey noises are, of course, permitted. Here is the description that only the three volunteers should receive:

- The research biologist is performing a simple experiment. She teaches the monkeys that, when she hands each individual monkey a pen, it will receive **a piece of cucumber** (represented by the pieces of paper with the picture or word "cucumber") when it hands the pen back to her. So all the researcher does is hand each monkey a pen, wait for the monkey to hand it back, and then give the monkey a cucumber treat in reward for its "work."
- The monkeys mirror these acts (they can improvise a bit on the learning process, if they like) and take and then return the pen, perhaps at first unclear on the intentions of the researcher, but eventually catching on to the experiment. Capuchin monkeys are very collaborative and learn fast, so after a few iterations the process should run smoothly: receipt of the pen, handing it back, and receiving a cucumber treat.
- It is very important that throughout the first seven or eight iterations of the experiment, the monkeys act similarly, almost as exact copies of each other. They are excited to receive their cucumber piece and get into the game.
- Then, in round 8 or 9, inequality is introduced. Instead of both receiving their cucumber treat, one monkey gets **a grape** instead. Tell the student volunteers that, to monkeys, grapes are much more valuable than cucumbers. It is important that the students playing the monkeys understand that the monkey who is paid in cucumber currency will at first be simply jealous and eventually, as the other monkey continues to receive grapes for what is exactly the same effort (handing back the pen), completely outraged.
- The monkey who continues to receive the lowly cucumbers has to show this building outrage and can improvise, going from begging the other monkey to share, to refusing the cucumbers altogether or perhaps throwing them across the cage. The monkey receiving grapes should act excited about the grapes but show no or little concern about its unfairly treated counterpart.
- The researcher should continue the experiment for several more rounds, simply rewarding one monkey consistently with grapes and the other monkey with cucumbers. The experiment ends when the cucumber monkey simply refuses further cooperation.

After explaining their roles to the three student volunteers, give them the numbered list printed in Step 4 as a reminder of how the experiment will unfold. Point out to them that you will "freeze" the experiment halfway through, just as the researcher is giving one monkey a grape instead of a cucumber for the first time. At this point the rest of the class (the "research assistants") will be asked to predict what will happen next; once you have gathered suggestions from the class you can tell the volunteers to continue their acting.

Step 3   0:15–0:20 (5 minutes)
With the help of the three volunteers, set up the classroom as follows: The two students playing the part of the monkeys should be positioned next to each other facing the research biologist. If possible, build "cages" (using tables or chairs) around the monkeys so that they are separated both from each other and from the researcher and assistants. Though the monkeys cannot touch each other, they can clearly see what the other monkey is doing and they can toss things through the "bars" if they feel so inclined. The researcher has a stack of "grapes" and a stack of "cucumbers" (prepared as described under "Materials List"), both hidden from view of the monkeys. At the start of the exercise, the researcher is holding the two pens.

Step 4   0:20–0:30 (10 minutes)
Start the experiment, following the steps below:

1. The researcher approaches the monkey cages, holding out one pen to each monkey.
2. The capuchin monkeys, naturally curious and cooperative, each take a pen.
3. The researcher retreats and picks up pieces of cucumber.
4. The researcher approaches the cages with the two pieces of cucumber and holds out one piece to each monkey. The monkeys try to take the cucumber, but the researcher points at the pens and gesticulates to make clear that the monkeys will receive the cucumber only if they first hand back the pen.
5. The first exchange occurs: The monkeys each get the cucumber, and the researcher retrieves the pens.
6. This pattern is repeated several times until the monkeys know exactly what to expect. Cucumber is a favorite snack for capuchins and they eat every piece.
7. After about seven or eight pens-for-cucumber exchanges, a change is introduced by the researcher. The researcher waits until the last round of cucumber pieces have been consumed, hands the monkeys the pens, and the monkeys are immediately ready to hand back the pens in exchange for yet more cucumber. Everything is exactly the same, except that this time the researcher hands one monkey a grape in return for the pen, while the other monkey receives the standard piece of cucumber.

Step 5   0:30–0:40 (10 minutes)
At this point, tell the monkeys to "freeze" and ask the research assistants how they think the monkeys will respond. Mention that capuchin
monkeys consider grapes far more delicious than cucumbers. The students
may hesitate to assign humanlike behavior to the monkeys, but ask them
to guess anyway. At least some of the students will point to the fact that
it is not fair, from the "underpaid" monkey's perspective, that the other
monkey is receiving a grape for exactly the same effort. Nothing has
changed; they both have the same pens and go through the same routine,
yet suddenly the monkeys are receiving unequal rewards. Once this issue
has been raised, ask the research assistants how they think the "overpaid"
monkey will respond. Will it sense unfairness? How will both monkeys
react, and what will they do? Write the suggestions offered by the students
on the whiteboard so that you can return to them later.

Step 6   0:40–0:45 (5 minutes)
Tell the monkeys to unfreeze and tell the researcher to continue the
experiment:

8. The monkey offered the grape happily eats its prize, while the monkey
    offered the piece of cucumber just holds it, looking uncertainly from
    its neighbor to the researcher.
9. The researcher once again hands over the pens to the monkeys (the
    cucumber monkey dropping his snack in order to receive its pen) and
    hands another grape to the monkey who received a grape in the previ-
    ous iteration, while giving another piece of cucumber to the grape-
    deprived monkey.
10. The grape-receiving monkey immediately eats the grape again, while
    the cucumber-receiving monkey holds out its hand to the other
    monkey through the bars. No luck.
11. The experiment continues in exactly the same fashion, with the grape
    monkey receiving more grapes and the cucumber monkey receiv-
    ing more cucumbers in return for the pens. The cucumber monkey
    gets angry, starts throwing the pieces of cucumber in a fit of rage,
    and eventually just sits in the corner of its cage and sulks. The grape
    monkey unconcernedly supplements its diet of grapes with the occa-
    sional cucumber thrown through the bars by the angry cucumber
    monkey (free food!).

Step 7   0:45–1:00 (15 minutes)
Now that the experiment has been concluded, ask the research assistants
to discuss and answer the following questions:

- Capuchin monkeys like cucumbers and normally can't get enough of them. What, exactly, causes the cucumber monkey to stop eating the cucumber pieces it is offered?
- Can the students recall situations, whether from their childhood or more recently, that closely resemble the experiment?
- What are the parallels in the business world to this kind of behavior? Who are the human "grape monkeys," and who are the human "cucumber monkeys"?
- The monkey receiving the cucumbers is outraged, while the monkey receiving the grapes is unperturbed and even eats some of the cucumber pieces lying around. What does this tell us about the monkey concept of fairness? Is there any particular reference to entrepreneurship?
- Fairness does not seem to be of much concern to the grape monkey – it does not offer to share its grapes with the cucumber monkey even when the cucumber monkey holds out its hand to the grape monkey and begs. Where do we see this double standard in the human world? Think of examples to show that fairness tends to be a concern primarily for those who feel short-changed or even violated, while those benefiting from unfairness may not even stop to think about their privileged position (let alone be motivated to "share the wealth").
- When creating a business, or any kind of organization, when and how do you plan for the degree of fairness you want to show to people within your organization? Outside the organization?
- If you were in the process of bringing on two employees with equal qualifications to your new venture and did not have the resources to pay both equally, how would you treat them fairly if you had to pay them differently in terms of amount of money and timing of payments?
- How does the concept of fairness in business vary around the world?

Teaching Tips

This exercise works best if the volunteers are excited about their roles – enthusiastic monkeys and a serious or studious researcher are crucial to getting a good response from the rest of the group. If any students make it clear that they think this exercise is a little silly, that does not need to be a problem. The fact that there is some silliness inherent in the exercise helps students open up about the very serious issue of fairness; introducing the concept in this way gets around the paralysis that can result from a heavy theoretical lecture on the subject. Just make sure to impress on the students that this experiment, simple as it is, shows us something very fundamental: outrage in the face of unfairness is so fundamental that it is ingrained not just in humans but in our close evolutionary cousins. Resistance to unfairness is part of our nature, and this insight is important to our attempts to frame what counts as fair and unfair in entrepreneurship practice. The notion of fairness applies especially when building a management team and considering incentives for how to encourage team members to work together in the early stages. Early-stage organizations or ventures, especially those that are resource constrained, often have to make trade-offs about rewards and incentives for employees and team members. This exercise helps students to weigh the implications of these decisions.

Attribution

This exercise is my creation but is based on an experiment conducted on capuchin monkeys by biologist Frans de Waal and described in his books *Our Inner Ape* (New York: Riverhead Books, 2005) and *Primates and Philosophers: How Morality Evolved* (Princeton, NJ: Princeton University Press, 2006).

EXERCISE: SEQUENCED AND ESCALATED PEER COACHING EXERCISES

AUTHOR: MARY GALE

Description

This set of three in-class exercises involves the use of peer feedback for individual or team student entrepreneurial business initiatives in small, experience-based courses. Initiatives might include entrepreneurial business creation or consulting assignments or projects. The set includes exercises designed for different project stages: initial project or concept development; hurdles and opportunities; and draft final presentations. The feedback technique for each session is stage specific. These are described in more detail in "Specific exercises" (below). At the conclusion of the session, students will communicate their immediate impressions to the entire class and subsequent reflections in an on-line discussion board or wiki.

A major formative goal is for students to practice giving and receiving stage-specific feedback to improve insights and outcomes for their own and others' benefit. Additionally, these exercises help students develop the habit of constructive evaluation and reflection at all project stages.

Peer feedback is used widely by colleges and universities for assessment (grading) and formative (learning) purposes. In their review of the literature on this topic, Liu and Carless present a case for the latter purpose, which they term "learning-oriented assessment" (Liu and Carless, 2006). A study done at the Manufacturing and Operations Engineering Department at the University of Limerick concludes that students who participate in peer feedback and critiques develop "cognitive sophistication" as a project module progresses, encouraging students to "intuitively engage at the higher levels of Bloom's Taxonomy" (Lynch et al., 2010). The benefits of "bringing others along" (in a variety of ways, including advisory and creative thinking) are a by-product of peer feedback (Schlesinger and Kiefer, 2012).

Specific exercises

1. **Initial project or concept questions: questioning to help others enrich their initial ideas**. Individuals or teams are paired into breakout groups. The students or teams take turns presenting their ideas and asking questions about the others' concepts. The questioners gain practice looking for the needed elements of sound business ideas such as target market, distinctive advantage, and product or service concept. Presenters have an early opportunity to elaborate their ideas

and discover where there may be gaps in concept or logic. Breakout groups offer an informal and less public venue for the first exercise. A subsequent class debrief will focus on personal reactions to the experience, lessons learned, and thoughts about the nature of constructive questions.

2. **Hurdles and opportunities: creative, group-based idea generation**. Each week, one or two students or student teams present a three-minute summary of their project or business, including hurdles and areas where fresh thinking is needed. The class is invited to offer suggestions and ideas or build on each other's comments.

3. **Draft final presentation critique: direct feedback on presentation topics, delivery, and slides**. A week prior to final course presentations, individuals or teams are divided into two groups. Students or teams in Group 1 present a draft of the final presentation to those in Group 2 without interruption. Afterwards, Group 1 project teams set up "booths" (table or desk with a computer) at different locations in the classroom. Group 2 students visit the booths and offer specific feedback and suggestions on the presentations. Then the groups change places and the process is repeated. The final step is a class debrief in which students generate conclusions about effective and ineffective presentation techniques and slide development. During the following week, students incorporate suggestions into a final presentation. Final presentations take place in class and are evaluated by the instructor and students. Instructors may also choose to invite experts to help with assessment.

Usage Suggestions

This is designed for all students in small, experience-based, and project courses, who will participate alternately as givers and receivers of peer feedback on initiatives. To avoid student report fatigue (from a long series of in-class presentations), these sessions are suggested for smaller courses: workshops or smaller teams of students, eight to ten individual students, or three to eight teams.

In a 13-week course, it is recommended that each exercise in the feedback set take place in the following sequence:

Initial project or concept questions   Week 3
Hurdle and opportunity sessions   Weeks 5–10
Draft final presentation critique   Week 12

Learning Objectives

1. Learn how to give and receive objective, fresh, stage-specific advising.

2. Gain practical appreciation for the importance of advisors from the beginning of an entrepreneurial initiative.
3. Practice techniques for providing feedback and advice in a constructive, objective, and generative manner.
4. Evaluate and integrate feedback as an asset in the entrepreneurship method.

Materials Required

- "Peer Coaching Guidelines" (at the end of this exercise).
- "Self-Reflection Guidelines for Students or Teams Post-exercise" (at the end of this exercise).

Pre-Work Required by Students

It is suggested that the peer feedback component of the course be included in the course description and syllabus and explained in detail in the first class. Handout 1 ("Peer Coaching Guidelines") should be distributed the week prior to the feedback sessions and explained in that class. The goal of this pre-work is to help students understand how to deliver objective feedback and understand how helpful critiques, ideas, and suggestions can help entrepreneurs overcome problems and deliver richer, more successful outcomes.

Theoretical Foundations

The following publications are useful for deeper understanding of the role and process of student peer advisors in projects and other initiatives such as entrepreneurship:

Boud, D., Cohen, R., and Sampson, J. 1999. Peer learning and assessment. *Assessment and Evaluation in Higher Education*, 24(4), 413–26.
Jurado, Juan A. 2011. Group projects in interior design studio classes: Peer feedback benefits. *Journal of Family and Consumer Sciences*, 103(1), 34–9.
Lam, R. 2010. A peer review training workshop: Coaching students to give and evaluate peer feedback. *TESL Canada*, 27(2), 114–26.
Liu, N., and Carless, D. 2006. Peer feedback: The learning element of peer assessment. *Teaching in Higher Education*, 11(3), 279–90.
Lynch, R., Seery, N., and Gordon, S. 2010. The formative value of peer feedback in project based assessment. 3rd International Symposium for Engineering Education, University College Cork, Ireland.
Schlesinger, L., and Kiefer, C. 2012. *Just Start*. Boston, MA: Harvard Business School Publishing.

Time Plan

1. Initial project or concept questions (35–40 minutes)
First presentation: 3 minutes
Questions: 5 minutes
Second presentation: 3 minutes
Questions: 5 minutes
Class debrief: 15 minutes

2. Hurdle and opportunity sessions (15–20 minutes each)
Presentation (3 minutes each)
Class ideation, suggestions (10–15 minutes each)

3. Draft final presentation critique (60–90 minutes)
Group 1 presentations: 5–8 minutes each.
Group 2 student feedback at Group 1 "booths": 10 minutes.
Group 2 presentations: 5–8 minutes each.
Group 1 student feedback at Group 2 "booths": 10 minutes.
Class debrief: 10–15 minutes.

Post-Work

1. **Initial project or concept questions**: At the end of this exercise, the class will debrief their feelings, ideas, and lessons learned. In the following week, teams or individuals will develop a collective, categorized list of lessons learned and reflections and post these on a discussion board or wiki.
2. **Hurdle and opportunity sessions**: Each presenter will give immediate feedback to the class about what was useful to solving the problem or advancing the initiative.
3. **Draft final presentation critique**:
  a. Post-class debrief: The class discusses how they felt about this exercise and what they learned from this process relative to their presentation and roles as advisors and advisees.
  b. As part of the final presentation, each individual or team discusses what they learned from their critics and gives credit to individuals and teams for their help.

Key Takeaways

- Constructive, objective criticism improves the outcome of entrepreneurial initiatives if the recipient decides to be open to new – and perhaps contrary – opinions.

- Delivering constructive, objective criticism is a learned skill that is based on fundamental ground rules that maximize value to the recipient and the provider.
- The abilities to deliver and receive constructive, objective feedback are critical leadership skills.

Teaching Tips

These exercises are best used in classes where the instructor has established a "safe zone" for expressing feelings, beliefs, and ideas. It is possible that individuals or teams competing for grades or recognition on the same initiative may be reluctant to share their insights and suggestions with others.

Peer Coaching Guidelines Handout

- Share observations, e.g. "I've noticed that . . . and I'm concerned/ interested to know/wondering . . . "
- Use positive statements.
- Speak in a friendly tone.
- Ask questions that lead to reflection.
- Encourage two-way conversations.
- Summarize and verbally verify.
- End on a positive note/close the session with a friendly comment.

Self-Reflection Guidelines for Students or Teams Post-Exercise Handout

- Summarize comments and suggestions.
- Identify the underlying messages.
- Categorize these messages as:
  - concerns;
  - affirmations;
  - suggestions;
  - creative ideas.
- Decide the disposition of the message:
  - clarify;
  - adopt (all or part);
  - reject (all or part).
- Identify key lessons learned from the feedback.
- Characterize your major feelings and surprises (or lack of surprises) from the feedback overall.

EXERCISE: INTERVIEWING AN ENTREPRENEUR AND SELF-ASSESSMENT

AUTHOR: ANDREW ZACHARAKIS

Description

In this exercise, students interview an entrepreneur of their choice. The goal is to get students to engage a "real life" entrepreneur, ideally in an industry in which they are interested. The interviewed entrepreneur not only provides new learning for the student, but hopefully will become a mentor, possibly provide a job or internship, and so on. The interview should take place in person and last 30–60 minutes. After the interview, students should prepare field notes, which then become the primary research for an analytical paper. The students should use the interview and subsequent analysis to assess their own entrepreneurial potential.

Usage Suggestions

This exercise is appropriate for all audiences, undergraduate, graduate, executive education, and high school. The exercise can occur in any class, but most often is in the introductory entrepreneurship elective. It is often best to assign it early in the course, because it not only provides outside contacts, but also is a great learning tool for the industry space in which the student is interested.

Learning Objectives

- Learn from an actual entrepreneur strategies for succeeding in a new venture.
- Gain insight into an industry space.
- Build a network and acquire a potential mentor.
- Evaluate personal entrepreneurial potential.

Materials List

While students should be encouraged to develop their own questions, the instructor can provide a sample questionnaire that can be useful in coming up with ideas of the types of questions. To encourage an analytical paper, assign students to address the following points:

- Who is the entrepreneur?
- What is the entrepreneur's professional experience or background?
- What process did the entrepreneur use to develop the business?
- Was the process successful?
- By what criteria can the venture be viewed as successful?
- What have you learned from speaking with the entrepreneur?
- Based upon the interview and your own self-assessment, what is your entrepreneurial potential?
- What skills do you need to develop to achieve success, whether it is in an entrepreneurial setting or not?
- Develop a preliminary schedule to help you build these skills.

Pre-Work Required by Students

Assign the interview in the very first class and expect the students to hand in their final paper three to four weeks later. It is important that students call prospective entrepreneurs early. Most entrepreneurs are willing to meet with students, but have very busy schedules. Thus, the sooner students schedule an interview, the more likely they can meet the deadline for the paper. A couple of requirements:

1. The entrepreneur cannot be a family member or friend. This is an opportunity for students to add to their network.
2. Encourage students to aim high, so possibly put metrics around appropriate entrepreneurs, such as company age and revenues. Otherwise, students may interview a classmate who has no revenues or a very small business.

Theoretical Foundations

Bygrave, W., and Zacharakis, A. 2014. *Entrepreneurship*, 3rd ed. Hoboken, NJ: Wiley.

- Chapter 2, "The entrepreneurial process" (which discusses the Timmons Model).
- Chapter 6, "Building the founding team" (which discusses personal assessment and where the student might fit in a founding team).

Time Plan (60 minutes)

The in-class exercise debrief typically takes 60–75 minutes.

Step 1
Three days prior to the class session where students turn in their paper. Students post on the blackboard (or other classroom electronic platform) and discuss two issues:

1. the most surprising quote;
2. the most important lesson learned.

All students are expected to review the various posts and build connections to their own self-assessment and the Timmons Model in preparation for class.

Step 2   0:00–0:10 (10 minutes)
During the face-to-face class, the instructor should lead off with several of the key quotes and have a few of them written on the board or a PowerPoint slide. Get reactions from the students.

Step 3   0:10–0:40 (30 minutes)
In small groups, have students make explicit connections to various learning objectives covered in the class to date, for example how these examples tie to the Timmons Framework of opportunity, resources and team.

Step 4   0:40–0:60 (20 minutes)
Debrief the small group discussions. Ask groups to share some of their connections to the class topics.

Post-Work

Within a week of conducting the interview, students should send a handwritten thank-you with a promise that they will follow up with a copy of their paper. There are two goals in this process. A handwritten thank-you in today's electronic world is more likely to be noticed and remembered, because so few people do them anymore. Following up with the paper a week or two later reinforces the relationship and gives the students a chance to improve or correct weaknesses that have been found in the paper, creating a stronger impression. Students should be encouraged to continue regular contact with the entrepreneur with the goal of having the entrepreneur become a mentor. Thus, they should use LinkedIn to connect with the entrepreneur and also try to have an occasional face-to-face meeting in informal settings, such as over coffee.

Key Takeaways

1. Reinforce theory as students make connections from current entrepreneurs and their process to class concepts.
2. Enable students to assess their own entrepreneurial potential.
3. Create a student action plan to enhance their entrepreneurial potential.

Teaching Tips

Students often find this exercise intimidating, especially undergraduate and high school students. They are fearful of rejection, which leads them to ask the instructor to introduce them to suitable entrepreneurs, or they interview family members, friends, and other people already within their network. Force students outside of their comfort zone. Require them to identify and approach an entrepreneur they don't know (again, most entrepreneurs are willing to spend time with students; it is just a function of finding a convenient time). Suggest students search the alumni database to find a suitable entrepreneur who is likely to be friendly to a current student, which can ease the student's anxiety.

Setting parameters around applicable entrepreneurs is useful. Setting revenue criteria and age of venture forces students to stretch and reach out to more successful entrepreneurs.

Check in with students each class prior to the assignment due date and see how many have scheduled and conducted their interviews. This reminds students not to wait until the last minute (meaning they're more likely to get a quality interview) and applies subtle peer pressure on the procrastinators.

Make sure to check with the university's institutional review board (IRB) on conducting interviews with subjects. The IRB may need to approve the exercise.

Attribution

J. Timmons and S. Spinelli, *New Venture Creation: Entrepreneurship for the 21st Century*, 8th edn. (New York: McGraw-Hill/Irwin, 2008).

EXERCISE: PERFECT PITCH

AUTHORS: ANGELO SANTINELLI AND CANDIDA BRUSH

Description

This exercise offers students an opportunity to develop and reflect on approaches for communicating their venture effectively and clearly through a simple interactive exercise. Students will consider different techniques to communicate the essence of their opportunity to an audience of potential investors. Because students are pitching to each other, they will learn from the experiences of others, and have empathy for the on-the-spot situation this exercise requires. A "perfect pitch" is composed of two elements: the content – aspects of problem being solved, solution, value proposition, business model, and resources required; and the communication – the delivery of the message in terms of voice, body language, appearance, and eye contact. Both the content and the communication are essential to a "perfect pitch".

Research has shown that people make up their minds in less than 90 seconds as to whether they want to know more about an idea. It often takes between 7 and 20 seconds to create a first impression, and nearly 93 percent of a first impression is based on non-verbal communication (sitting, standing, eye contact, body language, tone of voice, and physical aspects such as clothing). Investors can be put off very quickly when entrepreneurs speak too fast or too softly, lack enthusiasm, read slides, avoid eye contact, rely on technical jargon, or excessively gesture. The reality is that entrepreneurs who manage impressions and convey confidence and social adaptability are more likely to be persuasive (Hoehn-Weiss et al., 2004).

Usage Suggestions

The exercise works for all audiences, undergraduate, graduate, executive, or practitioner. It is appropriate for new venture creation courses, entrepreneurship bootcamps, or workshops. The session can be positioned to bookend a course, where the students are first asked to stand up and deliver a short description of their idea after having identified a venture concept, project, or family or corporate initiative, but prior to any other learning. The exercise can be used again toward the end of the course after students have developed an understanding of the opportunity, team, resources, and business model and can more clearly articulate the value proposition.

Learning Objectives

● Learn the basics of constructing the content and communication of a pitch for a venture idea.
● Consider the importance of understanding the expectations and motivations of their audience.
● Assess the amount of research and thought that go into effective communication of a business opportunity.

Materials List

● "Babson Rocket Pitch Evaluation" (at the end of this exercise).
● Stopwatch (preferably with an alarm).

Pre-Work Required by Students

If the exercise is delivered in two parts, as suggested above, there is no pre-work required. If conducted toward the end of the class, one or both of the readings below are recommended.

Theoretical Foundations

Hoehn-Weiss, Manuela N., Brush, Candida G., and Baron, Robert A. 2004. Putting your best foot forward? *Journal of Private Equity*, 7(4), 17–26.
Santinelli, A., and Brush, C.G. 2013. Designing and delivering the perfect pitch. Babson College.

Time Plan (60 minutes)

This exercise can be adapted to fit various time schedules, including an entire class. For the purposes of this teaching note, the exercise requires one hour.

Step 1   0:00–0:20 (20 minutes)
Begin the exercise by asking for a volunteer to present his or her idea to the class. Let the student know that he or she will be given only 3 minutes to present the idea. No other instructions should be given. The student should be promptly stopped after 3 minutes.

Ask the students in the class to take a few minutes to jot down their thoughts and impressions, and then ask for another volunteer. Continue in this fashion until three to five students have presented.

Step 2   0:20–1:00 (40 minutes)
Hand out the "Babson Rocket Pitch Evaluation" and ask the students to
compare it to their notes and complete the evaluation form for each of the
pitches. Now you are ready to conduct a conversation using the following
questions as a guide:

- Let's start with the first pitch: Can anyone describe what the product
  or service is and how it works?
- Who is the target audience and what is the problem that is being
  solved?
- Is this a good opportunity? Why?
- Are there any contextual factors that lead you to believe that this is
  a good opportunity?
- How is the product unique or different from the competition and
  other alternatives?
- How does the company plan to make money?
- Do the skills of the team match the needs of the business?
- What resources are required to launch the business?
- What did you think of the manner in which the information was
  communicated?
- What could the presenter have done within the given time con-
  straints to improve the content and the communication?

Continue with each of the pitches asking similar questions. Ask how the
students' evaluation compared to the evaluation criteria on the form.

The discussion will surface many of the holes in the idea at its current
stage. From this discussion a work plan for further analysis of the idea
should emerge.

The first time through this exercise the students will only have an idea,
little knowledge of whether the idea is indeed an opportunity, and no
props.

The second time through the exercise at the end of the course, the students will have more of the answers to the questions above. The presentation should still be kept to three to five minutes, or you can require that
it is shorter, even two minutes, depending on the overall time allocated
for the session. The presenter may use slides, a flip chart, or a device of
his or her choosing as a communications aid. It is important that the time
constraint be kept, so as to keep the presenter focused on answering the
critical questions.

A variation of the exercise could be to have a few judges, who are
familiar with the pitch pedagogy, provide immediate written and verbal
feedback using the "Babson Rocket Pitch Evaluation." For the purpose

of staying on time, no time should be allowed for questions and answers, just feedback.

A third variation of the exercise could be to allow for a question-and-answer period by the judges and/or classmates. This is totally dependent upon the amount of time you have allotted for the exercise.

Post-Work

If the exercise is used at the beginning of a course, an interesting follow-up exercise is to have students individually or in teams use the feedback as a guide for creating a work plan for conducting further research into the feasibility of their ideas. The initial presentation usually exposes open issues and questions about the idea that require further feasibility testing.

Teaching Tips

Students often begin this exercise with much apprehension. It is best to allow the class to stew for a while, calling up volunteers and keeping strict adherence to the time constraint. Students will begin to realize the seriousness of the pitch when asking investors for money. Once you get into the discussion a bit, you can calm their nerves by noting some very favorable aspects of the content of the ideas as well as positive communication skills demonstrated. The students will also be pleased to find out that, as the course unfolds, they will be learning the skills, tools, and techniques necessary to improve their performance by the end of the course.

Allowing individual or group time to assess the pitch from the perspective of exposed holes in the idea, questions raised, and necessary data and analysis required is another way to frame the arch of your entrepreneurship course and allow students to create their own work plan to follow as the course unfolds.

Key Takeaways

- The importance of communicating the key content items to your audience: value proposition, team, market opportunity, product descriptions, competitive environment, business model, key milestones, and finances.
- The role and importance of preparation and communication in how people and ideas are perceived.

Babson Rocket Pitch Evaluation

Project name:

		False				True
Idea	What is it? How does it work? (clear and well-understood description of the product or service)	1	2	3	4	5
Comments:						
Customer	Who is it for? (initial target market is clearly described and sized)	1	2	3	4	5
Comments:						
Need	Why do they need it? (the problem or opportunity fit is clearly stated and understood)	1	2	3	4	5
Comments:						
Business model	How do you make money? (the various elements of the business model are clearly understood)	1	2	3	4	5
Comments:						
Differentiation	What makes it unique and different? (certain unique aspects that *resonate* with the target have been identified and *substantiated*)	1	2	3	4	5
Comments:						
People	The team has or has identified needed skills, contacts, and experience	1	2	3	4	5
Comments:						
The ask	The financing plan is sensible and a specific amount of funding identified	1	2	3	4	5
Comments:						

EXERCISE: WHO'S ON FIRST?

AUTHOR: ELAINE EISENMAN

Description

This exercise is designed to highlight the ways that entrepreneurial teams approach problem-solving challenges. In particular, it highlights team skills in decision making, delegation, leadership effectiveness, and leader control, and ways in which teams make sense of uncertainty and ambiguity.

Usage Suggestions

It can be used for multiple purposes to highlight issues around owner–employee relationships, and to understand the differing dynamics in intact, functional teams, but tends to work better with a more experienced audience

Learning Objectives

- Experience how group dynamics and leader behaviors play a critical role in defining and solving challenges.
- Practice defining the problem and asking the right questions before rushing to a solution before the challenge is fully defined.
- Recognize that the approach to problem-solving chosen can impact both process and outcomes.

Materials List

Flip charts, markers, a copy of the worksheet "Group Problem-Solving Challenge: 'Who's On First?'" (included at the end of this exercise) for each participant, and a timer.

Pre-Work Required by Students

None.

Theoretical Foundations

Katzenbach, Jon, and Smith, Douglas. 2005. The discipline of teams. *Harvard Business Review*, July.
Bradford, D.L., and Cohen, A.R. 1998. *Power Up: Transforming Organizations Through Shared Leadership*. Hoboken, NJ: Wiley.

Time Plan (60 minutes)

1. **Set Up**   0:00–0:15 (15 minutes)
   Read the challenge and distribute the "Group Problem-Solving
   Challenge: 'Who's On First?'" challenge worksheet. Give students
   time to read the challenge and think silently.
2. **Group challenge**   0:15–0:40 (25 minutes)
   Ideally, set the timer to ring at the end of 20 minutes; allow 5 additional minutes for completion. If the group completes the task before
   20 minutes, begin the debrief.
3. **Report out**   0:40–0:45 (5 minutes)
   Each group must read their answers aloud. After all groups have
   reported the instructor should then present the correct answers.
   Answer Key

Catcher:	Allen
Pitcher:	Harry
1st baseman:	Paul
2nd baseman:	Jerry
3rd baseman:	Andy
Shortstop:	Ed
Left field:	Sam
Center field:	Bill
Right Field:	Mike

4. **Debrief:**   0:45–1:00 (15 minutes)
   Discussion about the process used, challenges, learnings, and areas of
   application to the actual work setting.

   - Ask the group to identify who the leader was, how the leader
     emerged, what the group did that was effective and ineffective,
     and what when faced with a similar challenge, given hindsight,
     they would do differently.
   - Review the decision-making styles set out in the handout
     "Decision-Making Styles" (at the end of the exercise). Ask:
     What decision-making styles were used? Which were most effec-
     tive? Which were least effective? Give examples. Why was one
     style more effective than the others?
   - For intact groups, ask how much felt like business as usual, and
     then ask the above questions. Pay particular attention to issues
     arising from one person going off, figuring it out, and coming
     back with the answer. Ask about the impact on the team and if
     this is a regular occurrence.

Key Takeaways

- Time spent on problem definition is critical to achieve successful resolution.
- Decision-making styles vary in effectiveness depending on context and challenge.
- Openly reflecting as a group on group dynamics is important to team development.

Post-Work

Ask how they can apply the insights from this exercise back at work. What might they do differently, or how can they remind people of the effective and ineffective roles when they see them going forward?

Teaching Tips

- Remind the students that the challenge can be solved without knowing anything about baseball. The one recurring question is what positions constitute the Battery, and that information is provided on the worksheet ("Group Problem-Solving Challenge: 'Who's On First?'").
- The ideal size is no more than ten members per group, and the minimum size is five.
- If the group is not a previously intact group, tell them that it is required that this be solved as a total group.
- If there are multiple groups, make it a competition and have a small prize for the winning team. Ask the winning team to share their process and strategy.
- If it is intact, say nothing and watch how the process plays out. Do some members go off and solve it on their own?
- What subgroups form? How do the group solve the challenge? Do they draw a baseball diamond? If they do, how much time is spent on it before realizing that it doesn't help solve the questions?
- The most effective solution is to create a matrix of all the names on one axis with all the positions on the other. Then the names are checked off as the statements are read and the impossible combinations are eliminated.
- Most groups finish in 15–20 minutes. If the group hasn't finished, end the exercise at 25 minutes after giving a 5-minute warning at 20 minutes.
- When they are finished, have them read the answers to you, and you check the answer sheet.
- In general, reasons for not completing are not drawing a matrix on

the flip chart, not having a person who is in charge of eliminating names, allowing tangential discussion, subgrouping, and over-analyzing before beginning to work on the challenge itself.

Group Problem-Solving Challenge: "Who's On First?"

Goal
As a team, identify the individual who plays each of the following positions on the baseball team described below.

Positions to identify
Catcher _____
Pitcher _____
First baseman _____
Second baseman _____
Third baseman _____
Shortstop _____
Left field _____
Right field _____

Note: "The Battery" is the pitcher and the catcher.

Information available:

1. Andy dislikes the catcher.
2. Ed's sister is engaged to the second baseman.
3. The center fielder is taller than the right fielder.
4. Harry and the third baseman live in the same building.
5. Paul and Allen won $20 from the pitcher at pinochle.
6. Ed and the outfielders play poker during their spare time.
7. The pitcher's wife is the third baseman's sister.
8. All the battery and the infield, except Allen, Harry and Andy are shorter than Sam.
9. Paul, Andy and the shortstop lost $150 each at the racetrack.
10. Paul, Harry and Bill and the catcher got trounced by the second baseman at pool.
11. Sam is undergoing a divorce suit.
12. The catcher and the third baseman each have two children.
13. Ed, Paul, Jerry, the right fielder and the center fielder are bachelors: the others are married.
14. The shortstop, the third baseman, and Bill each made $100 betting on the fights.

15. One of the outfielders is either Mike or Andy.
16. Jerry is taller than Bill. Mike is shorter than Bill. Each is heavier than the third baseman.

Decision-Making Styles

There are four general decision-making styles that leaders (and teams) use:

1. **Autonomous**: The leader alone makes the decision, although data collection from others is possible. Data collection can be either one-on-one or in a group. In the group, the leader might seek information (e.g. "How would various customers respond to . . .?") but does not otherwise involve the other(s) in the decision-making process.
2. **Consultative**: The leader involves others in the decision making itself. (Again this can be done one-on-one or in the group.) In the group, members can influence the decision (and often the leader will change his or her opinion by the weight of the arguments), but in the last analysis the decision will be the *leader's first choice*. (A variation is that, when the specific agenda item is within one person's area but impacts others, it might be consultative to that person (so the decision has to be his or her first choice).
3. **Joint**: Joint decision making is by consensus. This means all people have their say, are understood by everyone else, and collaboratively work toward a solution that all can actively support (even though it may not be any one individual's first choice). The leader should not accept a team decision he or she can't live with, but, since there is often more than one viable way to solve a problem, the leader will accept a decision that is not first choice as long as it is still supportable.
4. **Delegative**: In this case, the problem is delegated to an individual or subgroup *to make the decision*, often within predetermined parameters. The leader and the group agree to accept the subgroup's decision, so this is different from it being assigned to an individual or individuals to come back with a recommendation.

Effective leaders *use all four* decision-making styles. What differentiates leaders is *which style they want to use with each problem*. It is less an issue of right or wrong than of what benefits you seek and what costs you are willing to pay. Each has some drawbacks – there is no free lunch.
Source: Bradford and Cohen (1998).

Teaching entrepreneurship

EXERCISE: FAMILY SYSTEMS

AUTHOR: MATT ALLEN

Description

This exercise helps students to recognize the different viewpoints that influence decision making within a family business. Students will consider multiple viewpoints within a family system as well as the impact that these viewpoints might have on the decision-making process. In this exercise, students will have the opportunity to assume different roles within a family business. Using a case study situation, students will then work through issues related to the case based on their assigned role, thus helping them to see the complexity involved in the family business decision-making process.

This exercise is theoretically grounded in systems theory, which argues that in order to understand a concept or process it is important to understand the various systems that impact that process or concept (von Bertalanffy, 1968). Systems theory has been applied to the context of family businesses in order to clarify the complexity of multiple systems influencing decision making (Habbershon and Williams, 1999). Family businesses tend to be much more complex than their non-family counterparts because the family system, the management system, and the ownership system all play an influential role in decision-making processes. In addition, this exercise is useful in helping students to understand the importance of socioemotional wealth preservation for family businesses (Gómez-Mejía et al., 2007). Researchers have demonstrated that family businesses will often focus on preserving socioemotional wealth (family status, family ownership, community influence, etc.) even at the expense of financial well-being (Wiseman and Gómez-Mejía, 1998). Socioemotional wealth preservation provides an example of how different systems within the family business context might influence decision making in a way that makes family businesses distinct from other business forms.

Usage Suggestions

This exercise works well for all audiences, undergraduate, graduate, practitioner, or even high school students, though it is most effective for groups with some business education or experienced practitioners. It is appropriate for family business courses or family business discussions within an entrepreneurship course. The exercise is best positioned early on in a family business course or discussion of family business, as it helps students to better understand the general dynamics of the family business context.

Learning Objectives

- Apply family systems theory.
- Discover the complexity involved in family business decision making.
- Assess the implications of a dual focus on financial and socioemotional wealth.

Materials List

- "Business Case" (included at the end of this exercise).
- "Team Role Assignments" (included at the end of this exercise).

The business case included here is generic, but readily adaptable to fit the needs of the instructor. The instructor may choose to use his or her own case or alter the included case in order to meet specific needs of the class.

The roles assigned to students can vary based on the size of the class and the complexity desired in the classroom discussion.

Pre-Work Required by Students

Readings found in the theoretical foundations may be required for pre-work depending on the audience.

Theoretical Foundations

Bertalanffy, L. von. 1968. *General System Theory*. New York: Braziller.
Gómez-Mejía, L.R., Haynes, K.T., Núñez-Nickel, M., Jacobson, K.J.L., and Moyano-Fuentes, J. 2007. Socioemotional wealth and business risks in family-controlled firms: Evidence from Spanish olive oil mills. *Administrative Science Quarterly*, 52(1), 106–37.
Habbershon, T.G., and Williams, M.L. 1999. A unified systems perspective of family firm performance. *Journal of Business Venturing*, 18, 451–65.
Wiseman, R.M., and Gómez-Mejía, L.R. 1998. A behavioral agency model of managerial risk taking. *Academy of Management Review*, 23(1), 133–53.

Time Plan (30 minutes)

This exercise can be adapted to meet various time frames depending on how much time and effort are used for the discussion and debrief. For the purposes of this teaching note, the exercise requires 30 minutes. No reading or other preparation is required by the students prior to the exercise and, because of the length, the exercise can be employed as one component of a full class meeting focused on family businesses.

Step 1   0:00 to 0:10 (10 minutes)

- Begin the exercise by presenting the business case. This may be accomplished by allowing the students to read the short case description on a slide or handout or by explaining the business situation as part of a discussion in class. It is important that all students have a clear and common understanding of the situation faced by the business described in the case.
- Without discussing implications of the case described, divide the class into small groups of four to five students each and assign each group a role that relates to the business described in the case. It is important that participants clearly understand the role assigned. (If this is being done in a large class, you might have multiple groups assigned the same role. In a smaller class you would have one student group representing each assigned role.)
- Ask each group to consider both their role and the current situation of the business described in the case. Their assignment is to discuss what they consider to be their three greatest concerns. Again, this is based on both their assigned role and the situation of the business in the case. Allow teams to discuss these concerns for 5–7 minutes.

Step 2   0:10 to 0:20 (10 minutes)

- When discussion is complete, allow each team to share the different concerns that they came up with based on their assigned role. Write the concerns for each role on the board so that participants can see the concerns of other teams compared to their own.
- Once concerns from all teams have been listed, ask students to compare the concerns of each of the assigned roles.
  - How are they different? (Differences in this exercise are generally the result of differing needs and perspectives. Employees are concerned about their jobs, managers about their jobs as well as decision making, owners about the business and perhaps even their reputation, while spouses might be concerned about lifestyle or the health and well-being of their spouse.)
  - Why might they be different? (There are many reasons for these differences, and different groups will see different reasoning. One common reason for differences is based on dif-

ferent spheres of influence. As employees often feel that they cannot influence much beyond their individual role, their concerns might be more narrow in scope. Managers, on the other hand, might recognize their ability to influence change and, as a result, will also be thinking about decisions and consequences. Owners, with an even broader influence, would be concerned about the company and the larger implications. Spouses, with little leverage over the company, will tend to focus on what they do control in the situation, which might be children, spouse, or the effect of the business on the family.)

- How are they similar? (The obvious similarity is that, at one level or another, the situation is likely concerning to all.)
- Why might some of the concerns be similar? (All draw benefits from their involvement with the business, and all have something to lose, even if that something is not the same across all parties.)

• Once the concerns expressed by each of the assigned roles have been compared and contrasted, ask participants to consider the implications of the differences between roles for decision making.

- How might each of the assigned roles approach decision making for the business? (One way to look at different approaches to decisions is based on their knowledge and the experience that they can bring to the decision. Another is to look at their ability to impact the business.)
- How might the solutions to the current issues differ by role? Most answers here will be based on self-serving decisions from each role. Employees will want to do what is best for employees, owners for owners, and so on.
- How might they be the same? While different, it is also possible that there are some similarities in solutions. Clearly all will benefit if the business improves quickly; this is the complexity of the family business. Even when goals are somewhat aligned, significant differences exist in approach and motivation.

Step 3   0:20–0:30 (10 minutes)

• Point out to participants that the different roles assigned represent perspectives of different systems influencing decision making in the family business (family, management, ownership, etc.).
• Explain that it is important to understand each of the different systems in order to fully appreciate the complexity involved in family business decision making.

- You might choose to further highlight this complexity by allowing participants to debate which role expressed the "correct" or "right" concerns. The answer is generally that all are "right" based on their perspective or point of view. The difficulty is that most decisions will not be able to fully satisfy any of the different perspectives.

Key Takeaways

- Systems theory represents a useful perspective for understanding family businesses. In order to understand family businesses, it is important to understand the different systems that might influence a family business.
- While all businesses are influenced by different systems, family businesses tend to be more complex. A typical publicly traded company might focus mostly on management decisions, while a family business will be concerned with management, ownership, and family issues among others.
- When working in a family business it is important to recognize the influence of these various systems on decision making.
- When struggling to make change in a family business it might be because you are focusing on influencing the wrong system.

Post-Work

A follow-up to this exercise might include a discussion of the different family system perspectives for current issues faced by a real family business. If participants come from a family business background they might be asked to consider these issues in their own family business.

Teaching Tips

- Participants may find it difficult to fully consider some of the assigned roles such as "spouse of the owner." While discussion in the teams is taking place, it may be necessary to wander around the classroom in order to listen to the discussion and remind participants that they are to think from the perspective of their assigned role, not their own thoughts or opinions.
- Often there will be overlap in the concerns expressed by teams assigned to different roles. Here it might be useful to point out that, even though concerns are similar, the reasoning behind those concerns is often different. For example, managers and owners might both be concerned about the financial future of the company, but

managers might be thinking from an employment standpoint and owners from a personal risk and wealth standpoint. These nuances can be developed by asking teams to explain the reasoning behind the concerns they express.

Business Case

(This described situation can be adapted in many ways to fit specific needs in the classroom.)

- Situation – small business (manufacturing company) struggling financially.
- Expenses have exceeded income for six months.
- Cash reserves will be depleted within three months.
- Minimal debt is available because of the recession.
- Demand is down from normal, leading to the company operating at only 57 percent of capacity.
- Aside from reducing orders for supplies in order to match reduced demand, the company has yet to implement any major budget cuts, layoffs, or other measures to cope with the situation.
- As with most businesses in today's environment, it is not known when demand will improve.

Employees are worried, and motivation across the company is poor, leading to a decrease in performance, quality, and customer service.

Team Role Assignments

(This list of roles is not exhaustive, and additional or alternative roles may be assigned in order to fit the needs of the discussion.)

- **Owner**: The person who owns the majority of the shares of the business described.
- **Manager**: A non-owner manager responsible for management of employees within the organization.
- **Spouse of owner**: A non-owner spouse who has no involvement in the business and does not own shares.
- **Employee**: An employee who does not own shares and does not have responsibility for the management of others.

EXERCISE: UNDERSTANDING THE ENTREPRENEURIAL SIDE OF GOVERNMENT

AUTHORS: JULIAN LANGE AND CRAIG BENSON

Description

This exercise illustrates the application of entrepreneurial thinking to the challenge of providing excellent customer service in the public sector. Through class discussion students analyze the implications of regarding people served by government as customers. Students also explore the similarities and differences in the processes and motivations affecting private and public sector stakeholders. In addition, students identify the major categories of the customers of a town government and the opportunities and challenges presented by providing excellent service to these diverse groups. Next, students are divided into teams, each of which takes on the role of a town government customer service team. The teams develop recommendations for improving and implementing excellent customer service, and these recommendations are presented to the class and discussed by the students in a plenary session. Finally, class discussion turns to the analysis of implementation issues, including resource availability, customer feedback, and the development of metrics.

Usage Suggestions

This exercise works well with various student audiences including MBA, undergraduate and executive. It is desirable but not necessary for MBAs and undergraduates to have completed at least one core entrepreneurship course. We suggest positioning the exercise as a special topic in a basic survey course on entrepreneurship; as a topic area in an entrepreneurial marketing course; or as an example of entrepreneurial approaches in a public policy entrepreneurship course, combined with a guest speaker or speakers from the public sector.

Learning Objectives

- Identify entrepreneurial approaches in the public sector environment.
- Compare similarities and differences between "customers" in the private and public sectors.
- Define the key actors, stakeholders, and decision makers in an entrepreneurial government initiative.

- Explore the opportunities and challenges involved in implementing a customer service initiative in government.

Materials List

None.

Pre-Work Required by Students

You may want to assign or excerpt Blanchard, Kenneth H. and Bowles, Sheldon. 1993. *Raving Fans: A Revolutionary Approach to Customer Service*. New York: William Morrow.

Theoretical Foundations

Case: Lange, Julian E. and Benson, Craig R. 2013. *Entrepreneurial Thought and Action® in Wellesley: Customer Service*. Wellesley, MA: Babson College
Baumol, W.J. 1990. Entrepreneurship: Productive, unproductive, and destructive. *Journal of Political Economy*, 98(5), 893–921.
Minniti, Maria. 2008. The role of government policy on entrepreneurial activity: Productive, unproductive, or destructive. *Entrepreneurship Theory and Practice*, 32(5), 779–90.
Davenport, Tom and Lange, Julian. 2011. Prediction logic: Analytics for entrepreneurial thinking. In Danna Greenberg, Kate McKone-Sweet, and James Wilson (eds.), *The New Entrepreneurial Leader: Developing Leaders Who Shape Social and Economic Opportunity* (pp. 62–76). San Francisco: Berrett-Koehler.

Time Plan (90 minutes)

This exercise is designed for 90 minutes, but it can be adapted for shorter time schedules as well. Prior to the class, students will have completed a reading assignment on customer service. It is recommended that students read the classic book *Raving Fans* (Blanchard and Bowles, 1993) in preparation for this exercise, but the instructor may substitute a reading of his or her choice that provides an introduction to customer service principles.

Step 1   0:00–0:20 (20 minutes)
A useful way to begin is for the instructor to say: "Historically, in many venues, government officials and employees have not thought of the people they serve as customers. Does this view make sense?" The instructor should then ask students to vote "yes" or "no," and count the votes. After the vote, the discussion can proceed as follows:

- Choose students who voted each way and ask them to explain their vote. During the ensuing discussion, the instructor should make two lists on the board of the students' reasons for voting "yes" and for voting "no."
- Next, the instructor should ask the students: "What are the major components of effective customer service?" and list these on the board.
- The instructor can then turn the class's attention to a comparison of customer service in the private and public sectors by posing the following questions:
  - Has anyone in the class ever been involved in public sector activities?
  - What are the differences, if any, between the customers of a retail business and the customers of a local or state government?
  - What are the similarities and differences in providing excellent customer service in the private sector and the public sector?
  - Does it make sense to adopt a strategy of attempting early "quick wins" on smaller projects in order to build momentum for larger long-term projects?

Step 2   0:20–0:50 (30 minutes)
The instructor should then divide the class into groups of five to six students and introduce the assignment for the teams, which is as follows:

- As members of the Town Centralized Customer Service Team, create a list of your recommendations for improving customer service in town government.
- From this list, *choose the five most important recommendations.*
- Be prepared to present your recommendations to the class.

During this time period, each group should choose a scribe and develop their recommendations.

Step 3 (groups report out and class discussion)   0:50–1:15 (25 minutes)
The instructor should choose one group to write their recommendations on the board and present them to the class. The instructor should then ask each of the other groups to add one recommendation to the list.

At this point, the instructor should ask the class:

- What are the major resources that the town will need to implement effective customer service?

- How should the town obtain feedback about customer service?
- How should the effectiveness of customer service be measured?

Step 4 (wrap-up)   1:15–1:30 (15 minutes)
The instructor should ask the students to vote again on the initial question, "Should the people served by government be thought of as customers?" and count the votes and note the similarity or difference between this vote and the initial vote. The instructor should then ask the students to explain why their vote stayed the same or changed. Finally, the instructor should ask the students what their first actions would be in implementing excellent customer service in government and lead students to observe that small first steps can be an important component of implementing excellent customer service in the longer run.

Post-Work

If desired, the instructor can assign a short two-page/500-word paper in which students discuss their lessons learned about providing excellent customer service in the public sector.

Key Takeaways

- Although many people think entrepreneurial government is an oxymoron, in fact there are many opportunities to apply entrepreneurial approaches to government activities.
- Thinking of the people served by government as customers helps government decision makers to recognize the importance of providing excellent customer service.
- Effective analytical decision-making processes are similar in the public and private sectors.
- The achievement of "quick wins" on smaller projects can build momentum toward implementing effective longer-term solutions.

Teaching Tips

- Don't get bogged down in minutiae or in politics: Keep the discussion non-political.
- Ask students follow-on questions about how they would implement their ideas.
- Ask students to focus on the similarities as well as the differences between thinking and acting entrepreneurially in the private sector and the public sector.

EXERCISE: CREATING CUSTOMER PERSONAS

AUTHOR: DONNA KELLEY

Description

Early-stage entrepreneurship requires a connection between a novel opportunity and a customer who sees its value. So how do entrepreneurs stretch their imaginations, think beyond what has already been done, yet also create something that people will actually buy? They do this by learning about their customers. The Creating Customer Personas exercise helps students walk in their customers' shoes and develop an empathetic understanding about who they are, how they think, what they do, where they go and when, and ultimately the problems they have that may reveal opportunities.

Usage Suggestions

Students, entrepreneurs, and managers can benefit from this exercise. It can be used in feasibility or new venture courses, and entrepreneurship workshops. It is also relevant for classes or seminars on entrepreneurial marketing, particularly since this is an early-stage technique aimed at developing fresh market insights under high uncertainty and less clarity about the product or market mix (in contrast to more traditional corporate marketing practices). It can be used after ethnography or observation exercises and customer interviews to develop a picture of the customer that pulls together all that has been learned so far. It can also help the students develop testable assumptions about their target market.

This exercise is particularly effective for international entrepreneurship courses, where students are taking a class or expressing a desire around doing business in another region of the world. By stepping in the shoes of someone who lives in a very different place, with dissimilar lifestyles, foods, customs, and so on, the students can develop empathy for those living in an unfamiliar culture.

Learning Objectives

- Adopt a customer learning perspective to build customer-driven opportunities.
- Employ early-stage market research techniques.
- Build a customer profile around an entrepreneurial opportunity.
- Visualize the core customer segment.

Materials List

"Customer Persona Worksheet" (included at the end of the exercise).

Pre-Work Required by Students

If the students have conducted ethnography or observation exercises or customer interviews in previous classes, they can review their field notes or any written assignments or presentations. If they haven't, it's helpful to have some contact with customers or people representing their customers. They can be assigned a short pre-class exercise where they talk with someone who is a customer, or at least representative of one. This can be either in person (preferably) or over the phone and doesn't need to be longer than 30 minutes.

The interview should focus on understanding the customer's behavior and preferences relative to the opportunity space. Caution the students that this is about learning and exploring, not validating; they should therefore *not* be presenting a concept and asking the customers if they like it, how they would change or enhance it, when they would use it, and how much they would pay for it. Those are later-stage questions and not reliable or valid in the early phases of shaping the opportunity.

Another approach to the interview exercise involves spending about 30 minutes taking a potential customer through a customer decision-making map: walking him or her through a "day in the life" map of a usage situation (go through the decision, purchase, and usage process with the customer – ideally an actual recent situation). The student can be on the lookout for problems, particular actions, or perceptions the customer identifies, and even unexpected remarks arising during this process. These can be probed further to gain better understanding about customer behavior and preferences.

For either the interview or the decision-making map, it would be best if everyone did this individually so they build their skills talking to customers and bring different experiences to the group discussion.

Theoretical Foundations

Cooper, Alan. 2004. *The Inmates Are Running the Asylum: Why High Tech Products Drive Us Crazy and How to Restore the Sanity*. Indianapolis, IN: Sams Publishing.

Kelley, Donna. 2013. *Conducting an Early-Stage Feasibility Analysis for an Entrepreneurial Opportunity*. Wellesley, MA: Babson College.

Pruitt, John, and Grudin, Jonathan. *Personas: Practice and Theory*, http://research.microsoft.com/en-us/um/redmond/groups/coet/grudin/personas/old%

20versions/pruitt-grudinrev2.pdf; http://research.microsoft.com/en-us/UM/Peo
ple/jgrudin/publications/personas/DesignChapter.pdf (accessed September 30,
2013).
Seiger, Alicia, and Chess, Robert. 2003. *Stanford Note on Market Research*. E-165.
Stanford University.

Time Plan (60–70 minutes)

Generally, the students will have been working on a business concept
for a course. If this is a seminar or shorter course, they could apply this
exercise to a current or familiar business (for example, working MBAs or
executives). It helps for them to have some knowledge or learning about
the customer, and this can take place in prior classes or exercises like ethnography or observations, customer decision-making maps, and customer
interviews. The exercise is best done in teams, so there can be group interactions around the elements of the storyboard in small groups, before the
class discussion.

Step 1   0:00–0:10 (10 minutes)
Introduce the storyboard, handing out the worksheet. Review the objectives of the exercise, and in particular how it fits into the particular framework for the course. Let them know what they will or should get out of
this exercise. For example, if it is an international entrepreneurship course,
they should be able to view the opportunity space from the standpoint of
a customer in a different culture; they should develop a type of empathy
for the situation and perspective of someone who may otherwise seem
very unfamiliar to them. In addition, talk about how it links with the other
exercises they have done, for instance how they are pulling together all
they have learned into creating a profile of the customer. Mention how it
will fit with, and inform, their next steps in the course.

Step 2   0:10–0:30 (20 minutes)
Introduce the components of the exercise. This can be done all at once;
move around the room observing the teamwork and answering questions.
Alternatively, the components can be introduced one at a time; the class
can pause between each to have a few teams share what they developed.
Some teams may be faster at some parts of the process and want to spend
more time on one of the four aspects, so be aware of this. If teams have an
opportunity to get together outside class, the instructor could assign this
as a homework exercise for the teams to go through; this will save time and
move the focus toward discussing the outcomes and implications.
    It may be useful to use flip charts, flip chart paper taped to the walls,

or white- or blackboards. The students will enjoy drawing big pictures
of their customer, and it's fun to look around the room at these profiles.
Teams can present their storyboards to the class. (If there are a lot of
teams, different teams can present particular parts of their storyboard.)

Step 3   0:30–0:50 (20 minutes)
Initiate the report-out and class discussion. Some questions can include:

1. What have you learned about your customer so far? How has your
    view of your customer changed?
2. What surprised you? What did you not anticipate? (Students should
    move beyond their preconceived notions to more objective observa-
    tions and insights, and a view toward capturing the unexpected.)
3. What assumptions are you making? Do you have evidence to back
    this up? Can you find a way to test these assumptions?
4. What issues or uncertainties are evident here? What questions might
    you ask a customer to probe further on these and to get valid and reli-
    able answers?
5. What would be the most logical next step you would take to continue
    understanding your customer?
6. What benefits does the customer seem to be looking for (convenience,
    simplicity, status, durability, and speed, for example)? Which are
    more important than others?

The instructor should be sure to engage others in the class about each
team's storyboard. In this way, teams get feedback, their opportunities
are exposed to a greater diversity of perspectives, and they learn from
the diverse array of customer stories and opportunities, ideally applying
what was learned from the other storyboards to their own opportunities
or businesses.

Summary and close   0:50–1:00/1:10 (10–20 minutes)
Ask the students to identify what they learned with regard to their opportunities, and how this changes their approach. Looking forward, they can
identify what they should do next in their investigation, or use what was
learned to plan the next class exercise. The instructor can close with some
summary points.

Post-Work

Students can use what they learn to identify assumptions to test or questions to explore further. The instructor may assign a market test exercise,

where they test one of their assumptions (for example, counting bicycle traffic at different locations at various points of the day, setting up a rough prototype test).

Additionally, the students should be encouraged to incorporate these qualitative elements in their feasibility analyses, marketing analyses, or business plans. Business plans in particular tend to over focus on quantitative data on the market, and students aren't always comfortable describing their customers. By encouraging them to include these qualitative descriptions, instructors can help students learn to project in-depth understanding about who they are targeting their opportunity toward.

Key Takeaways

- Traditional market research techniques like surveys and concept testing are less relevant for early-stage opportunity development. In-depth, qualitative techniques like customer personas can help entrepreneurs obtain a more sophisticated "gut feel" about their customers and shape their opportunities to better address existing or latent customer needs. It is more effective than either attempting to convince customers that an opportunity the entrepreneur developed (in isolation) is valuable to them, or missing the mark with the market.
- The customer understanding gained in this type of research can also be useful in making a convincing case to the audience for the opportunity (for example, the reader of a business plan, or an investor or stakeholder in a presentation or meeting). It is thus valuable to accompany numbers and charts with qualitative descriptions of customers.
- Customer understanding is a skill that can be learned, and is best learned through practice. The persona exercise puts a face on the customer and, in so doing, helps make what seems like a vague, intangible process more tangible.
- This exercise should emphasize the importance of being open to surprises and allowing assumptions to be disproved. This process should lead to a revision of assumptions and help plan the next steps with regard to investigating and developing the opportunity.

Teaching Tips

Students may possibly approach this exercise with apprehension, owing to its creative nature (i.e. creating a fictional customer). Doing this in teams is helpful, and often there are some team members who are more comfortable with the artistic, creative aspects. The instructor, however, may need to assess initial progress and help get teams started. It's also useful to have made the students aware of this exercise in advance so they have time to think about this, particularly when they are performing other exercises (ethnographies, interviews, etc.) that will contribute to the storyboard.

The other challenge may center on connecting the profile and usage patterns to the problem. Ideally, the problem should arise from understanding who the customer is and how he or she behaves. Students may have a preconceived problem that doesn't really connect to what they are seeing. The instructor should therefore encourage students *not* to narrow in on a specific problem and to allow the problem they address to evolve or change. In addition, during the group work or class discussion, the instructor can really probe on this connection between the profile or usage and the problem. (For example, at what point during usage does the customer have this problem? Why? Where is the customer? Who is he or she with?)

Sometimes the students have a hard time identifying a problem from the profile and usage situation. Often, it starts as some version of "The customer doesn't have what we offer." That's not really a problem. The instructor will therefore need to coach them to identify problems in the usage situation. (Where in the process was there a real or perceived issue? Why does the customer use particular products and not others? Does the customer modify or compromise usage in any way?)

Customer Persona Worksheet

Describe (draw) a typical customer; give him or her a name. How old is the customer? Where does the customer live and what is his or her family like? What does the customer do (work, school, etc.) and where? What's the customer's background (experience, education)? Does the customer have certain interests or hobbies? What about the customer's beliefs? Can you say something else about the customer?	
How does the customer spend his or her time relative to the opportunity? Tell a story about a typical usage situation.	
What problem does the customer have relative to your opportunity and why?	What are the different ways the customer solves this problem? How does the customer feel about these different solutions?

9. Exercises to practice creation

EXERCISE: MIND DUMPING FOR IDEATION

AUTHORS: HEIDI NECK AND DENNIS CERU

Description

The Mind Dumping exercise jump starts the creative aspect of the entrepreneurial process – specifically ideation as a non-judgmental exercise designed to generate many ideas, some non-practical, from which to build and branch out to more practical potential ideas for new ventures, as well as to promote corporate innovation through new in-house initiatives and new corporate-sponsored ventures.

Usage Suggestions

This exercise works well for many audiences across the undergraduate, graduate, and practitioner arena. It is appropriate for new venture creation and entrepreneurship courses, workshops, and programs. This may be positioned as a first class exercise, ice-breaker, or warm-up exercise preceding more in-depth exploration of the idea creation and entrepreneurial thinking process.

Learning Objectives

- Practice techniques for creating and developing new ideas.
- Build skills in free association that are necessary for the creative process.
- Get comfortable with starting with "raw" or "seed" ideas rather than feeling the pressure to produce big opportunities.

Materials List

- "Student Mind Dump Worksheet" (see Figure 9.1). Each student should be given at least three worksheets.

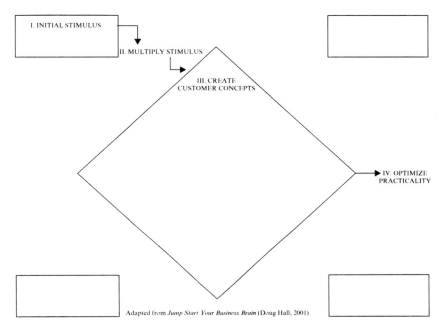

I. INITIAL STIMULUS

II. MULTIPLY STIMULUS

III. CREATE
CUSTOMER CONCEPTS

IV. OPTIMIZE
PRACTICALITY

Adapted from *Jump Start Your Business Brain* (Doug Hall, 2001)

Source: Adapted from Hall (2001).

Figure 9.1   Student Mind Dump Worksheet

- Small (1 inch × 2 inch) "sticky notes" – a variety of colors, one packet per student.

Pre-Work Required by Students

None.

Theoretical Foundations

Hall, D. 2001. *Jump Start Your Business Brain*. Cincinnati, OH: Clerisy Press.

Time Plan (2 hours)

The exercise has six parts: 1) set up the challenge, 2) gather stimuli, 3) multiply the stimuli, 4) develop raw or seed ideas, 5) elaborate one solution, and 6) debrief.

1. Set up the challenge   0:00–0:15 (15 minutes)
The instructor may identify one challenge for all students to work on or
students may work on individual challenges. Examples of challenges that
all students can work on are: How might we reimagine business education?
How might we solve the problem of waste on campus? Or how might we
create a better coffee mug? Whatever the challenge, students must write
down the challenge on a sticky note and place it in front of them. Once the
challenge is clearly written on a sticky note, hand out three "Student Mind
Dump Worksheets" to each student.

2. Gather stimuli   0:15–0:25 (10 minutes)

a. Address the types of stimuli and their importance to the idea genera-
    tion process.
    i. What is the role of stimuli and why are they important?
    ii. Ask: "If you were developing a new coffee mug, what could
        your stimuli be?" Answers will probably be sitting in a coffee
        shop, drinking coffee, testing out various mugs, reading coffee
        trade publications, and so on.
b. The purpose of stimuli is to surround yourself with artifacts that can
    help you stimulate new ideas. Artifacts do not have to be things or
    people – words work.
c. Quickly play a word association game: "If I say boy, you say . . .? I
    say cat; you say . . .? I say red; you say . . .?" This is called word asso-
    ciation, and it uses words as stimuli to get to the next word. We'll do
    something similar in this exercise.
d. For the next 3 minutes write down one word or very short phrase that
    comes to mind when you think about the challenge that sits before
    you. *This is not the time to be thinking about ideas* – only words. You
    are simply free-associating based on the challenge. You need to write
    down whatever comes to mind – even if you don't think it relates to
    the challenge. Important: Only one word or phrase should be written
    on each sticky note.
    i. Again you may want to give an example and revisit the coffee
        mug challenge. What are all the words that you think of when
        you think about developing a new coffee mug? Hot, leakage,
        driving to work, environment, taste, relaxation, home, and so
        on. Given that students should be writing one word or phrase per
        sticky note, the goal is to generate lots of written sticky notes.
e. *Note*: The people who are not generating a lot of completed stickies
    are those who are thinking too much. These are typically the left-
    brainers in the room, who often self-judge their own ideas.

f. After 3 minutes stop and have participants count how many stickies were filled out. Ask for high and low numbers so you can get a range. You can expect a high of around 30 or more and a low of eight or even less. Write this range on the board and ask the group for their thoughts.

3. Multiply stimuli   0:25–0:40 (15 minutes)

a. The free association that was used above is considered "habit" for many. It's part of most brainstorming sessions that we do in groups or simply as individuals. The next step however – multiplying the stimuli – is what makes this exercise unique. Multiplying the stimuli is *not* habit. Similar to what we did in the previous round we will free-associate again, but we will free-associate not on the challenge but on what we free-associated! You may need to repeat and clarify this a few times. In essence, the students are associating on their associations.

b. Randomly pick four stickies and place one in each of the four corners of the mind dump worksheet.

c. Free-associate on these four stimuli for 1–2 minutes.

d. Repeat at least three times (using three different mind dump worksheets) using a variety of methods. Options are:

    i. Free-associate on one corner at a time for 30 seconds each.

    ii. Free-associate using all four corners. You may look at one word, two, three, or all four (2 minutes per page).

    iii. Switch with a neighbor and free-associate on his or her corners.

e. Regardless of method the participants should be writing the words directly on the mind dump worksheet – not on stickies. They can write anywhere on the mind dump worksheet except inside the diamond. The diamond space will be used in the next stage.

4. Create raw or seed ideas   0:40–0:55 (15 minutes)

a. Now it's time to create seed – or raw – ideas. The goal is to create as many ideas as possible that will satisfy the original challenge. These ideas do not need to be complete or even feasible. They can be big or small, boring, exciting, bold, crazy, or fanciful. It doesn't matter as long as you are generating lots of ideas.

b. You have to let the words work for you and contribute to the idea generation process. Don't just write an idea that you probably had before you started – the seed ideas must come from the words on the page. Revisit the coffee mug example. Consider a mind dump worksheet with the following words: leakage, hot, morning drive, traffic, sleepy, radio talk show, Starbucks, Colombia, car, drink holder, sugar, sweet, calories, ice cream. What ideas for a new coffee mug can be derived from these words? One raw or seed idea could be a coffee mug that is a drink holder in one so you never have to worry about a space for the mug. Another idea could be a 100 percent lifetime warranty mug with a leak-proof lid. Are these great ideas? No, but it's a start. In later stages ideas can be combined or shaped into real opportunities, but now we're just concerned with seed ideas.

c. Do *not* consider feasibility or focus on a fully fleshed-out idea – this is a preliminary concept only.
d. Continue doing this until you have "seeded" at least three ideas per completed mind dump sheet.

5. Elaborate one solution   0:55–1:40 (45 minutes including break)
If time permits students may begin working together to develop stronger concepts. We encourage you to give students a break before moving to this stage in the same class session.

a. Break into groups of four to five. Each team member should share their favorite idea.
b. After sharing ideas the team must work together to combine the seed concepts into a bolder, more innovative idea. Encourage the students to try combining the best aspects of each idea. Note: This part of the exercise will not work if students are working on individual challenges rather than the entire class working on one shared challenge.
b. Each group then has 1 minute to present its final idea.
c. The instructor lists each "solution" on the board. When all presentations are completed ask the group to vote for the one solution they would choose to advance to the next stage of concept development. Then have a discussion of what those "next steps" could be. This is important to encourage an action orientation on new ideas.

6. Wrap up – what did you learn?   1:40–2:00 (15 minutes)

a. Reflections? What was easy and what was difficult for you?
b. What is the role of creativity in entrepreneurship? How important is creativity to the entrepreneurial mindset? And what is the role of structure and process in creativity? Can structure and process stifle or enable creativity?

Post-Work

The next steps might include using the results of this exercise as input for a preliminary feasibility blueprint or "quick screen" to explore the further qualification, quantification, and shaping inherent in the entrepreneurial process.

Key Takeaways

- Judgment slows down or stops the creative process – by side-stepping judgment or evaluation, the mind is opened to new and fresh thinking.
- "Wild ideas" provide the building blocks for more practical ideas and are necessary to fuel true lateral thinking, which is the source of creative problem solving.
- Ideation is an iterative process where nascent ideas are transformed into concepts that are ultimately shaped into "working practical possibilities," which are the foundation of innovation and entrepreneurial thinking and acting.

Teaching Tips

- Pay careful attention to timing – it is essential to move students through the "mind dumping" quickly to promote rapid-fire non-judgmental ideation.
- The number of "stickies" generated in the first part of the exercise (free association on the challenge) is directly and positively correlated with the number of ideas generated through the exercise. If time was not a constraint in the classroom, students would continue to fill out mind dump worksheets until all stickies were used.
- When students are building to one solution together encourage them to create "wild" or "out-there" solutions to show the reach of the ideation process"

Attribution

Derived and adapted from: Doug Hall, *Jump Start Your Business Brain* (Cincinnati, OH: Clerisy Press, 2001).

EXERCISE: IDEASPACE

AUTHOR: HEIDI NECK

Description

The Ideaspace exercise is designed to help students shape new ideas into more innovative and interesting opportunities. There are three types or categories of ideas in the exercise: grounded, blue sky, and spaced-out. Grounded ideas are safe, incremental, obvious, imitable, plain, and predictable. Blue sky ideas are forward-looking, novel, different, unique, exciting, risky, progressive, and thought-provoking. Spaced-out ideas are those ideas that are crazy, absurd, whacky, magical, and nonsensical. In other words, spaced-out ideas are not possible (at least in the short term).

Ideaspace is an exercise in lateral thinking. Specific principles of lateral thinking emerge during the exercise:

- Changing direction and nonlinearity are often necessary to develop innovative solutions to problems.
- Steps are not sequential, and iteration is expected.
- Willingness to explore the least obvious (such as spaced-out ideas) can be a better pathway to something useful and novel.

Usage Suggestions

This exercise works for all audiences, undergraduate, graduate, and practitioner. Ideaspace is best positioned after a general brainstorming or other type of ideation session where "seed" ideas are generated. This is an important follow-up exercise that helps students focus on quality of ideas rather than quantity of ideas generated in earlier brainstorming. The exercise should be done in small groups.

Learning Objectives

- Develop and shape ideas into stronger opportunities.
- Acquire a level of comfort with "crazy" ideas.
- Practice lateral thinking.

Materials List

- Ideaspace image (shown in Figure 9.2; should be used as a handout).
- Flip chart paper or whiteboard space.

It's okay to have your feet on the ground, but your eyes should be on the big blue sky. Try some space exploration and reenter with a more attractive, bigger blue sky.

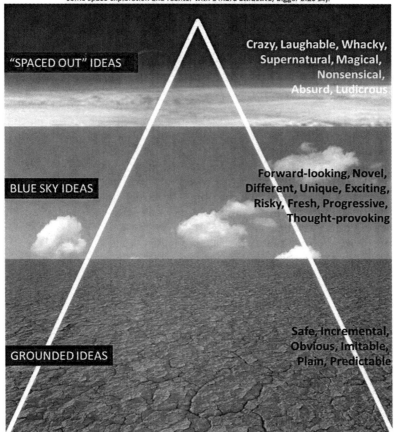

Figure 9.2   Ideaspace image

- Sticky notes.
- Pens or markers.

Pre-Work Required by Students

It is expected that students have gone through some type of general ideation exercise or have at least three ideas they want to shape for the exercise.

For example, students could do the Mind Dumping for Ideation exercise (page 194) prior to Ideaspace.

Theoretical Foundations

Bono, E. de. 1970. *Lateral Thinking*. New York: Harper & Row.
Bono, E. de. 1993. *Serious Creativity: Using the Power of Lateral Thinking to Create New Ideas*. New York: HarperBusiness.

Time Plan (40 minutes)

The minimum time needed is 40 minutes (as depicted in the timing below), but 60 minutes is suggested to benefit from a more immersive practice.

Introduction and exercise setup   0:00–0:10 (10 minutes)
Introduce the exercise by showing the Ideaspace graphic (Figure 9.2), either in handout form or as a PowerPoint graphic. Explain the three categories of ideas and emphasize that the target space is blue sky. It is important also to give an example of how the exercise works, because it's a shaping rather than generating exercise.
    Here is an example that can be shared with students:

- **Problem**: Students not reading and analyzing lengthy case studies.
  Grounded idea: Video cases.
  A video case is not a bad idea – grounded ideas are not bad ideas. Rather, the video case is not very innovative and it's currently being done. Because it can be very difficult to turn a grounded idea into a blue sky idea, it is suggested that students first transform the grounded idea into a spaced-out idea.
- **Transformation of the grounded idea to a spaced-out idea**: Teleport to the decision consequence.
  The great thing about case studies is that students are forced to analyze the information presented in the case and make a decision. The problem is that students never really see their decision in action. The crazy, spaced-out idea is to travel into the future and see the actual consequence of the decision. As a result, the spaced-out idea is "teleporting to the decision consequence" (rather like the holo-deck in *Star Trek*). Though this is not possible, there is a kernel of a great idea here. How can students really *see* the impact of their decision? Now the problem is not necessarily reinventing the case study, but rather identifying new ways that students can see and feel the impact of their decisions.

● **Transformation of the spaced-out idea to a blue sky idea**: Mega-
multiplayer video game. Imagine a business video game filled with
avatars and real interaction in a virtual world.
Emphasize again that the exercise is about moving and shaping
ideas into blue sky opportunities. As illustrated in the example, the
idea moved from grounded (video case) to spaced-out (teleport)
down to blue sky (video game).

Exercise   0:10–0:30 (20 minutes)
Before starting the exercise, it is assumed that students have a few ideas
they are working on to solve some type of problem. There are many different approaches to using the Ideaspace, but the following guidelines can be
used and given in handout form to the students. This exercise works best
in teams of four to five.

Student instructions

● **Step 1**: Groups should decide on one to three ideas they would like
to shape. Write each idea on a sticky note provided. Please don't
evaluate your ideas at this point. They are just ideas and that's what
they should be. They can be small ideas, big ideas, partial ideas, or
absolutely crazy ideas. Actually, go for the crazy ideas if at all possible. The feasibility of the idea is not important at this juncture.
What does matter is the specificity of the idea. In other words, don't
simply write "Open a restaurant." In order to be specific you should
write "Open a fast-casual vegan restaurant in Cambridge."
● **Step 2**: On the flip chart provided draw a triangle with three different areas similar to the Ideaspace handout (Figure 9.2). Quickly talk
through the ideas brought into the exercise and place them in one of
the three spaces on the Ideaspace triangle. For each idea the group
must determine if it's a grounded, blue sky, or spaced-out idea.
Note: Most of the ideas at this stage will be grounded or spaced-out.
Critically challenge your peers if they think they have a blue sky idea
at this point.
● **Step 3**: Now the fun starts! This step separates the Ideaspace exercise
from more traditional brainstorming approaches. This step is where
the bulk of your allotted time should be spent! Start moving ideas
across the various levels (ground, sky, space). Shape a **grounded** idea
into a **spaced-out**, magical idea and then back to a more innovative,
blue sky idea. Or take an idea that may already be in your spaced-
out area and shape to move toward the blue sky. Taking an idea and
moving it through different levels is integral to this exercise.

Presentations   0:30–0:40 (10 minutes)
Have select teams present their new, blue sky ideas and illustrate how the idea was shaped.

Key Takeaways

- Lateral thinking is a way of shaping ideas into bolder, more innovative solutions.
- Lateral thinking takes practice. The nonlinearity of the process and movement up and down the triangle are not easy and require time.
- It can be very difficult to identify the spaced-out ideas, but this is the key ingredient to success with Ideaspace.

Teaching Tips

This is not an easy exercise; therefore, the instructor needs to interact with the groups to help them move from one area to the next. Creating blue sky ideas is not easy, which is why this exercise is so important. Bringing an idea down from spaced-out is much easier than turning a grounded idea into a blue sky idea. The most important path for students to experience is taking a grounded idea and turning it into a spaced-out idea and then turning the spaced-out idea into a blue sky idea. Instructors should pay particular attention to where students place their initial ideas. Students have a tendency to place their seemingly grounded ideas in the blue sky space!

EXERCISE: FUTURE TRENDS AND ENTREPRENEURIAL OPPORTUNITIES

AUTHOR: CAROLINE DANIELS

Description

Many students building new ventures focus on building a business for today's customers and markets. The time it takes an entrepreneur to shape an opportunity, gather resources, and build a dynamic team varies, but an initial planning-to-operational time frame is usually from one to three years. During that time, customer needs and markets can change.

This exercise lifts the focus of the entrepreneurial student from today's customers and markets to a perspective that includes future customers and markets from the present to a few years from now, to ten years from now, and beyond. Focusing on the future allows entrepreneurs to build an innovative approach to developing opportunities and to think about emerging opportunity spaces, which are often less fraught with existing competitors.

The objective of this exercise is to explore the impact of trends and markets on entrepreneurial activity in general and on students' business ideas in particular from concept to launch. The exercise makes use of a video by National Geographic on how the world's population will shift from now through to 2050 and how that shift will cause changes in the way we live. The video transports the students into the future and is a beginning point to discussing the future trends students envision that will influence customers and markets.

Usage Suggestions

This exercise challenges students of all kinds (graduate, undergraduate, and practitioners) to think in new ways about how trends can expand opportunity spaces, influence the determination of key customer segments, and focus the designs of products and services to reach customers.

The session can be positioned after idea generation exercises, when the students have a clear idea of the opportunities they are beginning to pursue.

Learning Objectives

- Design and assess opportunities with a view toward future trends and competitive forces.

- Critique the implications of future trends for business opportunities.
- Expose students to working in the complete unknown.

Materials List

- Flip chart paper.
- Markers.
- Tape.

Pre-Work Required by Students

- The instructor can assign relevant and timely short articles and videos, such as:
  - Reading: Landry, Laura. 2012. Revolutionary technologies that have spun out of MIT's Media Lab. June. *BostInno.com*, Boston, http://bostinno.com/2012/06/18/10-revolutionary-technologies-that-have-spun-out-of-mits-media-lab/#ss__170 540_1_4__ss.
  - Review the video: Changing the way we live: Designed by nature, biomimicry. *Innovators Program*, Bloomberg TV, April 29, 2010, New York, http://www.bloomberg.com/video/ 63600024-innovators-episode-3-designed-by-nature.html.

Theoretical Foundations

Geus, Arie de. 2002. *The Living Company*. Boston, MA: Harvard Business Review Press.
Schwartz, Peter. 1991. *The Art of the Long View: Planning for the Future in an Uncertain World*. New York: Doubleday.
Toffler, Alvin. 1970. *Future Shock*. New York: Bantam Books.

Time Plan (90 minutes)

This 90-minute exercise can be adapted to fit various time schedules, including an entire class. For the purposes of this teaching note, the exercise requires 90 minutes, but can be tailored to the amount of class time the instructor has.

Step 1 (introduction)   0:00–0:15 (15 minutes)

- This introduction serves as a bridge back to idea generation. Student teams present their proposed solutions and ideas for testing those solutions. This is a key part of the entrepreneurial process and will likely require faculty feedback to encourage a) the pursuit of forward thinking solutions and b) the actual testing of those solutions.

- Faculty will link this process to any brainstorming exercise.

Step 2 (trends and markets)   0:15–0:35 (20 minutes)
A trend is a change in the general direction in the way we live.

- Show the *7 Billion* video produced by National Geographic to get the students to think about powerful changes that are occurring that will influence how we live, the products and services that will be in demand, and how business processes will change to deliver those products and services. Discuss what trends the students see occurring by beginning with the trends suggested in the *7 Billion* video and in the Landry (2012) article about the MIT Media Lab in the pre-work. The video can be found here: http://video.nationalgeographic. com/video/the-magazine/the-magazine-latest/ngm-7billion/.
- Generate a list of trends with the class. It is important to generate a robust list of trends. A typical list could include: rebalancing of world resources, mobile, alternative energy sources, ubiquitous delivery, 3D communication anytime and anyplace, diversification of food sources, social media, proliferation of learning tools through the internet, holographic printing, miniaturization, robotics, and so on. The list will include overlaps: that's fine – the important objective is to get the students thinking about where the demands for goods and services will go in the future, five, ten, 20 years from the present, and that aiming at that future is a way to expand the demand for their opportunities.

Step 3 (student exercise)   0:35–1:10 (35 minutes)

- Student teams each select three trends from the list of trends generated and spend time discussing what the scenario for the future, based on the three trends they select, will be. Allow time for the teams to develop their picture of that future world. Student teams will place their opportunities in their scenarios of the future and discuss how they could shape their opportunities to take advantage of emerging trends. They should consider how the trends will affect customer segments and relationships, the design of their products or services, and new ways of organizing their business processes, for example distribution of their products or services. Student teams will draw their scenario of the future on flip chart paper.

- Student teams report back their three trends, scenarios for the future, and how they will leverage the emerging trends and opportunity spaces (i.e. how their thinking about their opportunities has changed as a result of considering emerging trends).

Step 4 (wrap-up)   1:10–1:30 (20 minutes)

- It is important to make sure that students understand that the trends create markets, markets that will be described in more detail in a future session.
- Ask students to describe how it felt creating for the future.

Key Takeaways

- Entrepreneurs who are building a business today need to take into account the future needs and wants of customers and markets.
- Trends, changes in the directions of how we live, influence customers and markets.
- Keeping an eye on future trends and developing scenarios for the venture's products and services focus the venture on innovation and new markets.

Teaching Tips

- Walk around the room and talk with the students about their choices of trends. It is important for the students to select the trends to focus on fairly quickly, that is, within the first 10 minutes or so, so that they can imagine the future and the impact of the trends as well as shape their opportunities with the trends in mind. The instructor can remind the students that they can repeat this exercise with different trends to their hearts' content later on if they would like to include the influence of more than three trends.
- Watch the timing of the class. Ensure that there is adequate time for all teams to present and share their work.

EXERCISE: SELF-UNDERSTANDING FOR OPPORTUNITY CREATION

AUTHORS: ANDREW CORBETT AND CANDIDA BRUSH

Description

A strong understanding of self is critical for entrepreneurs. Being able to not only recognize but also synthesize one's interests, desires, skills, and network is a critical building block for entrepreneurial activity (Fiet, 2002; Nixon et al., 2006). This exercise offers students an opportunity for introspection and allows them to reflect upon both what makes them who they are and what they can be as entrepreneurs. It is a great exercise to get groups working on venture concepts that they will explore for feasibility or business planning during a semester. It is ideal for some of the first sharing sessions for teams looking to develop a venture concept or class venturing project.

Usage Suggestions

This exercise works well for just about all audiences: nascent entrepreneurs searching for an idea, undergraduates, graduate students, and executives. It is geared for a session early in the semester of any entrepreneurship courses focused on creativity, feasibility, or new venture creation. It also works well at the beginning of a bootcamp, workshop, or any entrepreneurship intensive training program.

Learning Objectives

- Reflect on your accomplishments, things you are proud of, and think about what knowledge, skills, and capabilities were gained from these accomplishments.
- Discuss the process of determining these accomplishments.
- Connect your knowledge, abilities, and desires as a foundation for venture ideas.

Materials List

The instructor needs to develop two relatively short-form handouts that ask students to think about 1) their personal accomplishments and 2) their knowledge, skills, and abilities. Details for each of these are below:

1. **Accomplishments**: "Please list at least five of your most significant personal accomplishments. Since we are using these accomplishments as the basis for entrepreneurial idea generation and potentially a future business, all accomplishments should be based upon something that you 1) are proud to have accomplished, 2) enjoyed accomplishing, and 3) think that you did very well.

   The accomplishments should not only be work related (developing a new product or rolling out a large software transition or upgrade) but also include hobbies and other related interests (e.g. teaching Girl Scouts how to sell, or running a marathon). They can be recent or from back in your childhood, but they must satisfy the three criteria in the above paragraph."

   After the students have listed their accomplishments, ask them to rank the accomplishments based on significance to themselves (not what others think). The most significant accomplishment will be ranked number one, then two, and so on.

2. **KSAs**: Knowledge, skills, and abilities (KSAs) are classic concepts deconstructed and used throughout management education and training. In this case we want to break down the KSAs that led to the listed accomplishments. The second handout simply makes space for each student to list the accomplishments from the first handout and leaves room for a detailed description of the knowledge, skills, and abilities that were needed to achieve the accomplishment. Students should complete this for each accomplishment.

   Students should now spend some time reflecting on the accomplishments and KSAs that underlie them by highlighting or circling the KSAs that they believe had the most influence on their success.

"Take a look at all you have done in these two short exercises. You are likely to see overlap, connections, or interesting combinations. Are there indicators of categories where you think you possess unique experience? Do you have special understanding of a specific activity or set of activities or a specific category of knowledge that has been a recurring theme throughout your accomplishments?"

From this, students make a list of three or four different themes. For example, a list might include: 1) social media expertise, 2) creative writing, 3) working well under tight time lines, and 4) team leader. Students should bring this list of themes along with all of their completed worksheets to class.

Pre-Work Required by Students

Students need to complete the above-noted self-understanding handouts prior to coming to class. Upon arrival the students should have a foundation from which they can begin to develop entrepreneurial ideas based upon who they are, what they can do, and what they desire. They should bring all completed worksheets to class.

Theoretical Foundations

Fiet, J. 1996. The informational basis for entrepreneurial discovery. *Small Business Economics*, 8, 419–30.
Fiet, J. 2002. *The Systematic Search for Entrepreneurial Discoveries.* Westport, CT: Quorum Books.
Kiefer, C., Schlesinger, L., and Brown, P. 2012. *Just Start: Take Action, Embrace Uncertainty and Create the Future.* Cambridge, MA: Harvard Business Press Books.
Nixon, R.D., Bishop, K., Clouse, Van G.H., and Kemelgor, B. 2006. Prior knowledge and entrepreneurial discovery: A classroom methodology for idea generation. *International Journal of Entrepreneurship Education*, 4, 19–36.
Sarasvathy, S.D. 2001. Causation and effectuation: Toward a theoretical shift from economic inevitability to entrepreneurial contingency. *Academy of Management Review*, 26(2), 243–63.

Time Plan (75 minutes)

Introduction and reflection   0:00–0:05 (5 minutes)
Start the session by introducing the objectives of the session; then provide 2–3 minutes for the students silently and individually to reexamine their worksheets in class to familiarize themselves with what they did and to get their minds back into the exercise.

Discussion   0:05–0:20 (15 minutes)
Begin the discussion by asking students to share their observations about their reflections:

- Who found this process difficult? Why?
- Who found it easy?
- Enjoyable?
- How did you approach this exercise?
- Was it hard to identify skills, capabilities, or knowledge? What criteria did you use to determine the capabilities, skills, or knowledge?
- As you reflected on the exercise, did you find patterns?
- Were there any surprises?
- Who would like to share what they found?

Transition   0:20–0:25 (5 minutes)
To make a connection between self-understanding and entrepreneur-ship, ask: What are the connections between self-understanding and entrepreneurship?

Group work   0:25–0:45 (20 minutes)
Students should then be put into groups to share their themes, KSAs, and desires. Many entrepreneurship courses require students to work in teams on either feasibility plans or business planning. This class session serves as a great way for students to kick off their work together and develop their "group means." Groups can be composed randomly or, if students have emailed their key themes to the instructor in advance of the class, they can be predetermined based on commonalities in KSAs. The group assign-ment should cover the following:

- Discuss the themes and find commonalities in areas of expertise and skills.
- Identify one or two skills or themes each person is passionate about.
- What ideas for new businesses or initiatives can you think of that build on your expertise, knowledge, or skills?
- Narrow to the top two ideas you like the best and be prepared to present when you return to class.

Report-out from group work   0:45–1:05 (20 minutes)
The group report may include the following activities and discussion questions:

- Ask all the teams to present their ideas without discussion.
- Debrief on the process: How long did it take to identify similarities or differences?
- How did you identify the business idea (education, experience, hobbies, talents, things you really care about!)?
- Why did you think this was a good business idea?
- Why do you think you could make this idea work (team capabilities)?

Wrap-up   1:05–1:15 (10 minutes)
A final wrap-up should focus again on the importance of self-understanding and how it provides the foundation for entrepreneurial activity, especially venture idea development. The session may end with a short video or TED talk, or examples of entrepreneurs who have built successful ventures based on their KSAs.

Key Takeaways

- This exercise helps students to reflect on the importance of understanding oneself in relation to entrepreneurial activity.
- Underlying themes and patterns related to life accomplishments can be the foundation for new venture ideas that better align and fit with student entrepreneurs.

Teaching Tips

Ideally, if students can email their three key themes to the instructor before class, this can serve as the basis for forming groups (based on common KSAs), which is often more productive.

In making the connection between self-understanding and entrepreneurial ventures, instructors can bring in a few brief slides to explain the bird-in-hand principle from Sarasvathy's (2001) effectuation work. The goal is to reinforce that anyone can develop and create by starting with their means: Who am I? What do I know? Who do I know?

You should remind your students prior to completing their handouts that awards are *not* accomplishments. As you consider your accomplishments, focus on the tasks accomplished rather than the rewards that might have resulted from those tasks. Similarly when working on KSAs remind students that personality traits or characteristics are not knowledge, skills, or abilities.

It is also important to note that more mature students do better with this assignment simply because they have more life experience and tend to have more accomplishments (and a better filter to understand a broad array of accomplishments). Therefore, some undergraduates can struggle with this assignment, and it is probably not ideal for high school students.

Attribution

Adapted by Candida Brush, Heidi Neck, and Andrew Corbett from: R.D. Nixon, K. Bishop, Van G.H. Clouse, and B. Kemelgor, Prior knowledge and entrepreneurial discovery: A classroom methodology for idea generation, *International Journal of Entrepreneurship Education* (2006), 4, 19–36.

EXERCISE: RESOURCE ACQUISITION GAME

AUTHORS: MATT ALLEN AND CANDIDA BRUSH

Description

This exercise offers students an opportunity to develop and reflect on approaches for resource acquisition through a simple interactive exercise. Students will consider different types and properties of resources, as well as strategies for resource development. This exercise is rooted in resource-based theory, which argues that firm resources include all assets, capabilities, organizational processes, firm attributes, and so on that are controlled by a firm to enable it to conceive of and implement strategies that improve its efficiency and effectiveness (Barney, 1991). Resources types are human, social, financial, physical, technological and organizational (Brush et al., 2001). Resources can be a source of competitive advantage if they are valuable, rare, and inimitable. New ventures are launched with a small base of generic resources that come from the entrepreneurial team and general human and social capital. At this time, entrepreneurial teams need to identify and acquire resources that can be leveraged, combined, or traded to develop a foundation for competitive advantage.

Usage Suggestions

This exercise works for all audiences, undergraduate, graduate, executive, or practitioner. It is appropriate for new venture creation courses, entrepreneurship bootcamps, or workshops. The session is best positioned after students have identified a venture concept, project, or family or corporate initiative to pursue.

Learning Objectives

- Develop approaches for acquiring resources.
- Assess the value and scarcity of different resources.
- Identify the basics of resource development strategy.

Materials List

- Resource list handout (see "In-Class Exercise – Resource Acquisition Handout" at the end of this exercise).
- Each resource can be characterized by type (human, social, tech-

nological, financial, organizational, physical) and by the degree to which it is valuable or a commodity, rare, or easy to imitate.

Pre-Work Required by Students

The readings below may be required for pre-work, depending on the audience.

Theoretical Foundations (Citations, Suggestions for Further Reading)

Barney, J. 1991. Firm resources and sustained competitive advantage. *Journal of Management*, 17(1), 99–120.
Brush, C.G., Greene, P.G., and Hart, M.M. 2001. From initial idea to unique advantage: The entrepreneurial challenge of constructing a resource base. *Academy of Management Executive*, 15(1), 64–80.

Time Plan (30 minutes)

Begin the exercise by asking the students to write down two key resources needed to launch their venture.

Discussion   0:00–0:10 (10 minutes)

- What do we mean by resources?
- How are they defined?

Resource exercise instructions)   0:10–0:15 (5 minutes)
(pass out the resource list handout

- Find a person (in this classroom) who possesses one of the resources on the list.
- Have that person sign his or her name next to the resource he or she possesses.
- You cannot use the same person for multiple resources on your own sheet, but the same person can sign multiple sheets for the same resource.
- You can use yourself for one resource.
- You will have 3 minutes.

Ask one person to sit still and not get up during the exercise. The person is still participating but does not move around the room.

Exercise debrief 0:15–0:30 (15 minutes)

- What happened during this exercise?
- Were some resources easier to obtain? Harder to obtain?
    - Which were harder? Why?
    - Easiest – those most common?
    - Hardest – those with expertise, culturally significant, most valuable?
- Which were most valuable?
    - How did you determine whether resources were valuable or rare?
    - Valuable – built webpage, has more than 500 LinkedIn contacts.
    - Rare – has a patent, speaks more than four languages.
    - Was "value" obvious?
- What was your strategy for acquisition?
    - Easy first? Hardest first? Mixed?
    - Went to those you knew who possessed the resource?
    - Did you trade signatures?
    - Advertising – shouting?
    - Listening to others shout?
    - Where did you place yourself in the room?
    - Were there viral aspects to this exercise (word spread as people moved around)?
    - Time – did the 3-minute time limit influence your approach?
- Types of resources:
    - What types of resources are represented in these items?
    - Which types of resources did you go after first? Most likely to acquire?
- Total resources acquired:
    - How many total resources did you acquire?
    - What would be different if these resources had a price?
    - One person was asked to sit still. How many resources did this person acquire? (This person usually acquires fewer resources because he/she did not take an active role in acquisition.)
- Resource development strategy.

Key Takeaways

- New ventures should begin by conducting a resource assessment: what they have, what they need (human, social, organizational, technological, physical, and financial), and where they might get these resources.

- Resources differ in their quantity and availability.
- Resources differ by ease of identification.
- Resource acquisition is a social process, and it takes time to determine source and availability.
- Resource acquisition requires action (entrepreneurial thought and action).

Post-Work

A follow-up to this exercise might include group work to assess which resources relative to their venture are possessed by the team, which they need, and sources. They might draft an acquisition strategy and timetable for acquisition. Borrowing, trading, or combining strategies for resources might be considered.

Teaching Tips

Students often begin quietly, without moving around very much; then, as they realize that they are time constrained, they move around. Some students become competitive, others will shout out, while others will move around very little. They will often forget that the instructor can be part of the exercise and frequently possesses some of the more rare or inimitable resources. They never think to leave the room even if some of the resources are possessed by people nearby. In this case, all resources are "free" and, therefore, there is no cost.

The resources on this list may be adapted as needed. *Note*: For an executive audience, you might include items like: has patented or trademarked something (technology resource – valuable, rare, and hard to imitate); manages more than 20 people (human capital – valuable); and has changed jobs more than four times (social – valuable).

Attribution

This is a common icebreaker game that can be found in many variations online (e.g. human bingo), but has been adapted here to demonstrate various resources that can be shared and leveraged by students in a classroom.

Resource Acquisition Handout

Try to find the person who possesses this resource. Have that person sign his or her name. Try to obtain as many resources as you can. A person can sign for only one resource. You may use yourself for only one resource.

1. Has built a webpage _____
2. Has travelled to Asia on business _____
3. Speaks more than four languages _____
4. Is part of a family business_____
5. Is a good golfer _____
6. Has $100 in his or her wallet _____
7. Has investing experience _____
8. Has a degree in psychology _____
9. Belongs to a club or membership organization _____
10. Owns a piece of real estate _____
11. Has investing experience _____
12. Has more than 500 LinkedIn contacts _____
13. Owns an iPhone_____
14. Plays chess _____
15. Owns a motorcycle _____
16. Has won an art or design contest _____
17. Plays a musical instrument_____
18. Has a dog _____
19. Has published an article in the newspaper _____
20. Has been sky diving _____

EXERCISE: BUILDING A STRATEGIC NETWORK

AUTHORS: CANDIDA BRUSH AND PATRICIA GREENE

Description

Networks provide a conduit for the exchange of information and resources that can enhance your personal success as well as the survival and success of an entrepreneurial venture. Through networks, entrepreneurs gain access to opportunities and resources, save time, and tap into advice and moral support that may otherwise be unavailable. Networks can affect entrepreneurs' social, emotional, and material well-being (Ibarra, 1996). Entrepreneurs not only use their existing networks, but, as they acquire information and resources, they build new ones (Dubini and Aldrich, 1991). Networks are sets of relationships important to the accomplishment of your entrepreneurial activities and your personal development (Uzzi and Dunlap, 2005). They are generally described as three types, task networks which involve an exchange of job-related information resources, career networks, which are composed of relationships with various people who can provide career and entrepreneurial direction and guidance, and social networks, which are relationships characterized by higher levels of closeness and trust, outside of job- or career-related networks (Ibarra, 1996). Networking behaviors are those activities involved in two-way communication whereby contacts are developed and information is communicated, in either formal or informal settings. This exercise is designed to help students better understand the importance of networking generally, examine the composition of their current network, practice networking techniques, and think about how they might expand their network. Expansion of the network requires the ability to make a short "pitch" about what one has to offer and what help is needed.

Usage Suggestions

This exercise can be used in any entrepreneurship class, workshop, or training session, and for any level of student (college to practitioner). It often works best earlier on in an entrepreneurship course or workshop in that it assists with the process of venture feasibility assessment, market research, raising funding, or building a management team.

Learning Objectives

- Assess your current network.
- Practice networking techniques.
- Design a strategic network.

Materials List

- "Networking Assessment Form" (included at the end of this exercise).
- "Networking Development Form" (included at the end of this exercise).

Pre-Work Required by Students

Complete the networking assessment form.

Theoretical Foundations

Dubini, P., and Aldrich, H. 1991. Personal and extended networks are central to the entrepreneurial process. *Journal of Business Venturing*, 6, 305–13.

Greve, J.W., and Salaff, A. 2003. Social networks and entrepreneurship. *Entrepreneurship Theory and Practice*, 28(1), 1–22.

Ibarra, H. 1996. *Managerial Networks*. Cambridge, MA: Harvard Business School Publishing.

Santinelli, A., and Brush, C. 2013. *Designing and Delivering the Perfect Pitch*. Wellesley, MA: Babson College Case Collection.

Uzzi, B., and Dunlap, S. 2005. *How to Build Your Network*. Cambridge, MA: Harvard Business School Publishing.

Time Plan (80 minutes)

The session is divided into several segments, some of which are discussion based, while the rest are experiential. This plan is for a 1 hour 20 minute session, but it can be expanded depending on size of group.

Introduction   0:00–0:15 (15 minutes)

Introduce the topic, the purpose of the session, discussion of what networking is, and why networking is important. (*Note*: There are statistics available online; search on *networking statistics*.)

Examples of good networking and not-so-good networking   0:15–0:25 (10 minutes)

What are networks and types of networks, how are networks and networking connected, and what is the strategic process of networking?

a. Network assessment.
b. Creating an approach.
c. Developing a pitch.
d. Practicing.
e. Outreach and follow-up.

Discuss your network assessment (pre-work)   0:25–0:35 (10 minutes)

- Composition of your network – what observations do you have?
- Are there any particular patterns?
- What is the composition of men and women in your network?
- How often do you ask for help?
- Do you see opportunity for building your network?

Complete the network development form   0:35–0:45 (10 minutes)

In pairs – practice your pitch to each other   0:45–1:00 (15 minutes)

Debrief the entire group   1:00–1:15 (15 minutes)

- Were you able to say your pitch in less than a minute?
- Concise? Memorable?
- Ask for volunteers to share their "pitches" – group feedback.

Post-Work

Write down a plan, and set a date to meet the person. In the next class session, follow up and ask for the results of the meeting. Students should keep a "journal" that identifies their network development, and work on revising their pitch as they move forward.

Key Takeaways

- Network assessment can yield insights into whom you rely on for business, emotional, and career support.
- Network development should be strategic.

Teaching Tips

Examples of networking: there are some good videos on YouTube which are either good or bad examples. Another idea is to ask for real life experiences when they were "put off" or developed a good relationship. Alternatively, role-playing situations can work too.

Networking Assessment Form

Please complete the following form regarding your personal network.

Name	Male/ female	How long known?	Frequency of interaction?	Context: where/how interact?	Topics discussed		
1							
2							
3							
4							
5							
6							
7							
8							
9							
10							

Networking Development Form

Write down a project, opportunity, or activity you are presently working on or plan to work on.

List five people who might be helpful to you in this project	Who in your present network can facilitate an introduction?	How can you help that person?	What will your "pitch" be?

EXERCISE: CREATING AS AN ARTIST

AUTHOR: PHYLLIS SCHLESINGER

Description

Creating as an Artist is a series of student workshops, directed by artists, designed for students to experience and model artists' thinking and process. This exercise is appropriate for any number of students, provided they are divided into teams of 10–12 students. Each team is paired with an artist representing any of a number of different media (object theater, painting, sculpture, mixed media, poetry, music, improvisation, etc.), who teaches the students the basics of that discipline. The artist and student team meet at least weekly. At the end of several weeks of working together, students deliver a live performance to the class utilizing their medium. Each performance is followed by a question-and-answer session on the creating process, with specific connections made to entrepreneurship.

Usage Suggestions

Creating can be done with undergraduate or graduate students, or practitioners. Creating should be positioned at the beginning of a course or program; we use creating at the beginning of the Babson 2-year MBA program. Student teams are assigned and meet with their artist the afternoon of the first day of class. The presentations occur over the course of a day (depending on the number of teams, of course) about three weeks into the course. Attendance at each presentation is required. As this exercise is designed to encourage participants to be out of their comfort zone, the minimal class time is four sessions. Participants need to get to know their team and the medium, and experiment with ideas. Shorter time frames minimize that process.

Learning Objectives

1. Discover one's innate creativity.
2. Assess one's capacity for risk.
3. Develop team process and relationship-building skills.
4. Develop a tolerance for and ability to handle ambiguity.
5. Create a performance.
6. Employ creative strategies to acquire resources from unexpected places.
7. Connect the creative process to the method of entrepreneurship.

Materials List

Artists generally bring their own supplies. We do not supply anything for students except rehearsal space and time in the course to practice.

Pre-Work Required by Students

None.

Theoretical Foundations

Csikszentmihalyi, M. 1996. *Creativity: Flow and the Psychology of Discovery and Invention.* New York: HarperCollins.
Dewey, J. 1934. *Art as Experience.* New York: Minton, Balch & Company.
Eisner, E.W. 2002. *The Arts and the Creation of Mind.* New Haven, CT: Yale University Press.
Levy, J. 2005. Reflections on how the theatre teaches. *Journal of Aesthetic Education*, 39(4), 20–30.

Time Plan (3 weeks)

Session 1
Students are introduced to the project by faculty, and are assigned to a creating team, medium, and artist. Immediately after the introduction, teams join their artist for a three-hour introductory session. The artist is responsible for designing and delivering the session. Students are given instructions. An example of instructions given to MBA students is as follows:

> Creating is the first step in entrepreneurial thought and action. In this stream we invite you to explore, experience, and share creating over the next few weeks: Take risks; make a difference; be innovative and unconventional; see in new ways. You and your group are responsible for developing a creativity presentation for your first-year MBA peers, faculty, and the Babson community on [date].
>
> On [the first day], you will be assigned a creativity consultant – an artist or practitioner of one of a variety of arts, including object theater, movement, new approaches to music, dramatic writing, improvisation, mixed media, and drawing. Your consultant will introduce to you the principles of her or his art, offer suggestions for how to apply them, and provide general guidance about the creative process. You and your group, however, are entirely responsible for generating, shaping, arranging, rehearsing, and presenting the product(s) of your creating. At the end of the course, after the presentations, you will be asked to evaluate yourself and your peers, and you will as a group be evaluated by your consultant based on a set of criteria for passing or failing the assignment. Please discuss evaluation with your consultant. The following guidelines offer a way of thinking about your project and the creative process:

- See in a new way – recontextualize the familiar and the unfamiliar.
- Build an understanding of yourself and others.
- Trust the process, your peers, and surprise – have fun too.
- Experience ambiguity and stay open to discovery.
- Be innovative and/or unconventional, and embrace risk.
- Take responsibility for concrete results.
- Stretch the talents and inventiveness of your group members.
- Add value and provide a learning experience for your class.

Instructions:
On the day of your presentation your group will have 20 minutes to present, plus an additional 10 minutes for your own comments, and Q&A from the audience. Please plan ahead to be available on this day – **you are required to attend all presentations**. Actively witnessing your peers' presentations is a significant part of the learning process for this stream. After all the presentations are completed, your group will meet with your consultant to discuss the experience and fill out evaluations; after your meeting with your consultant, everyone will reconvene for general debriefing in [the auditorium].

The first afternoon is designed for you to meet your creativity consultant to begin your adventure with creative process. You should plan on meeting with your consultant at least twice after today and with your group as many times as is necessary. Note that there are designated times listed on your schedule for creativity work – please use them for this purpose. Allow for some extra rehearsal time during the week prior to your presentation.

Weekly (sessions 2, 3, and 4)
Students are expected to meet on their own and/or with their artist for approximately 5 hours per week or however long the artist and team decide they need for an effective performance. Artists "teach" their team(s) as they see fit.

Final performance day (at the beginning of week 4)
Each team is required to perform using their medium in front of the entire class and community members. Each performance is approximately 20 minutes in length, which includes questions from the audience.

Key Takeaways

- Everyone is creative: a maker of the means for order, survival, and pleasure. While artists are often thought to be the "creative ones" in our culture, the act of creating is in fact a natural human impulse available to all.
- Creating is a process involving a range of elements and experiences: for example, the use of the senses, imagination, trust, intuition, desire, risk taking, playfulness, and courage, as well as the willing-

ness to be vulnerable and make mistakes and the ability to see differently and deeply.

- Creating must be experienced first-hand rather than through just reading or hearing about it. Because there are fewer and fewer opportunities for individuals and groups to experience creating, especially in the business world today, engagement with the elements of creating must be stimulated or challenged.
- The links between business and art – and entrepreneurs and artists – are compelling and rich. Artists can offer a unique perspective to the business community about the expressive and energizing potential of the creating process.
- Creativity is an introduction to entrepreneurial thought and action, grounded in personal engagement and an understanding of who one is, who one is not, and what one wants to risk in any venture.

Post-Work

Students are required to submit a two-page (minimum) reflection that answers the following questions:

- What kind of assumptions did you have related to producing work in this artistic medium before you began? How do you feel about producing work in this medium now?
- Describe an aspect of or moment in the creating process that challenged you.
- How do you think this artistic experience relates to thinking and acting entrepreneurially?

Teaching Tips

- Students go from being a bit skeptical at the beginning of the exercise to being excited and stimulated by the creativity they see. Instructors should be ready to trust the process and encourage students to do the same. The wealth of talent and resources in a class are truly amazing to see.
- Consultants can be paid an honorarium. Consultants can be from the local artistic community, or can be previous participants, faculty from other schools or colleges, or internal faculty with appropriate expertise. The nature of the exercise and outcomes should be explained to each consultant. The consultants generally act independently within the above guidelines.
- This exercise is difficult to accomplish in a compressed time period.

Participants need time to reflect and generate ideas. The more compressed the time, the more limited the ideas can be, and that does defeat the purpose of the exercise.

Attribution

Phyllis Schlesinger, Mary Pinard, J.B. Kassarjian, and Kate Buckman at Babson College.

EXERCISE: THE RESOURCE CHALLENGE

AUTHOR: HEIDI NECK

Description

The Resource Challenge requires student teams (five to seven per team) to generate as much profit as they can with two hours and $5 (Seelig, 2009). The challenge is a great lesson in bootstrapping and starting something with seemingly nothing. However, students quickly learn that cash is not their greatest asset and starting with what they have rather than what they need increases their probability of success (Sarasvathy, 2008).

Usage Suggestions

This exercise works best for undergraduate and graduate students. It is particularly useful when addressing resource acquisition and bootstrapping, but can also be assigned at the beginning of a course to stimulate entrepreneurial thinking.

Learning Objectives

- Demonstrate that value can be generated with very little.
- Apply an entrepreneurial mindset to resource acquisition.
- Encourage nascent entrepreneurs to "think cash last."

Materials List

- One envelope per team that includes a $5 bill within a folded 8.5 inch × 11 inch piece of paper. The piece of paper has one sentence in the middle: *How do you start something with nothing?*
- Resource Challenge directions (one set per team attached to the outside of the envelope). See Box 9.1.

Pre-Work Required by Students

None.

Theoretical Foundations (Citations, Suggestions for Further Reading)

Godin, S. 2013. *The Bootstrapper's Bible.* August. Retrieved from http://www.sethgodin.com/sg/docs/bootstrap.pdf.

Sarasvathy, S. 2008. *Effectuation: Elements of Entrepreneurial Expertise.* Cheltenham, UK and Northampton, MA, USA: Edward Elgar Publishing.
Seelig, T. 2009. *What I Wish I Knew When I Was 20: A Crash Course on Making Your Place in the World.* New York: HarperOne.

Time Plan (60 minutes)

Assignment
The Resource Challenge should be assigned to students two to five days in advance. An envelope (as described in the "Materials List" section) should be given to each team, with the instructions in Box 9.1 attached to the envelope.

In class   approximately 1 hour, depending on number of teams

Presentations   *0:00–0:35 (35 minutes)*
Each team is allocated 3 minutes to present their one PowerPoint slide, followed by 3 minutes of questions and answers from students and/or instructor. After each presentation the instructor should record the idea and the profit earned on the board.

Debrief   *0:35–0:55 (20 minutes)*
There are two aspects to debriefing: 1) an overall discussion and reflection on the assignment; and 2) a discussion on bootstrapping.

1. Reflection: The following questions are suggested:
    a. How did you feel when you were given the assignment?
    b. Describe the process your team used to arrive at "the idea" that you would implement. What role did the $5 play?
    c. What surprised you most about the experience and why?
2. Bootstrapping: It's important to explain to the students that what they experienced was classic bootstrapping. Bootstrapping is starting a new venture with minimal capital, and doing so requires a heightened level of resourcefulness. The instructor should summarize different ways that bootstrapping emerged in the teams. For example, it's likely that students asked for free things, enrolled others to help them execute, delayed payment for materials until cash was generated, or even collaborated with other teams. A great resource for bootstrapping is Seth Godin's *Bootstrapping Bible* (see "Theoretical Foundations").

Awards ceremony   0:55–1:00 (5 minutes)
The most profitable team earns a certificate. The instructor should also identify the most creative team (if different) and give a certificate. The

BOX 9.1 WELCOME TO THE RESOURCE CHALLENGE

How much profit can you generate with only $5 and 2 hours? This envelope contains seed money. Your team can spend as much time as you want planning, but once you open the envelope you have only *2 hours* to make as much money as possible (using only the seed money provided) by the start of class on [date].

How much money is in the envelope?
Answer. $5.

Can you use additional money obtained elsewhere to get started? *Answer.* No, absolutely not. This is the only seed money you have. $5. That's it.

Is there anything not allowed?

- You cannot participate in illegal activities.
- Raffles are not allowed, because that's boring and lacks imagination.
- Buying lottery tickets is not allowed, because that's just lazy.
- Other forms of gambling are not allowed . . . because I say so!
- You cannot collect cash before or after your two-hour period.
- You cannot execute anything after your two-hour period.

Deliverable
Be prepared to present *one* PowerPoint during class on [date] that answers the following questions:

- What did you do?
- How much profit did you earn? (Remember: Profit = Revenues – Expenses)!
- What did you learn about resources?

Profit must be in the form of cash on hand at the time of your presentation. Nothing collected or earned after the presentation will be accepted.

Grading
Group grade will be determined by 1) amount of profit earned and 2) creativity.

   Assuming you turn a profit, you may keep whatever money you earn *after* you pay back the original $5 of seed funding to [instructor's name]. It's a *loan* without interest – not an equity investment! If you don't turn a profit, it's [instructor's name]'s acceptable loss.

---

most creative team can be determined by student vote (while not voting for their own team).

Key Takeaways

- The resource base of entrepreneurs is initially determined by who they are, what they know, what they currently have, and whom they know. Cash is not necessarily the most needed asset to start something new.
- Generally the most successful teams are those who never use the $5. Their resourcefulness and creativity allow them to compete on an entirely different level. Most teams will articulate that the cash actually constrained them.
- From Seelig (2009): "They understood that five dollars is essentially nothing and decided to reinterpret the problem more broadly. What can we do to make money if we start with absolutely nothing? They ramped up their observation skills, tapped into their talents, and unlocked their creativity to identify problems in their midst – problems they experienced or noticed others experiencing – problems they might have seen before but had never thought to solve" (p. 2).

Teaching Tips

This exercise was adapted from Tina Seelig at Stanford University. Tina gives very little direction to her students. The modified version here includes specific directions that were created through trial and error. Once grading was introduced to the assignment, more directions were needed. The Resource Challenge can be even more illuminating and fun with less direction – Tina's way!

   There is also a video from Tina Seelig that can be used for instructor preparation or to show to students in the class. See http://ecorner.stan ford.edu/authorMaterialInfo.html?mid=2268.

Attribution

Tina Seelig, Professor of Practice, Stanford University.

EXERCISE: YOUR STRATEGIC ALLIANCE

AUTHORS: EDWARD MARRAM AND LES CHARM

Description

As a company grows, alliances have the potential to make an impact on its ability to prosper. Participants in this exercise will explore strategic partnerships and begin to understand some of the consequences of growth. By using their own companies, participants determine potential strategic partners. Students learn what the characteristic of the strategic alliance should be and the pros and cons for partners. A discussion is held on whether it is a realistic alliance and whether it can be implemented.

Usage Suggestions

This exercise is conducted with students who have work experience and executives. It will take approximately 1.5 hours.

Learning Objectives

- Assess the value of strategic partners and learn how a small company can dance with elephants!
- Evaluate the importance of strategic partners for growing companies.
- Analyze what makes a good strategic partner.
- Practice how to manage strategic partners.

Materials List

Each group should be provided with a flip chart and markers.

Pre-Work Required by Students

None.

Theoretical Foundations

Evora Software Case, prepared by Sheryl and Larry Overland under the direction of Edward P. Marram with the assistance of Glenn Kaplus.
Kanter, R. 1994. Collaborative advantage: The art of alliances. *Harvard Business Review*, 99(7/8), 102–07.

Lambert, D.M., and Knemeyer, A.M. 2004. We're in this together. *Harvard Business Review*, 82(12), 114–22.

Time Plan (60 minutes)

Group Organization   0:00–0:02 (2 minutes)
Divide the class into groups of four to five individuals (2 minutes).

Identify Strategic Partners   0:02–0:10 (8 minutes)
The group is asked to take one of its companies and identify a potential strategic partner for the company.

Creating the Alliance   0:10–0:30 (20 minutes)
On a flip chart the students come up with the "gives" and the "gets" from forming the alliance with the chosen partner.

Debrief   0:30–1:00 (30 minutes)
The class is then brought back together, flip charts are posted, and the class discusses why the strategic partnership is good for a growing company (30 minutes). Some discussion questions include:
- What are the requirements to make a satisfactory strategic alliance?
- What determines what is strategic for *both* parties?
- What are the parameters that make a strategic alliance work well?

Post Work

None

Teaching Tips

Other questions to consider addressing with students include:

- Is this strategic to the big company?
- How are you going to manage this?
- Who owns the intellectual property?
- Timing – how long is this relationship?
- Conclusions:
  - The company has to decide on its point of view about exclusivity (which will get altered).
  - Before you approach a strategic partner you need to ask "What is in it for them?"

10. Exercises to practice experimentation

EXERCISE: FEASIBILITY BLUEPRINT

AUTHOR: HEIDI NECK

Description

The feasibility blueprint exercise is a final team assignment requiring a 10- to 12-slide deck that answers early viability questions related to new business concepts. The exercise gives students practice in analyzing market and customer needs, gathering industry data, and using competitive information. Where there is no available data (which is usually the case with novel ideas), students are expected to collect their own data through action and experimentation.

Usage Suggestions

This exercise works for all audiences, undergraduate, graduate, and practitioner. The feasibility blueprint is most helpful for opportunity evaluation and discovery classes and sessions. The blueprint is designed to be done rather quickly. The version of the assignment presented here is an integrated, multidisciplinary assignment used in an MBA program. Teams of MBA students (6–7 students per team) have approximately four weeks to complete the blueprint.

Learning Objectives

- Gather and evaluate relevant data.
- Assess early viability of new venture concepts.
- Clearly present new venture concepts.

Materials List

Assignment (see the "Feasibility blueprint guidelines" below).

Theoretical Foundations

Mullins, J. 2010. *The New Business Road Test: What Entrepreneurs and Executives Should Do before Writing a Business Plan*, 3rd edn. New York: FT Press.
Osterwalder, A., and Pigneur, Y. 2010. *Business Model Generation*. Hoboken, NJ: Wiley.

Time Plan (4–5 weeks)

Students are able to complete the feasibility blueprint in as little as one week depending on the depth expected by the instructor. Teams are generally given 4–5 weeks to complete the assignment. The assignment guidelines are reproduced below.

Feasibility blueprint guidelines
Deliverable   Student teams are required to complete and present a feasibility blueprint to a faculty panel. You will have 15 minutes for the presentation, followed by approximately 15 minutes to answer questions posed by panel members.

The feasibility blueprint consists of a 10- to 12-slide PowerPoint presentation that includes the content outlined in this document. In addition:

- Include in the 'notes' section of the document a coherently developed set of talking points to explain the rationale, and elaborate and highlight the most important information.
- Your visuals should illustrate and graphically reinforce your major ideas, and not be merely a succession of bullet points.
- Qualities expected include an introduction that clearly frames your overall presentation, a coherent narrative from beginning to end, smooth transitions from point to point, clear speaking and delivery, teamwork, and a conclusion that effectively reinforces your main idea.

Both the presentation content and the presentation quality will be evaluated. The question-and-answer session should demonstrate a full understanding of the blueprint by all team members and full participation by the members.

Objectives   The goal of a feasibility blueprint is to assess the viability of a proposed business concept. The purpose of the exercise is to give you experience in analyzing market and customer needs, gathering industry data, and using competitive information. Where there is no available data (which is usually the case with innovative ideas), you are expected to collect your own data through action. The resulting effort is a basis for determining whether or not you should continue to pursue the concept and, if so, what business model might make sense. The practice of developing a feasibility blueprint will reduce uncertainty and provide input for the decision as to whether or not to move forward.

Feasibility overview and requirements   The feasibility blueprint addresses the most critical elements one needs to consider during the initial conceptualization of a new venture. To accomplish this, the entrepreneur (regardless of type of venture[1] or initiative) must answer the fundamental questions inherent in all new initiatives:

- What is the key problem or need that this concept will solve?
- How will you solve this problem or meet this need with your product or service concept and for whom?
- What is your customer value proposition (i.e. how do you propose to create value for your customer)?
- What is the competitive positioning of your concept?
- How do you propose to deliver value to the customer?
- What is the size or extent of the market for this product or service idea now and in the future?
- What is the revenue or income model?
- What capabilities does the team have to execute on the venture?

In addition to addressing the questions above, the team should draw some conclusions about whether this opportunity is feasible and worthwhile. If not, describe what the major constraints are. Remember, unlike the case for a business plan presentation, the primary audience for the feasibility blueprint is *you*. You want to be as honest as possible in deciding whether or not the proposed business is worthy of further investigation. This decision will be based on the particular desires or aspirations of each entrepreneur. Whether the decision is a "go" or a "no go," state the reasons.

A "go" decision means that the next step is to begin developing a launch plan, and may include developing and testing prototypes, filling out the management team, and seeking to raise the necessary funding and garner internal and external resources and support.

A "no go" decision is also a valid and valuable result of a feasibility blueprint, which will save the entrepreneur's time and expense that might have been incurred on a concept that does not have the potential to succeed in the market.

Feasibility process   The feasibility process is highly reliant on information gathering and analysis. While these initial stages are highly uncertain, the goal is to reduce this uncertainty and gain greater confidence about the opportunity and your approach. The process can be conceptualized as containing three key steps that are followed iteratively as the opportunity is defined, tested, and shaped over time. These include: 1) understanding the problem you are solving and for whom; 2) generation of ideas to solve the problem; and 3) testing assumptions, collecting more data, and iterating.

While these steps appear sequential, it's far from a linear process. The steps should be taken repeatedly, not necessarily in order, but always informed by prior information gathering, analysis, and so on. Think of the process as spiraling up to a higher level of understanding about the venture because at each iteration the need for new information is identified. When you begin the feasibility journey, however, avoid defining the opportunity too narrowly. Let the process shape the idea and venture. The goal is to explore multiple scenarios and recognize a potentially viable approach for your venture, rather than make explicit predictions or forecasts.

Action trumps everything. Don't rely solely on secondary data to inform your decision making. It's very important to demonstrate that you have taken real action in order to learn about the viability and feasibility of your idea. Some library research is all right for foundational material, but an overreliance on historical data is likely to lead to misguided decision making in entrepreneurial contexts.

Factors to consider   Below are some factors or guidelines that may help you address the fundamental questions demanded of a feasibility blueprint:

- early action and experimentation to test and shape the idea;
- primary and secondary research to demonstrate customer understanding;
- financial benchmarking using common-sized and comparable income statements;
- a one-year income statement to demonstrate potential economic viability as well as understanding of primary revenue and cost drivers;
- breakeven analysis;
- industry attractiveness;
- value creation, delivery, and capture analyses;
- team and individual self-assessment.

Key Takeaways

- Feasibility blueprints are not persuasive documents; they are evaluative and provide a quick screen to make decisions about proceeding to the next stage.
- Primary data collection is essential in early validation of new concepts. Don't wait until a "plan" is in place to take action.
- The generation of a feasibility blueprint emphasizes entrepreneurship as an integrated, multidisciplinary experience.

Teaching Tips

The feasibility blueprint is not a business plan but some instructors may have a tendency to treat it as such. Everything is very rough but grounded in data. Think of the feasibility blueprint as the next step up from the napkin drawing. The pro forma income statement should not extend past one year, and cash flows are not anticipated at this state. The faster students are expected to complete the assignment, the less of a business plan it will become. Fast, quick analysis of multiple ideas using the blueprint format is encouraged.

Attribution

The assignment has had many authors and iterations. Special attribution needs to be given to Donna Kelley, Dennis Ceru, and Bradley George – all faculty at Babson.

EXERCISE: COMPETITIVE CUP STACKING

AUTHOR: ERIK NOYES

Description

This exercise offers students a hands-on opportunity to reflect on the operational challenges of managing entrepreneurial growth. When ventures grow rapidly, entrepreneurs are often forced to adapt their business processes and create entirely new systems to support expansion; existing operations can become stressed and scale poorly. Through the physical challenge of competitive cup stacking, students learn how they need to design and implement new processes to enable growth.

Usage Suggestions

This exercise is appropriate for all audiences – existing entrepreneurs as well as undergraduate and graduate students. It can be used at various points in entrepreneurship courses but has particular value when students are considering growth strategy, operational strategy, and expansion.

Learning Objectives

- Reflect on the operational challenges of managing entrepreneurial growth.
- Evaluate the importance of systems and processes in confronting competition.
- Analyze and implement new processes in a hands-on, competitive simulation.

Materials List

182 large plastic cups, available at most grocery stores (e.g. red Solo brand).

Pre-Work Required by Students

None.

Theoretical Foundations

This exercise is grounded in the strategy literature and particularly think-ing on dynamic capabilities and organizational learning. Some suggested readings are offered below:

Levitt, B., and March, J.G. 1988. Organizational learning. *Annual Review of Sociology*, 14, 319–40.
March, J. 1990. Exploration and exploitation in organizational learning. *Organization Science*, 3, 71–87.
Nelson, R., and Winter, S. 1982. Skills. In *An Evolutionary Theory of Economic Change* (pp. 72–95). Cambridge, MA: Belknap Press of Harvard University Press.
Nelson, R., and Winter, S. 1982. Organizational capabilities and behavior. In *An Evolutionary Theory of Economic Change* (pp. 96–136). Cambridge, MA: Belknap Press of Harvard University Press.
Porter, M. 1996. What is strategy? *Harvard Business Review*, November–December, 61–78.
Teece, D.J., Pisano, G., and Shuen, A. 1997. Dynamic capabilities and strategic management. *Strategic Management Journal*, 18, 509–33.

Time Plan (45 minutes)

The recommended time to run this exercise is 45 minutes. However, the exercise can take as few as 35 minutes, depending on the preferred length of the debriefs and the number of cup-stacking competitions run.

Step 1 (cup-stacking competition among four individual students) 0:00–0:10 (10 minutes)
Pick four students in the class and have them compete to build and col-lapse 28-cup pyramids where each successive row is one cup less than the one below it (see Figure 10.1). Each individual should start with the 28 cups in a *single* stack (column) on a table surface. An individual participant wins the competition by erecting the proper structure *and* collapsing it back down into a *single* stack on a table surface in the shortest time.

Count out the cups beforehand to ensure four starting stacks of 28 cups. The instructor should demonstrate the general process – building the exact pyramid depicted in Figure 10.1 – and confirm there is only *one* acceptable design for the final pyramid. It is essential to emphasize that *this is not a creative design challenge*, but rather the focus is on the speed with which each individual can erect and collapse the structure. A properly built 28-cup pyramid will be 7 cups tall ($7+6+5+4+3+2+1=28$ cups).

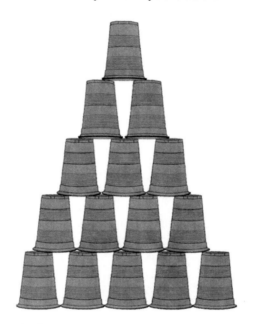

Figure 10.1   Stacked cups

Note: If you like, you can tell the competitors to imagine that they run competing wedding tent rental services. The aim is to erect "tents" correctly – rapidly – and then to take them down in an orderly fashion to enable more rentals and minimize labor costs.

Write down and review these important rules:

- To win, erect a pyramid *and* collapse it back down into a single stack in the shortest time.
- You must use *all* the cups.
- Each row must have one fewer cup than the row below it.
- All the cups must be in a line (no curves or 3D pyramids).
- Your pyramid must have a single peak.

The terminal height of a 28-cup pyramid is about 2.5–3 feet tall depending on the cups used. Pick competitors in highly visible parts of the room. When the competitors are clear on the task, count down and start the competition! Recognize the winner. Briefly comment on the range of strategies, outcomes, and speeds among the competitors.

Step 2 (class debrief)   0:10–0:20 (10 minutes)
Ask the class:

- "Why did [the winner] win?"
- "What about his or her process made him or her the fastest?"
- "What, if anything, did you notice about his or her approach?"
- "What approaches that you saw would you avoid?"

Ask the other contenders, "Is there anything you would do differently if you competed again?"

Incite competitiveness and if time allows rerun the competition to see how the competitors adapt their strategies in order to improve their speeds. Very quickly, on a flip chart, theme the full group's observations about what produced an efficient pyramid building and collapsing process. Are there a few key activities? Are there a few key mistakes to avoid? How fast could someone complete the task if he or she really studied and practiced the best methods?

Step 3 (cup-stacking competition among teams of two students – four people in total)   0:20–0:30 (10 minutes)
Invite the two fastest cup stackers to compete in a head-to-head competition, but tell them that this is now a *team* competition. Ask them each to pick a partner for the competition; they may choose one of the remaining competitors from the individual competition or they may choose someone else. Tell them that they will now compete in the same challenge – to erect and collapse pyramid structures. Again, the team that is able to erect *and* collapse and stack all the cups in a single stack will win the competition. Revisit the rules. Ask if there are any questions about the competition. Again, this is not a creative design challenge, but rather the focus is on the speed with which each individual can erect and collapse an identical pyramid.

After answering any questions, give each team 91 cups (counted out beforehand) to stack and collapse into the highest possible pyramid that obeys all the rules (i.e. the pyramid uses *all* the cups, each row has one fewer cup than the row below it, cups must be in a line, and the pyramid must have a single peak). As the instructor, you have dramatically changed the scale of the challenge; *offer no explanation and get the teams underway as soon as possible.*

A properly built 91-cup pyramid will be 13 cups tall ($13+12+11+10+9+8+7+6+5+4+3+2+1=91$ cups). The terminal height of a 91-cup pyramid may be up to 6 feet tall, and it will likely be necessary for competitors to get on chairs or a desk to complete and then collapse the pyramid.

Expect chaos. The height and the overall complexity introduce the prospect of time-wasting catastrophic errors during the erecting and collapsing of the pyramid. Again, the competition is not complete until one team has all cups in a single 91-cup stack.

Step 4 (class debrief and video)   0:30–0:45 (15 minutes)
Again, ask the class:

- "Why did [the winner] win?"
- "What about their process made this team the fastest?"
- "What, if anything, did you notice about their approach?"
- "Is there anything you would do or do differently if you competed in this competition?"

Key questions: "How did the fact it was 91 versus 28 cups affect the challenge? What are the lessons from the exercise?"
The students should point out that the scale of the challenge (91 cups) required vastly different processes to succeed. What worked for 28 cups only partially worked for 91 cups. Also, the team dynamics and potential for coordination were conspicuously different than in the individual competition. If students are creating a business plan in your class, you might ask the students to contemplate how their businesses or business processes would be different if they grew 5, 10, or 20 times in size? How would their company processes need to evolve to handle this growth?
For humor and to probe further, show and discuss the following two brief videos of competitive cup stackers (cup stacking is an emerging specialty sport where contenders stack and dismantle cup stacks at laser-like speeds). The first video (*Steven Purugganan Speed Stacking Champ*, http://www.youtube.com/watch?v=LyU5v0ZYMjI) shows Steven Purugganan, age 10, a world champion in cup stacking – what unique insights does he have about the process? The second video (*Slow Motion Cycle*, http://www.speedstacks.com/videos/slow_motion_cycle-31) shows a slow-motion demonstration of a competitive cup stacker – how does slowing down and analyzing the process give new context to understand best practices and opportunities for improvement?
The key questions above are important jumping-off points in considering the operational challenges of entrepreneurial growth. Particularly when a company grows, its existing processes and business operations may not scale efficiently. Things that worked well before no longer do. Systems get stressed and need to be evaluated and redesigned. Capture the main takeaways on a flip chart and use the exercise to frame discussions about growth strategy, operations, and expansion.

Post-Work

After running the entire cup-stacking exercise once, you may consider running the competition again – for example, a week later – to see if students compete with new strategies and processes.

Key Takeaways

To summarize, the exercise probes core entrepreneurial questions such as:

- How, if at all, do my business processes need to evolve?
- How do my existing business processes create (or destroy) value for my customer?
- Can my current business processes or operations scale to enable growth?
- How can a deeper understanding of my business's processes allow me to reduce my costs and/or increase the prices I charge my customer?

Teaching Tips

Carefully review and reinforce the rules of the cup-stacking competition – repeat the rules at least twice and answer any questions about the rules before stacking cups. Clarify that this is not a creativity challenge and that there is only *one* acceptable (i.e. winning) pyramid structure. Leverage the videos of expert cup stackers to drive finer points about tacit knowledge in operational processes as a wrap-up to the exercise.

EXERCISE: ESCALATING MARKET TESTS

AUTHOR: ANDREW ZACHARAKIS

Description

Launching a new venture involves risk. The goal of escalating market tests is to reduce the risk by running a series of low-cost experiments, building off the results of the previous experiment to shape and reshape the business model. Each escalating market test follows a similar pattern: plan, experiment, learn, reshape. The key is that each experiment should be as low-cost as possible, starting at $100 for the first experiment in the cycle and then escalating from there. After each experiment, entrepreneurs reshape the vision of their venture and move to a larger, incremental experiment.

Usage Suggestions

This basic concept works for audiences of all levels: undergraduates, MBAs, and executive education. Generally, this exercise encompasses one entire class and occurs early in a core entrepreneurship course.

Learning Objectives

- Test aspects of an opportunity at the lowest possible cost (affordable loss).
- Set metrics to measure the results of the test; key is to understand variance of outcome (either positive or negative) versus the metrics.
- Reshape opportunity and business model based upon learning from the experiment and then plan for the next test (escalating market test).
- Learn how entrepreneurs reduce overall risk.

Materials List

- Market Test Planning Worksheet (included at the end of the exercise).

Pre-Work Required by Students

Students should come prepared to class with an idea they are working on or want to start working on. It is also suggested they read Chapter 3,

"Opportunity Recognition, Shaping and Re-Shaping" from Bygrave and Zacharakis (2011) or another reading for background. Citation below.

Theoretical Foundations

Bygrave, W., and Zacharakis, A. 2010. *The Portable MBA in Entrepreneurship*, 4th edn. (chap. 3). Hoboken, NJ: Wiley. Or:
Bygrave, W., and Zacharakis, A. 2011. *Entrepreneurship*, 2nd edn. (chap. 3). Hoboken, NJ: Wiley.

Time Plan (60 minutes)

Step 1   0:00–0:15 (15 minutes)
Have students identify an opportunity for a new venture that they believe has merit. Hopefully this is an opportunity they have been working with in the class or the instructor may give the class a potential opportunity.

Step 2   0:15–0:45 (30 minutes)
Market Test Worksheet – Students can only learn so much from secondary research. Primary research with a purpose uncovers valuable insight. Have students devise the first 3 market tests they would run (with the assumption that the first test proves out and you move to the second test and so forth). The key is to come up with low cost first test. This exercise is suited to a group break out.

Step 3   0:45–1:00 (15 minutes)
Upon return, groups detail their first, lowest cost market tests which the instructor should put on the board. Have a rich discussion around order of tests, and how costs might be reduced even further. Give special recognition for the most creative, low cost tests.

Key Takeaways

1. Low cost and early experiments are essential for opportunity shaping.
2. Apply metrics to measure outcomes versus expectations.
3. Market testing is an iterative process that reduces risk and increases likelihood of survival.
4. Expect the opportunity to evolve or even pivot as market tests escalate.

Teaching Tips

Students assume that a lot of money is needed to conducts market tests, but a lot of information can be gleaned before major investment. Pay special attention to the types of experiments generated by the students. Note the action-based experiments versus broad data collection experiments (e.g. market surveys). Encourage the students to take action in order to learn at this stage.

Market Test Planning Worksheet

Market test description (briefly describe the market test. Remember to keep it as low-cost as possible. Also describe what you hope to learn from the test):

Key tasks (list the key tasks that need to be completed to run the market test):	**Person responsible:**	**Deadline:**
Resources needed (list resources, both financial and non-financial. Break down by use):	**How used:**	
Outcomes expected (what key learning do you expect?):	**Metric** (how will you measure the relative success of the test, e.g. number of customers served, customer reaction, etc.?):	**Variance from actual** (track whether your outcome was better or worse than predicted. Can you explain why?):

Overall learning from test:

How will you reshape your business and move to the next test?

Source: Bygrave and Zacharakis (2011).

EXERCISE: OPPORTUNITY SCREENING

AUTHOR: ANDREW ZACHARAKIS

Description

Not all ideas are powerful, commercial opportunities. How can students gauge which ideas have more potential? One method is to evaluate multiple ideas on an opportunity checklist (Table 10.1). The opportunity checklist provides metrics across a number of categories. Better opportunities are attractive on more metrics than less powerful opportunities.

Usage Suggestions

This basic concept works for multiple audiences: undergraduates, MBAs, and executive education. Generally, this exercise encompasses one entire class and occurs early in a core entrepreneurship course.

Learning Objectives

- Define criteria that are potential strengths and weaknesses of a particular idea.
- Evaluate opportunities on the metrics.
- Identify areas of further research to better understand how the idea measures on a particular metric.

Materials List

- Any new venture creation case where the core issue in the case is the evaluation of the venture opportunity.
- Opportunity checklist (Table 10.1).

Pre-Work Required by Students

Can be done without any pre-work (most often with an executive education audience), but Chapter 3, "Opportunity recognition, shaping and re-shaping" from Bygrave and Zacharakis (2011) provides background (see Theoretical Foundations). Students should also read the case and evaluate the opportunity based on the criteria from the checklist (Table 10.1). Students should bring the checklist to class and be prepared to discuss. Alternatively you can have the students complete the checklist in groups during the early part of the class session.

Table 10.1   Opportunity checklist

Customer	Better opportunities	Weaker opportunities
Identifiable	Defined core customer	Undefined customer
Demographics	Clearly defined and focused	Fuzzy definition and unfocused
Psychographics	Clearly defined and focused	Fuzzy definition and unfocused
Trends:		
Macro market	Multiple and converging	Few and disparate
Target market	Multiple and converging	Few and disparate
Window of opportunity	Opening	Closing
Market structure	Emerging or fragmented	Mature or declining
Market size:		
How many	Large core customer group	Small, unclear customer groups
Demand	Greater than supply	Less than supply
Market growth:		
Rate	20% or greater	Less than 20%
Price, frequency, and value:		
Price	Gross margin > 40%	Gross margin < 40%
Frequency	Often and repeated	One time
Value	Fully reflected in price	Penetration pricing
Operating expenses	Large and fixed	Low and variable
Net profit margin	>10%	<10%
Volume	Very high	Moderate
Distribution:		
Where are you in the value chain?	High margin, high power	Low margin, low power
Competition:		
Market structure	Emerging	Mature
Number of direct competitors	Few	Many
Number of indirect competitors	Few	Many
Number of substitutes	Few	Many
Stealth competitors	Unlikely	Likely
Strength of competitors	Weak	Strong
Key success factors:		
Relative position	Strong	Weak
Vendors:		
Relative power	Weak	Strong

Table 10.1　　(continued)

Customer	Better opportunities	Weaker opportunities
Gross margins they control in the value chain	Low	High
Government:		
Regulations	Low	High
Taxes	Low	High
Global environment:		
Customers	Interested and accessible	Not interested or not accessible
Competition	Nonexistent or weak	Existing and strong
Vendors	Eager	Unavailable

Source:　Bygrave and Zacharakis (2011).

Theoretical Foundations (Citations, Suggestions for Further Reading)

Bygrave, W., and Zacharakis, A. 2010. *The Portable MBA in Entrepreneurship*, 4th edn. (chap. 3). Hoboken, NJ: Wiley. Or:
Bygrave, W., and Zacharakis, A. 2011. *Entrepreneurship*, 2nd edn. (chap. 3). Hoboken, NJ: Wiley.

Time Plan (45 minutes)

Step 1   0:00–0:05 (5 minutes)
1. To start the case, have students vote on whether the opportunity is attractive or not, based upon how they completed the checklist. For each row on the checklist, students should circle the text that is either under better opportunities or weaker opportunities.
2. Students should then calculate how many circles exist in column 1 (better opportunities) and column 2 (weaker opportunities). As a quick screen, the column with the most circles determines whether the opportunity is strong or weak at the current stage.
3. It is important to remind students that no opportunity is strong on all criteria. Key is to evaluate those areas that are weaker and see if you can devise a business model to move those criteria to the "better" column or have a strategy that minimizes exposure on the weaker aspects while leveraging stronger aspects.

Step 2   0:05–0:35 (30 minutes)
As a class, discuss what factors make the opportunity:

1. attractive;
2. unattractive.

Spur debate. Different students are likely to evaluate the opportunity differently on the same criteria. For instance, one student may see the "graying of America" trend as a threat and another an opportunity. Talk about how perceptions drive decisions and action.

Step 3   0:35–0:45 (10 minutes)
Address frustration with the tool and encourage students to research further. The opportunity checklist is often used to evaluate multiple ideas side by side and so is done rather quickly with little information. Thus many question marks are likely, and students should consider what kind of information they need to feel comfortable in moving forward in launching the business.

Key Takeaways

1. Understand which ideas are stronger opportunities in the eyes of potential investors.
2. Guide further research. What are the gaps in the current opportunity?
3. An early screen of an idea is important to manage expectations and the amount of work that needs to be done during opportunity shaping.

Teaching Tips

Watch out for student bias. Entrepreneurs love their ideas and often evaluate in a biased manner that confirms their preconceived notions. One technique to overcome that natural bias is to have students or groups evaluate each other's ideas on the checklists. The differences between the two groups should serve as a launch point for further research and development around the business model.

EXERCISE: FEAR OF FAILURE

AUTHORS: YASUHIRO YAMAKAWA AND HEIDI NECK

Description

This exercise offers students the opportunity to raise awareness of "fear of failure." Through a simple activity, students will see how individuals vary in their notion of failure, and their tolerance to take risks. In addition to the discussion of fear and shame at the individual level (McGregor and Elliot, 2005), implications (e.g. similarities and differences) can be extended to the country, regional, and societal levels (Baumol, 1993; Lee et al., 2011).

Overall, the exercise allows students to discuss how varying degrees of risk tolerance may explain how entrepreneurial perception varies among individuals and how entrepreneurship development varies around the world (Xavier et al., 2012) or, instead, how generalizable and universal it is that we all fear failure. The debrief session can encourage discussions on how failure can be a relevant and important component of entrepreneurship education.

Usage Suggestions

This exercise can be used for any audience – undergraduate, graduate, or practitioner – and works particularly well with international audiences. The experience is appropriate and applicable for all entrepreneurship courses, especially for new venture creation. The session is best positioned toward the end of a course where there is enough trust in the classroom to have an authentic conversation around failure.

Learning Objectives

- Assess one's personal fear of failure (risk tolerance) at the individual level as well as at the country, regional, or societal levels.
- Identify sources of fear of failure.
- Compare similarities (generalizability) and differences (variance), and how they affect entrepreneurship.
- Contrast personal fear of failure with country-level norms.

Materials List

- A flip board, assessment sheets (included at the end of the exercise), and sticker dots (one for each student) for the exercise.

- Global Entrepreneurship Monitor (GEM) reports (http://www. gemconsortium.org/docs) for discussion (e.g. Xavier et al., 2012, Table 2.2, and the discussion of fear of failure on p. 23).

Pre-Work Required by Students

None.

Theoretical Foundations

Baumol, W.J. 1993. *Entrepreneurship, Management, and the Structure of Payoffs*. Cambridge, MA: MIT Press.

Houston, B.K., and Kelly, K.E. 1987. Type A behavior in housewives: Relations to work, marital adjustment, stress, tension, health, fear of failure and self-esteem. *Journal of Psychosomatic Research*, 31(1), 55–61.

Lee, S.-H., Yamakawa, Y., Peng, M.W., and Barney, J.B. 2011. How do bankruptcy laws affect entrepreneurship development around the world? *Journal of Business Venturing*, 26(5), 505–20.

McGregor, H.A., and Elliot, A.J. 2005. The shame of failure: Examining the link between fear of failure and shame. *Personality and Social Psychology Bulletin*, 31(2), 218–31.

Xavier, S.R., Kelley, D., Kew, J., Herrington, M., and Vorderwülbecke. 2012. *GEM 2012 Global Report* (Table 2.2, "Entrepreneurial attitudes and perceptions in the GEM countries in 2012 by geographic region"). Wellesley, MA: Babson College.

Time Plan (25 minutes)

Step 1   0:00–0:05 (5 minutes)
Begin the exercise by handing out and asking each student to fill out the
(one-page) assessment sheet. There are a total of nine items that need to
be rated (1: totally false to 6: totally true), and an average score to be
calculated at the end.

Step 2   0:05–0:10 (5 minutes)
When all students finish calculating their average score, ask each of them
to come down to the center of the room where a flip chart is located. On
the flip chart, ask each student to place a sticker dot to the corresponding
number (average score) (see Figure 10.2).

Step 3   0:10–0:15 (5 minutes)
Ask the students what the exercise was all about. What does the number
represent? What was measured? Reveal the answer – fear of failure and
risk tolerance.

Step 4   0:15–0:25 (10 minutes)
Discuss the implications. As a group, ask what students think about
the distribution (of sticker dot plot). Normal distribution? Outliers?
Risk tolerant or risk averse as a group? Individually, what are the
sources of the fear of failure? How would fear of failure affect entrepreneurship? Summarize and close with a notion that variation does
exist within individuals, groups, and countries (see "Option for an
additional exercise" below), but fear of failure is universal in the sense
that everyone fears making mistakes and that it affects entrepreneurial
action.

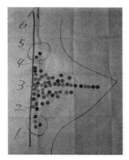

Figure 10.2   Example of class distribution on fear of failure

Option for an additional exercise
Depending on the demographics of the audience, students can be divided into teams based on their nationality, to discuss the implications for regional, cultural, or societal variations. How is risk tolerance in your country? The Global Entrepreneurship Monitor reports fear of failure by country. To download the most recent report go to http://www.gemcon sortium.org/docs.

Post-Work

If the Global Entrepreneurship Monitor was not used in class, then it is suggested you have students review the fear of failure statistics by country.

Key Takeaways

- Individuals vary in their tolerance of risk and fear of failure.
- Groups, teams, countries, and societies can vary in the same way.
- Despite the variation across individuals and nations, it is universal that we all do fear failure, and that this has implications for entre- preneurship development.
- Fear of failure is a major obstacle for nascent entrepreneurs.

Teaching Tips

As shown in Figure 10.2, responses will typically shape into a normal distribution. It may be natural to start from the outliers and then on to sharing with the whole audience that fear of failure is somewhat universal and that we do fear failure regardless of background, experience, and so on.

In-Class Exercise – Assessment Sheet

Please indicate how well the following statements describe you using the scoring key below. Please record your number (1–6) next to each statement, sum all scores to arrive at a total score, and then calculate the average score.

Answer:	Totally false	False	More false than true	More true than false	True	Totally true
Score:	1	2	3	4	5	6

Item	Statement	Score
1	In general, I prefer to work a puzzle that I know I can complete rather than try to do a puzzle that might be too hard for me.	
2	If I do poorly on something, I usually prefer to not let anyone else know or try to cover it up.	
3	I sometimes find myself carelessly doing things I find difficult.	
4	When I compete with someone who seems to be better than I am, I sort of give up trying.	
5	Sometimes when others are talking about their accomplishments, I find myself exaggerating things I have done in the past.	
6	I usually avoid telling a joke in public because people might not laugh.	
7	When I do something particularly well, I usually let my family and friends know.	
8	There are times when I worry about being a successful entrepreneur.	
9	When I feel uncertain about how I might perform compared to others in an activity, I prefer to watch rather than participate.	
	Total	
	Average = total score ÷ 9	

Source: Adapted from Houston and Kelly (1987).

EXERCISE: DRAWING BRIDGES

AUTHOR: CANDIDA BRUSH

Description

This exercise is designed to help students understand the difference between predictive and creative thinking. The predictive approach is rooted in what Neck and Greene (2011) refer to as a *process approach*, where entrepreneurship is taught in a linear fashion, by identifying an opportunity, developing the concept, assessing and acquiring resources, implementing the business, and then exiting. The creative approach leverages resources and relationships at hand and "within reach" both in the founding process and as a course for venture development versus finding and acquiring resources from a pre-created plan (e.g. human resources, financial resources, physical resources). Creative thinking includes entrepreneurial experimentation and creation of options, and considers how stakeholders can dramatically reshape a venture based on acquired experience (Sarasvathy, 2001). In this exercise, students experience both approaches by the simple exercise of drawing a bridge exactly (predictive approach) and drawing a solution to cross a river (creative approach).

Usage Suggestions

This exercise is best positioned as an introduction to entrepreneurial thinking. It works for any audience, youth, family enterprises, adults, or undergraduate or graduate students.

Learning Objectives

- Explore how predictive thinking leads to constrained and bounded outcomes, while creative thinking leads to more innovative outcomes.
- Discover how predictive logic is rooted in analysis, clear logic, and a known outcome.
- Discover how creative logic is rooted in experimentation, reflection on past experience, and unclear and evolving outcomes.

Materials List

Prepare two handouts. The first is a picture of a bridge over a river. Print the bridge on half the page, leaving the other half blank. The instructions at the top should say: "Take a few minutes to make a drawing of this bridge capturing most of the features." The second picture should be a similar picture of a river with no bridge, again with the picture on half the page and the other half blank. The instructions at the top should say: "Take a few minutes and draw a way to get across this river."

Prepare enough copies for the class, but half the class will receive handout 1 and the other half will receive handout 2.

Pre-Work Required by Students

None.

Theoretical Foundations

Kiefer, C., Schlesinger, L., and Brown, P. 2012. *Just Start: Take Action, Embrace Uncertainty and Create the Future*. Cambridge, MA: Harvard Business Press Books.

Neck, H., and Greene, P.G. 2011. Entrepreneurship education: Known worlds and new frontiers. *Journal of Small Business Management*, 49(1), 55–70.

Noyes, E., and Brush, C. 2012. Teaching entrepreneurial action: Application of creative logic. In J.A. Katz and A. Corbett (eds.), *Advances in Entrepreneurship, Firm Emergence and Growth*, Vol. 14: *Entrepreneurial Action* (pp. 253–80). Bingley, UK: Emerald Group Publishing.

Sarasvathy, S.D. 2001. Causation and effectuation: Toward a theoretical shift from economic inevitability to entrepreneurial contingency. *Academy of Management Review*, 26(2), 243–63.

Time Plan (40 minutes)

Drawing time   0:00–0:10 (10 minutes)
Pass handout 1 to half the class and handout 2 to the other half. Tell the students that this is an entrepreneurial thinking exercise. After a few minutes, ask the class some questions, starting with those drawing the bridge.

Questions for those drawing the bridge   0:10–0:20 (10 minutes)

- How did you start? What did you look at? (Analysis.)
- Was it clear what the possibilities were for starting?
- What assumptions did you make about materials, design, and functionality?
- Did you follow a prescribed formula? Draw the curve first? Look at the scale? Add the lines?
- Was the assignment clear or unclear?
- Was it helpful to have a model to follow?
- Did you know where you would end up?

Questions for those drawing a way to get across the river		0:20–0:30 (10 minutes)

- How did you start? What did you look at?
- Did you think about what you knew about bridges? (Reflection.)
- Was it clear what the possibilities were for starting?
- What assumptions did you make about materials, design, and functionality?
- Did you follow a prescribed formula? (No, because there was no model.)
- What type of bridge did you create? For people, animals, cars, trains?
- What assumptions did you make?
- Did you make more than one attempt? (Experimenting.)
- Was the assignment clear or unclear?
- Was it hard not to have a model to follow?
- Did you know the outcome – what your bridge would look like when you started?

Wrap-up								0:30–0:40 (10 minutes)
Use two slides that summarize the difference between creative thinking and predictive thinking and the logics that accompany these (Neck and Greene, 2011; Kiefer et al., 2012).

Predictive approach to entrepreneurial thinking

Action	Assumptions
1. Identify the opportunity	Known inputs
2. Identify and quantify the resources needed	Identified steps
3. Create the plan	Precision approach
4. Execute and measure results	Predictive, linear, and tested

Creative approach to entrepreneurial thinking

Action	Assumptions
1. Self-assessment and understanding	Skills and capabilities of individuals, unknown and unique inputs
2. Observation and reflection	Opportunities can be made or created
3. Experimentation	Interactive and iterative
4. Build on results	Means driven

Post-Work

None.

Key Takeaways

- Two different approaches for problem solving and entrepreneurial behavior.
- Both approaches are needed in entrepreneurial activities, depending on the situation and context.

Teaching Tips

This exercise makes the point quite well. Those receiving handout 1 may get frustrated if they think they are not artistic. This is a point to discuss as well: following a prescribed formula in entrepreneurship may not be possible or desirable. For those with handout 2, students might start several times and create multiple bridges. It is also nice to wrap up with pictures of unique bridges, which might be pulled from Google Images – water bridges, natural rock bridges, covered bridges, railroad bridges, and so on.

EXERCISE: $5, $50, AND $500 EXPERIMENTS

AUTHOR: ERIK NOYES

Description

This exercise challenges students to get out into the field and conduct creative "experiments" to explore entrepreneurial opportunities. Students are pushed to design and then run three sequential market experiments – first $5, then $50, and then $500 (or some other ascending scale of investment) – which broaden and shape understanding of an entrepreneurial opportunity.

A simple experiment might involve taking public transportation ($5) to meet face to face with a potential customer; a later, larger-scale experiment might involve creating a looks-like prototype of a product concept ($500) to seek feedback from other stakeholders (e.g. possible customers, investors, or suppliers). The chief aim is to have students pre-specify an acceptable maximum investment, or affordable loss, at each step to take a particular creative action and further investigate an entrepreneurial opportunity.

The exercise is built on empirical research in effectuation (Sarasvathy, 2001, 2008), where entrepreneurs take action with available resources they have at hand, often collaborating with self-selecting stakeholders who join in the opportunity development process. The concept of pre-setting a maximum investment for a market experiment lines up with Sarasvathy's concept of *affordable loss*, where an entrepreneur decides to move ahead when and where there is a known downside risk (e.g. $5, $50, or $500). This type of creative logic and exploration contrasts with entrepreneurial action based on a predictive logic where an entrepreneurial opportunity is pursued (or not) based on an analysis of estimated upside returns and pre-set attractiveness criteria.

Usage Suggestions

This exercise is appropriate for multiple audiences, including undergraduate and graduate students as well as existing entrepreneurs. The exercise can be run with individual students or with student teams. Students should have at least a loosely formed idea for an entrepreneurial opportunity which they are looking to develop or evaluate.

The exercise is particularly valuable for undergraduate students, who likely have greater anxiety around engaging (unknown) potential customers and stakeholders. The three-part exercise can guide and inform many phases in the entrepreneurial process, including opportunity evaluation or feasibility analysis, early-stage idea generation, and later-stage opportunity development. The exercise can be used in a wide range of entrepreneurship courses, including introduction to entrepreneurship, new venture creation, managing entrepreneurial growth, and/or entrepreneurial marketing.

Learning Objectives

- Apply the logic of affordable loss to an entrepreneurial action and learning challenge.
- Develop increased comfort acting in the face of high uncertainty.
- Engage opportunity stakeholders (e.g. target customers and/or users, suppliers, or potential partners) directly with three different approaches.
- Design market experiments with a fixed budget in mind, particularly to drive future entrepreneurial action.

Materials List

An "Experiment Worksheet" (included at the end of the exercise) offers students a format for summarizing each market experiment, including its rationale, methodology, outcomes, and most importantly implications. Conducting the exercise requires basic funds. However, funding amounts may vary depending on the length, nature, and budget of the particular entrepreneurship program. Even modest funds, for example $5–$25, funded by the program or students, can drive significant action, reflection, and learning.

Pre-Work Required by Students

As noted, to run the exercise, students should have at least a loosely formed idea for an entrepreneurial opportunity which they are looking to develop or evaluate. This idea establishes the context for critical questions such as:

- Who are the key stakeholders we are looking to engage and understand – and why?
- What are potential actions and strategies to seek input and feedback from these stakeholders?
- How can and should the entrepreneurial opportunity or opportunity concept be presented to these stakeholders (e.g. possibly as a written

opportunity statement, venture sketch on a poster board, or even a simulation or role-play with stakeholders)?

Theoretical Foundations

Sarasvathy, S. 2001. Causation and effectuation: Towards a theoretical shift from economic inevitability to entrepreneurial contingency. *Academy of Management Journal*, 2, 243–63.
Sarasvathy, S. 2008. *Effectuation: Elements of Entrepreneurial Expertise.* Cheltenham, UK and Northampton, MA, USA: Edward Elgar Publishing.

Time Plan (1–2 weeks)

Generally students require one to two weeks to run and document a single, thoughtful experiment using the worksheet handout. Higher-cost experiments and engagements (i.e. $500) require additional time to plan and conduct.

Step 1 (broad framing)
Challenge students to design and conduct three sequential market experiments (first $5, then $50, and then $500) to better understand the needs and wants of their target customers and, most importantly, to co-develop entrepreneurial opportunities with their targets. Students need to understand that their charge is to design creative interactions with stakeholders with the real potential for surprise and insight, not simply to validate or invalidate their business idea. Distribute the worksheet handout as the expectation for what constitutes a thoughtful experiment and experiment report.

Step 2 ($5 experiments)
Next, instruct the student teams to design and execute a simple experiment requiring no more than $5 to test their ideas or assumptions about an opportunity or space. Ask them: "What is a small creative investment, or type of untraditional market research, you might make to explore or test your concept? What can you explore, confirm, or challenge with only $5?" Experiments may include at first sharing a simple product or service concept as embodied in a two-dimensional sketch. You might ask: "How can you generate $10000 of learning or more with only $5?" Tell students that a chief goal of the exercise is to engage stakeholders in order to reshape and strengthen their entrepreneurial opportunity after each phase.

Step 3 ($50 experiments)
Only after students have completed their first experiments and submitted a complete worksheet – which you might grade – ask them to design and run a $50 experiment to test their (revised) ideas or assumptions about the opportunity. Instruct them that they may leverage secondary research, but they should use the $50 to engage potential customers directly and seek their critical input. You might ask: "How can you generate $100 000 of learning or more with only $50?"

Step 4 ($500 experiments)
Only after students have completed and again submitted a complete worksheet handout drawing out implications from their $50 experiments – which you might grade – ask them to design and execute a $500 experiment. You might ask: "How can you generate $1 000 000 of learning or more with only $500?" *Note*: Quantifying any particular dollar value of the learning is less important than having students engage with their potential customers or stakeholders and recalibrate based on the feedback and resources they discover along the way. Also, a decision not to launch a failing venture may be extraordinarily valuable!

Key Takeaways

- Experimentation, and specifically taking creative action, helps drive learning about entrepreneurial opportunities.
- Pre-setting an affordable loss, by itself, can incite entrepreneurial action by circumventing the requirement to work out all the elements of return on investment (i.e. predictive logic).
- Escalating market experimentation driven by the concept of affordable loss is a low-risk, cost-effective approach to exploring and evaluating entrepreneurial opportunities.

Teaching Tips

This exercise works best when students are asked to investigate very specific questions or assumptions about their opportunities – a narrow and deliberate focus for experimentation (see experiment worksheet). Moreover, the exercise is most effective when each experiment is run and debriefed sequentially, driving successive action. While entrepreneurs in fact juggle and connect numerous experiments and actions simultaneously, new entrepreneurship students are more likely to appreciate this through a phased approach. Using the worksheet handout, forces students to extract the maximum value from each experiment before designing the next, higher-investment action. In certain cases, the handout may not be needed for quick, initial experiments (i.e. $5) but it should be used to drive learning and reflection for higher-value experiments ($50 or $500).

Attribution

This core approach, and particularly the methodology of $5, $50, and $500 experiments, is credited to Andy Hargadon of UC Davis. Hargadon runs the UC Davis Center for Entrepreneurship.

Experiment Worksheet

Team member names:
Experiment level (circle one): $5 $50 $500
Abstract
Provide a one-paragraph abstract that captures the rationale, methodology, and results of your experiment. If possible, provide one to two images with captions as part of the abstract to communicate the nature of the experiment.
Introduction
What is the broader context of this experiment? When and where did the experiment take place and why? What did you set out to do?
Rationale
What core question(s) or assumption(s) did your experiment aim to address? What parts of your opportunity are you clarifying? What opportunity-shaping decisions will this experiment allow your team to make? Indicate both the importance and the elements of uncertainty that warranted investigation to increase confidence. Whether it is a $5, $50, or $500 experiment, summarize the experiment costs and briefly justify the return on investment.
Methodology
How was the experiment conducted and evaluated? What were the planning, setup, and detail to run the particular experiment? Briefly, what other types of experiments were considered?
Outcomes
Detail the results that were realized by carrying out this experiment. Include specific findings and insights gained.
Discussion
Reflect on the outcomes in the context of the decisions that you need to make to shape your entrepreneurial opportunity. What do the results reveal to you about the choices your team faces with its opportunity? Comment on the effectiveness of this experiment. Would you do this

experiment the same way again? Why or why not? *Based on these results, what is the next experiment you should run and why?*

Appendix

Include subsections for raw data, such as observation data, interview transcripts, pictures of the experiment, survey data, and so on, and other supporting information.

NOTE

1. Babson supports entrepreneurship in a variety of contexts. A "new venture" can be a for-profit new venture, nonprofit organization, licensing of technology as the foundation of a new venture, and a new venture inside an existing organization.

11. Exercises to practice reflection

EXERCISE: DEVELOPING A REFLECTIVE
PRACTICE

AUTHOR: PATRICIA GREENE

Description

This multi-part exercise can be offered in various time configurations. At its fullest form, it is conducted for 30 minutes each at seven different times across a semester, with the last offering given towards the end of the course. During the first exercise session a reflective framework is introduced that includes a set of dimensions to consider when reflecting. These dimensions serve as content guides. This is followed by a process guide, and for each of the first several sessions a different process for a reflective exercise is introduced. For 30 minutes the students are asked to reflect on their work in the class to date, using the assigned framework dimension and the process of the day. On the seventh time, the content assignment is changed to reflecting on the reflective experiences in order to consider which dimensions of the content framework and which reflective process best fit the learning style and promote the reflective practice of each individual student across a range of tactile and cognitive approaches. (For a summary of content framework dimensions and processes see Table 6.3 in Chapter 6.)

Shorter versions of this exercise may be developed to match the time allotted by selecting a subset of content framework dimensions and a smaller number of reflective processes.

While the benefits of reflection in education are largely based on the early work of John Dewey ([1916] 1985) and Alfred North Whitehead ([1938] 1966), more recently the discussion of reflection-in-practice and reflection-on-practice from Schön (1983, 1987) build an even stronger theoretical foundation and provides practical guidance for use in the classroom.

Usage Suggestions

This exercise is quite flexible and can be used with audiences ranging from high school students through experienced practitioners. The older the audience, the more likely the resistance to an authentic exploration of reflective practices and therefore the more encouragement may be needed.

Learning Objectives

- Develop a reflective practice to support ongoing critical thinking and learning.
- Engage in numerous styles of reflective practice.
- Evaluate a set of reflective practices to determine best fit for the person and the type of learning desired.
- Illustrate the importance of reflection in learning and expanding our knowledge base.

Materials List

- Access to individual Twitter accounts and a class hashtag.
- Creation materials for each table or small group of students (construction paper, markers, colored pencils and/or crayons, glue, pipe cleaners, stickers, etc.).
- Video capabilities on phones.
- Reflection dimensions – Table 6.3 in Chapter 6 (one per student).

Pre-Work Required by Students

None.

Theoretical Foundations

Brockbank, A., and McGill, I. 2007. *Facilitating Reflective Learning in Higher Education*, 2nd edn. New York: McGraw-Hill and Open University Press.
Dewey, J. [1916] 1985. *Democracy and Education*, ed. Jo Ann Boydston and Patricia Baysinger. Carbondale: Southern Illinois University Press.
Schön, D. 1983. *The Reflective Practitioner*. New York: Basic Books.
Schön, D. 1987. *Educating the Reflective Practitioner*. London: Jossey-Bass.
Whitehead, Alfred North. [1938] 1966. *Modes of Thought*. New York: Free Press.

Time Plan (30 minutes per Session – Seven Sessions over the Course of a Semester)

Reflection generally should take place at the end of a class and can follow any type of other class activity. Each reflection exercise begins with a short introduction of the questions of the day and the process of the day. (*Note*: It is up to the instructor whether or not he or she wants to present any overview of the content dimensions. One suggestion is to simply give the questions without any extra discussion and then share the framework (Table 6.3) on the final day to "reveal" the themes.) The sessions will generally run: 5 minutes for the introduction, 20 minutes for the reflective exercise, and 5 minutes for the discussion and debrief. Session 1 and Session 7 will be slightly different. Session 1 is best at 15 minutes for the introduction of the overall framework and 15 minutes for reflection, with no debrief. Session 7 works best with very little introduction, 15 minutes of reflection, and 15 minutes of final debrief with a focus on the content dimensions.

Session 1

Introduction   0:00–0:15 (15 minutes)
The instructor introduces the overall concept of reflection as it pertains to entrepreneurial learning by doing and then moves to describing the overall reflective exercise across the semester. The instructor can decide whether to share all processes that will be used at this time, or to introduce the process only on the day it is to be used.

Student reflection time   0:15–0:30 (15 minutes)
Instructions to the students: "Today we will be reflecting through journaling in whatever notebook, app, etc. in which you are comfortable, and answering the following questions." (Use questions from the narrative dimension.)

Session 2

Introduction   0:00–0:05 (5 minutes)
"Today we will be reflecting through haiku." (*Note*: For help on explaining haiku, see http://www.wikihow.com/Write-a-Haiku-Poem.) (Use questions from the emotional dimension.)

Reflective practice of the day   0:05–0:25 (20 minutes)

Debrief   0:25–0:30 (5 minutes)

Session 3

Introduction   0:00–0:05 (5 minutes)
"Today we will be reflecting through creation. Please use the construction paper, stickers, etc. on the table to answer the following questions." (Use questions from the percipient dimension.)

Reflective practice of the day   0:05–0:25 (20 minutes)

Debrief   0:25–0:30 (5 minutes)

Session 4

Introduction   0:00–0:05 (5 minutes)
"Today we will be reflecting with a partner. Please select someone in the class that you don't know very well and discuss the following questions." (Use questions from the analytical dimension.)

Reflective practice of the day   0:05–0:25 (20 minutes)

Debrief   0:25–0:30 (5 minutes)

Session 5

Introduction   0:00–0:05 (5 minutes)
"Today we will be reflecting through comics. Please use the paper and crayons in front of you to create a comic strip that answers the following questions." (Use questions from the evaluative dimension.)

Reflective practice of the day   0:05–0:25 (20 minutes)

Debrief   0:25–0:30 (5 minutes)

Session 6

Introduction   0:00–0:05 (5 minutes)
"Today we will be reflecting through Twitter. Please use the #class hashtag to submit your tweets." (Use questions from the critical reflection dimension.)

Reflective practice of the day   0:05–0:25 (20 minutes)

Debrief   0:25–0:30 (5 minutes)

Session 7

Introduction   0:00–0:00 (very quick)
"Today you get to choose how you want to reflect using any process we've used so far or any process you'd like to try. You may also use whatever questions [focus your content] you'd like to use."

Reflective practice of the day   0:00–0:15 (15 minutes)

Debrief   0:15–0:30 (15 minutes)
The final debrief may focus on the overall practice of reflection and how students see this helping them (or not) to advance their entrepreneurial mindset and skillset. If the instructor has not previously shared the overview of the content dimensions, this is a good time to share the chart for the scholars to see how it all fits together.

Teaching Tips

Some student groups will be less enthused than others about the ideas of drawing, building, tweeting, and so on. It is helpful to remind them that if, as teachers, we don't push them to try things about which they are uncomfortable we haven't pushed them hard enough.

The processes may be done in any order, and there are many others you might try, including asking them to video themselves on their phones. One suggestion is to mix up those that feel most different to the students and intersperse the types of things they may be more comfortable doing. Another suggestion is to start comfortable and then keep pushing.

Key Takeaways

1. It is particularly important when emphasizing the "doing" in learning that time is taken to reflect and think critically through what has been done and what should be done.
2. Reflecting (thinking) is a form of doing.

EXERCISE: REFLECTING ON ENTREPRENEURIAL EXPERIENCE

AUTHOR: ANNE DONNELLON

Description

This assignment encourages students to reflect on and interpret entrepreneurial experiences (such as exercises on opportunity identification or resource acquisition). This exercise is based on the theories of experiential learning, which argue that adult learners, in particular, learn most effectively from doing and reflecting on their experience. Current work in entrepreneurial learning also emphasizes that an educational experience of entrepreneurship coupled with reflective practice enables those without this type of experience or background to develop the self-insight, self-confidence, and enhanced interpersonal skills that entrepreneurs need.

Usage Suggestions

This exercise works for all audiences: undergraduate, graduate, or practitioner. It is appropriate for any entrepreneurship course that involves experiential learning activities, but particularly for new venture creation courses, entrepreneurship bootcamps, or workshops. The exercise should be positioned after students have completed an exercise of some type of entrepreneurial activity, particularly one that involves others. It can be used afterward as an individual assignment or it can be combined with a session in which these reflections are discussed in the classroom.

Learning Objectives

- Develop a reflective practice about one's own actions, feelings, and thoughts during an entrepreneurial experience.
- Codify knowledge for a deeper learning experience.
- Assess one's own competency, comfort, and commitment to entrepreneurial activity.

Materials List

"Reflecting on Entrepreneurial Experience Handout" (included at the end of this exercise).

Pre-Work Required by Students

None.

Theoretical Foundations

Cope, J., and Watts, G. 2000. Learning by doing: An exploration of experience, critical incidents and reflection in entrepreneurial learning. *International Journal of Entrepreneurial Behaviour and Research*, 6(3), 104–24.

Kolb, D. 1984. *Experiential Learning: Experience as a Source of Learning and Development*. Englewood Cliffs, NJ: Prentice-Hall.

Neck, H., and Greene, P. 2011. Entrepreneurship education: Known worlds and new frontiers. *Journal of Small Business Management*, 49(1), 55–70.

Rasmussen, E.A., and Sorheim, R. 2006. Action-based entrepreneurship education. *Technovation*, 26(2), 185–94.

Schön, D.A. 1983. *The Reflective Practitioner*. New York: Basic Books.

Time Plan (50 minutes)

As this assignment is designed to follow an entrepreneurial activity (such as opportunity identification or resource acquisition), the instructor can have students do it during the same class or afterward as a graded assignment. It can also be followed by a class discussion of the reflection experience. The plan below should be adapted accordingly.

Giving the assignment   0:00–0:30 (30 minutes)

Explain, if not already covered, that entrepreneurship is a journey into territory full of uncertainty, ambiguity, challenge, and interdependence. Further, such conditions create strong emotions, considerable self-assessment, intense interaction with others, and great opportunity for learning and self-development. Reflection immediately following such an experience enables students to explore what happened and how they acted and felt, and to consider what their experience means for them as entrepreneurs.

Ask the students to take 20–25 minutes to read the assignment and write their own reflection paper as directed on the handout.

Discussion   0:30–0:45 (15 minutes)

The instructor may choose to debrief this exercise in any of several ways: by discussing the students' reactions and lessons in a plenary session, in pairs, or in groups, or by giving students individual feedback on this assignment. See "Teaching Tips" below on giving feedback. If debriefing in class, the instructor should use questions like these:

- What was challenging about doing this reflection? Why? How did you overcome those challenges?
- What was valuable about this assignment?
- What did you learn about yourself from reflecting on this experience of entrepreneurship?
- What did you learn from thinking about how you felt during the exercise?
- What did you learn from thinking about how you interacted with others during the exercise?

Summary   0:45–0:50 (5 minutes)
The instructor should summarize the students' discussion and draw on the key takeaways (see below).

Key Takeaways

- Entrepreneurship is characterized by uncertainty, ambiguity, challenge, and interdependence. These conditions create strong emotions, considerable self-assessment, and intense interaction with others.
- To be successful as an entrepreneur, a person needs to be able to cope with and learn from such experience.
- Reflection soon after such an experience about one's thoughts, emotions, and behavior enables an entrepreneurial student to develop those coping skills and improve his or her own self-awareness and communication.

Post-Work

A follow-up activity might include assigning groups of students who worked together in the entrepreneurial activity to give each other feedback on their behavior. If doing this, the instructor should remind them that effective feedback is both candid and constructive in tone. Subsequent journaling is also recommended.

Teaching Tips

Students often resist the idea of writing reflection papers for course credit, feeling that they are being asked to make themselves too vulnerable. Pass–fail grades for such assignments can often overcome this resistance. Often, once they get started, many find the activity cathartic. The most valuable part of this exercise is the dialogue that follows, whether it is in written form from the instructor or verbally from a peer or even in general in a class discussion. Regardless of what they put on paper, experience with this type of reflective assignment shows that students typically take great value from doing it. They also often develop the habit of doing this for themselves on an ongoing basis.

Feedback is challenging because there is no right or wrong. Some instructors prefer not to provide feedback, but this prevents the dialogue that is highly valued by the students. I am told that the feedback most useful to my students has been in the form of questions that probe more deeply into what they were feeling or thinking, why they think their actions had a particular effect, and what the meaning of the whole experience was for them as prospective entrepreneurs.

Reflecting on Entrepreneurial Experience Handout

You have just experienced a facet of entrepreneurship. Typically, such experience causes a person to have numerous thoughts and feelings, including some about yourself as an entrepreneurial actor. Please use the following questions to stimulate your reflection on how you acted, felt, and thought during and after this experience. Feel free to write your reflections in any format you wish and to add more insights than these questions seek. You should write about one page on these topics.

1. How would I describe my actions during this entrepreneurial activity?
2. What kind of interactions did I have with others during the activity? What was my intention? What effect did my communication have on the activity or other people?
3. What kind of feedback did I get from others during or after the activity?
4. How well did I do at this activity? In what areas did I especially do well? In what areas did I do less than was needed or desired?
5. What emotions did I have during this experience or afterward?
6. What thoughts about myself as an entrepreneurial actor went through my mind as I was engaged in the activity?
7. What did I learn from this experience?
8. What did I learn from this reflection?
9. What questions do I have about myself or entrepreneurship now?

EXERCISE: CULTURAL ARTIFACTS

AUTHORS: ELAINE EISENMAN AND ANNE DONNELLON

Description

This session introduces the concept of reflecting on one's organizational culture and highlights the importance of intentionality in building and maintaining the desired organizational culture. Each student is assigned the task of bringing a cultural artifact to class that represents the culture of a selected organization to which they belong or, perhaps, would like to build. This exercise includes pre-work, a paired partner exercise, group work, and group discussion.

Usage Suggestions

This exercise can be used in programs for founders or CEOs of early-stage and growing companies to demonstrate the criticality of early identification of the core values and culture which serve as the foundation for continued growth. The exercise may also be used with undergraduate or graduate students to plan the ideas of intentionality around culture.

Learning Objectives

1. Recognize and assess an existing organizational culture.
2. Assess fit of organizational culture with an organization's vision and values.
3. Evaluate how to use culture as a resource to enhance performance and growth and to attract, motivate, and retain employees.

Materials List

YouTube video on Zappos culture (https://www.youtube.com/watch?v= 5CcLIPaUz3E).

Pre-Work Required by Students

First, participants should write a statement that identifies the values and rituals which best define their company. They should answer the question: "Twenty years from now, when your company is a global success, if a cultural anthropologist was interviewing the early employees of your company, how would they describe the culture in terms of what was important and what it was like to work there 'back then'?" In answering this question participants should consider:

- What are the things we could see at your company that help us know what kind of company you are (i.e. posters, pictures, awards, memorabilia, colors, type of workspace, food, etc.)?
- What rituals do your employees demonstrate (bagels on Fridays, birthday celebrations, volunteer work, parties, etc.)?
- What are the stories that are told to new employees about the founding and founders of the company?
- What types of clothing do people wear (casual, formal, a mix, special days, etc.)?

Second, participants should bring *anything* they want that best captures, represents, or symbolizes the answer that people would tell the cultural anthropologist about what the culture of the company was.

Theoretical Foundations

Barney, J.B. 1986. Organizational culture: Can it be a source of sustainable competitive advantage? *Academy of Management Review*, 11, 656–65.
Brush, C.G., Greene, P.G., and Hart, M.M. 2001. From initial idea to unique advantage: The entrepreneurial challenge of constructing a resource base. *Academy of Management Executive*, 15(1), 64–78.
Schein, E.H. 1983. The role of the founder in creating organizational culture. *Organizational Dynamics*, Summer, 13–28.

Time Plan (2 hours)

This exercise can be done in a time ranging from 90 to 120 minutes, depending on the length of the class. This teaching note uses the two-hour version. You might also consider splitting up the exercise over two class sessions.

Part 1 (introduction to culture)   0:00–0:15 (15 minutes)
The faculty member will lead a discussion on the definition of culture and where and how people recognize, or don't recognize, it. The underlying definition of culture for this exercise is the shared values, beliefs, and practices of a group whose members regularly interact with each other. Examples of cultures experienced in different organizations can be shared. The Zappos video on culture is a strong supporting tool.

Part 2 (family culture)   0:15–0:30 (15 minutes)
Tell the students, "Today, before we ask you to share the story of your cultural artifact with the group, we will ask you to think and talk a bit about two important cultures: the culture of the family you grew up in and the one you have today in your company (which your artifact represents).

This is an important exercise because culture has a major impact on the way people in groups think and act – so, as a whole or in part, it can help the performance of your business. One example is the culture at Zappos giving the employees room to take the initiative to serve customers. Or it can create problems for you that will limit your growth. Consider the old story about the employees who take it easy while the boss is away only to complain bitterly about being overworked when he or she is around."

Give the students 15 minutes in total to think about and discuss, in paired partners, the culture of the family they grew up in. Remind them to consider both the positive and the negative effects of some cultural values or practices. For example, did an overly strict parent cause rebellion or self-doubt in some siblings? Did family dinners help everyone get past arguments to preserve close relationships? And so on.

Part 3 (company culture)   0:30–0:45 (15 minutes)
Students will now have 15 minutes to apply the same approach to their company (or a select organization, including the possibility of the class) culture. Ask them to use their assignment – the write-up of their company culture as seen in the future. Remind them to consider both positive and negative aspects of the culture. As the discussion will show, some cultures develop a norm of conflict between groups, for example sales and production. Others develop strong connections among employees and values of everyone helping everyone else. Ask: What are the norms of behavior in your company? What practices help form positive bonds, foster creativity and/or high customer service, and so on? Is there anything in the culture that actually takes value away from your company or your customer's value proposition?

Tell the students to think about this for 5 minutes, and then exchange thoughts with another person at the table for 10 minutes.

Part 4 (debriefing culture)   0:45–1:00 (15 minutes)
Take 15 minutes to collect the common themes and individual reactions. Ask:

● Was it relatively easy to identify the positives and negatives of your family culture?

- What about answering the question about the positives and negatives of your company culture?
- Were there some similarities in your pair?
- Does anyone want to share a positive feature of their culture?
- Does anyone want to share a negative feature that you have identified?
- Are there differences because of types of businesses, for example industry, size, age, family ownership, and so on?

Part 5 (cultural artifact presentations)   1:00–1:45 (45 minutes)
Divide the class into small groups of no more than five members. Each participant then has the opportunity to present his or her artifact to the group and tell why he or she has chosen it and how and why it is symbolic or representative of his or her organizational culture.

Suggested questions for the group:

- Based on what you have seen and heard, how would you describe the culture of this organization?
- What are the rituals?
- Is the culture motivating to employees?
- What do you think customers experience with this company?
- What are the values of the organization?
- Do you think people would want to work at this organization? Why or why not?
- Would you want to work at this organization? Why or why not?

At the end, each group selects one member to present to the entire class, with the class then asking the questions.

Wrap-up   1:45–2:00 (15 minutes)
Group debrief: What are some of the important things that company culture does?

Your culture can be a rich resource for managing, leading, inspiring, and even compensating your employees. You will want to think about what kinds of practices you could create to build esprit de corps or problem-solving values into your culture. You may also need to think about how well the values you started with continue to be known, shared, and applied by newcomers. Finally, if you found that you have some problematic norms or practices, such as persistent lateness or sloppiness on the part of many of your employees, you will want to think about what it will take to change those cultural practices.

Key Takeaways

- It is important to intentionally create organizational culture during firm emergence.
- Organizational culture can be a positive or negative firm resource.
- Organizational culture needs to be a fit between the founder, the firm, and the environment.

Teaching Tips

Participants often push back at the idea of identifying an artifact in the belief that there is nothing that they have. It is important to help them brainstorm a bit to think about possibilities. Some examples help them to understand – artifacts have been as minimalist as silly putty, with the explanation that the company required everyone to be completely flexible and to change based on the demands of the environment, to the more complex plaque that was on the founder's grandfather's boat to represent the longevity and foundation of the company as one that could face rough times and survive in spite of rocky seas.

EXERCISE: PASSION CUBE

AUTHOR: BRADLEY GEORGE

Description

Passion has long been considered to be an important aspect of entre-preneurial behavior. More recently, researchers have built upon identity theory to develop a theoretical basis for better understanding the role of passion and its importance in various outcomes. Passion can foster crea-tivity and aid in identifying new information patterns that can lead to the discovery of entrepreneurial opportunities (Sundarajan and Peters, 2007; Baron, 2008). In empirical research, passion has been associated with entrepreneurs' ability to raise funds from investors (Sudek, 2006; Cardon et al., 2009; Mitteness et al., 2012) and to hire and motivate key employ-ees (Cardon, 2008). Cardon et al. (2009) conceptualize entrepreneurial passion as "a consciously accessible, intense positive feeling" that "results from engagement in activities with identity meaning and salience to the entrepreneur" (p. 515).

Despite the importance of passion to entrepreneurship, students often have a difficult time connecting their passion to potential opportunities or expanding their ideas to other areas that may provide the same emotional connection. Because self-identity is also associated with our perceptions of our unique skills, this exercise attempts to combine these factors to help students better understand their passions and identify areas in which they may discover new passions. This exercise addresses these issues by having students identify their passion, the drivers of their passion, and their own personal skills and strengths. These are captured on cards, which are then randomly mixed and assembled into a cube, which allows students to begin to think about what ideas or opportunities exist at the intersection of their passion and their skills.

Usage Suggestions

This exercise works for all audiences, undergraduate, graduate, or prac-titioner. It is appropriate for new venture creation courses, entrepreneur-ship bootcamps, or workshops. The session is best positioned early in the program during idea generation.

Learning Objectives

- Reflect on and assess personal passions.
- Expand thinking around potential opportunities related to personal passions.
- Connect passion to skills as part of opportunity creation.

Materials List (Include Handouts)

- Six squares of white paper (about 2 inch × 2 inch or 3 inch × 3 inch each) for each student – heavier paper such as construction paper or 3 inch × 5 inch cards works best.
- Several roles of transparent tape for the class to share.

Pre-Work Required by Students

There is no pre-work required for this exercise, but it can be used in combination with a discussion of the book *The Monk and The Riddle* (Komisar and Lineback, 2000) about the importance of passion for entrepreneurs.

Theoretical Foundations

Baron, R.A. 2008. The role of affect in the entrepreneurial process. *Academy of Management Review*, 33, 328–40.

Cardon, M.S. 2008. Is passion contagious? The transference of entrepreneurial emotion to employees. *Human Resource Management Review*, 18, 77–86.

Cardon, M.S., Wincent, J., Singh, J., and Drnovsek, M. 2009. The nature and experience of entrepreneurial passion. *Academy of Management Review*, 34(3), 511–32.

Komisar, R., and Lineback, K. 2000. *The Monk and the Riddle: The Art of Creating a Life While Making a Living*. Boston, MA: Harvard Business School Press.

Mitteness, C., Sudek, R., and Cardon, M.S. 2012. Angel investor characteristics that determine whether perceived passion leads to higher evaluations of funding potential. *Journal of Business Venturing*, 27(5), 592–606.

Sudek, R. 2006. Angel investment criteria. *Journal of Small Business Strategy*, 17, 89–103.

Sundarajan, M., and Peters, L. 2007. Role of emotions in the entrepreneur's opportunity recognition process. Paper presented at the annual meeting of the Academy of Management, Philadelphia.

Time Plan (25 minutes)

Step 1   0:00–0:03 (3 minutes)
Start by passing around the square cards and have each student take six
cards. You can also pass around some tape and tell them to tear off eight
small pieces of tape.

Step 2   0:03–0:05 (2 minutes)
Instruct the students to take one of the cards and write down something
they are passionate about. This can sometimes require some encouragement on your part. Ask them to think of something that excites them and
that they really enjoy doing.

Step 3   0:05–0:10 (5 minutes)
Have students put that card aside and take two more cards. On each card
have them write one thing that describes why they are passionate about
what they wrote on the first card. You should give them a few minutes for
this, as students have often not been asked to reflect on what drives their
passion. You can prompt them with examples. Undergraduate students
are often passionate about a sport, so ask them to think about why that is.
Is it the performance in front of a crowd? Is it the sense of competition? Is
it the camaraderie of a team?

Step 4   0:10–0:12 (2 minutes)
Once they have completed the two cards, have them put them aside and
take the final three cards. On each card they should write a skill or strength
that they feel they have.

Step 5   0:12–0:14 (2 minutes)
Next, have students take all six cards and put them face down so that they
cannot read what is on them and have them mix them up. Once they have
done that, have them lay the cards out (still face down) in a "T" or cross
pattern, as shown in Figure 11.1, and tape the edges.

Step 6   0:14–0:15 (1 minute)
Have students make a cube with all of the writing on the outside by folding
the "T" into a box and taping the final edges.

Step 7   0:15–0:20 (5 minutes)
Ask students to examine the various intersections of their skills, passion,
and the drivers of their passion where the sides of the cube meet. Ask them
to pick an intersection at random and come up with at least one business

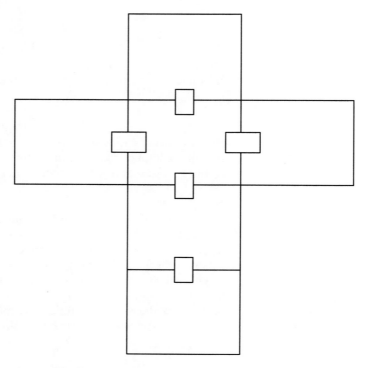

Figure 11.1   Layout of cards

idea that incorporates both sides of the cube that meet at that junction.
You can have them repeat this for other edges of the cube if you want to
spend more time.

Debrief   0:20–0:25 (5 minutes)
Ask a student for an example from his or her cube. It is often helpful
to build on this and add other business ideas that take advantage of the
two aspects the student identifies. Ask if anyone had trouble coming up
with an idea (there are usually a few of them). Call on one of them and
ask him or her to pick two random adjoining sides (note that you want
to be careful in this stage, because some students may be hesitant to share
something very personal in front of the class). Ask the class for ideas that
utilize those two aspects.

Don't spend too much time on this. It can take some time for students to reflect on this and really develop good ideas related to their passions and strengths – particularly for younger students. Emphasize that
they should take the cube with them and use it to generate further ideas.

They can also modify the cube as they reflect more on their passions. Point out that, by considering the drivers of their passion, they may come up with numerous ideas they hadn't considered that may give them that same feeling and inspiration.

Post-Work

As post-work the students can be asked to develop business concepts that build on what they have captured on their cube.

Key Takeaways

- Understanding what drives your passion can open up a host of new ideas you might find attractive.
- There are numerous ways to combine your passion(s) and strengths.
- Following your passion can lead in numerous directions.

Teaching Tips

The biggest thing to keep in mind in running this exercise is to emphasize that only the students will see what they write unless they choose to share it with others. It is also important to encourage them to feel free to write down what they feel they are good at, not what they feel others think they are good at – emphasize that this is a personal exercise for them and a way to help them better understand their passions and opportunities related to it.

Another common issue that arises is that students often take the idea of following their passion too literally (this is where the combination of skills and passion can be helpful for discussion). For example, I had a finance student who was passionate about sailing and felt that it was ridiculous for him to think that he should follow his passion and become a sailboat captain. This led to a discussion around how he could use his finance skills combined with his desire to be around boats and boating in potential business opportunities in yacht financing or investment and financial management for clients who live aboard their boats, sail the world, and do not have a fixed address. I now often use this example to illustrate how the cube can be used.

Attribution

This is a variation of an exercise originally created by Mary Pinard at Babson College.

EXERCISE: OPPORTUNITY WALK

AUTHOR: BRADLEY GEORGE

Description

Students often struggle with where to start with respect to finding opportunities. This exercise gets students thinking about the world around them in terms of potential opportunities. Students are taken outside (this can be done inside as well, but it is usually a good break from their normal routine to leave the building) and asked about what they see around them. They are then pushed to think about what they see in terms of the businesses that are responsible for what they see, and they compete to see who can identify the largest number of businesses. They are then asked to consider how they might make some of those businesses better in a way that improves people's lives. Students will begin to realize that there is an abundance of potential opportunities around them at all times, and they will begin thinking about how they can build on these initial ideas to develop potential business concepts.

This exercise is based on the idea of entrepreneurial alertness espoused in the Austrian Economic School of thought regarding opportunities. Kirzner (1973), for example, proposes that opportunities are present and merely waiting for an alert individual to pick them up. The basis of this argument is the fact that information is not equally distributed, leading different individuals to recognize different opportunities. While supporters of this theory suggest that these individuals will recognize opportunities without the need for deliberate search (Eckhardt and Shane, 2003), the process still requires the individual to be cognizant of his or her environment in order to take notice of these potential opportunities. Some scholars have suggested that people with better scanning behavior, among other skills, are more likely to discover opportunities (Shaver and Scott, 1991; Baron, 2006).

The exercise also builds on the idea of entrepreneurial opportunities being those in which new goods, services, or markets can be introduced through new means–ends relationships or new ends–means relationships (Shane and Venkataraman, 2000). By first becoming more aware of their external environment, students can then begin examining ways in which they may be able to change existing means–ends relationships to reveal potential entrepreneurial opportunities.

Usage Suggestions

This exercise works for all audiences, undergraduate, graduate, or practitioner. It is appropriate for new venture creation courses, entrepreneurship bootcamps, or workshops. The session is best positioned before students have identified a venture concept, project, or corporate initiative to pursue.

Learning Objectives

- Practice being observant about potential opportunities.
- Reflect on personal differences in viewing and perceiving the world.
- Improve the ability to generate new ideas.
- Improve the understanding of the relationship between ideas and value.

Materials List

None.

Pre-Work Required by Students

None.

Theoretical Foundations

Baron, R.A. 2006. Opportunity recognition as pattern recognition: How entrepreneurs "connect the dots" to identify new business opportunities. *Academy of Management Perspectives*, February, 104–19.

Eckhardt, J.T., and Shane, S.A. 2003. Opportunities and entrepreneurship. *Journal of Management*, 29(3), 333–49.

Kirzner, Israel M. 1973. *Competition and Entrepreneurship*. Chicago: University of Chicago Press.

Shane, S., and Venkataraman, S. 2000. The promise of entrepreneurship as a field of study. *Academy of Management Review*, 25(1), 217–26.

Shaver, K.G., and Scott, L.R. 1991. Person, process, choice: The psychology of new venture creation. *Entrepreneurship Theory and Practice*, 16(2), 23–45.

Time Plan

This exercise can be adapted to fit various time schedules depending on whether or not the instructor wants to spend more time on issues such as value propositions or creative idea generation. For the purposes of this teaching note, the exercise requires 40 minutes.

Step 1   0:00–0:05 (5 minutes)
Begin by telling the students to get out paper and something to write
with. Once they appear to be ready, tell them to stand up and follow
you outside. (If weather is a problem, the exercise can also be conducted
indoors in an open space.) Choose a location that is nearby to reduce the
time it takes to get the class moved and assembled.

Once everyone is gathered together, ask the students to tell you what
they see. Typically they will respond with things like "grass," "trees,"
"buildings," "sky," and so on.

Step 2   0:05–0:15 (10 minutes)
Now, ask them to look around and try to think of as many businesses
as possible that are necessary for them to see everything around them. It
sometimes helps to give them examples related to what they initially saw.
For example, if they indicate trees and grass, then you might suggest that
this involves businesses that grow grass seed, landscaping companies that
keep the grass mowed, nurseries for the plants and trees, and so on.

Give them about 5 minutes to identify the businesses. You can motivate
them by telling them that they should be able to come up with at least 20
and as many as 50 or more. The highest students are usually in the 40–50
range. Keep an eye on those who seem to be struggling and encourage
them. Give them a 1-minute warning and encourage them to try to hurry
to get as many more as they can in the last minute.

Return to the classroom and have the students count up how many
businesses they came up with. You can have a small prize for the one who
comes up with the most.

Step 3   0:15–0:20 (5 minutes)
Select a few students to tell the class some of the businesses they identified. Capture these on the board. You can push them further by asking
about what other businesses are related and necessary to support that
business. For example, if a student mentions a company that makes and
builds outdoor light posts, you could ask about the companies that make
the electrical wire or the mining companies that provide the metal ore and
so on.

Step 4   0:20–0:25 (5 minutes)
Have the students pair up and pick one business from their list and come
up with a way to do it better or differently. It is important here to encourage them not to limit themselves to what they think may be possible.
Remind them that there may be technologies that they are not aware of,
so they should try to think of ways in which it could be ideal. This allows

them to be more creative and then they can think about ways in which to provide the same value. After 5 minutes, call on one or two of the groups to share their ideas.

Step 5 0:25–0:35 (10 minutes)
Have students discuss what the value of their new concept is to the potential customers and think about ways they could actually provide that value. This helps them to think about their value proposition and then ground this back to reality and ways in which they could provide this same value (even if their original ideas were pretty far-fetched). Give an example that seems unrealistic at first. Some students have suggested a key chain that would make their car disappear and then reappear in order to avoid trying to find a parking space. You can ask them what the value is in this new idea (reducing the time to find parking). Then illustrate how this same value can be provided in numerous ways (for example, by showing a picture of an automated garage in Japan that stacks hundreds of cars – the key fob could signal the garage to pick up the car and store the location information for pickup). The point here is creative thinking in providing the value in a manner that is actually technically feasible – not necessarily financially feasible at this point.

Step 6 0:35–0:40 (5 minutes)
Finally, have students take their idea and think about how it improves people's lives. This helps them to understand whether or not they will truly provide value that customers will want and gets them thinking about businesses' role in society. For example, you could argue that Walmart improves people's lives by providing them with more disposable income or that Starbucks provides a gathering place and encourages social interaction. The key point here is to get students to begin thinking about their business in relation to the value it brings to the customer and society. Discuss a few of these.

Try to close by emphasizing that potential ideas and opportunities are around them all the time, so coming up with ideas should never be a problem. However, they need to consider whether their ideas truly bring value to their customers and society as a first step towards determining if the ideas constitute entrepreneurial opportunities.

Key Takeaways

- Potential business ideas are everywhere around us all the time.
- Understanding your value proposition will help you refine your ideas.

- It is important to consider whether your business provides positive benefits to customers *and* society and how that affects the viability of an idea.

Teaching Tips

Students generally need to be encouraged to think about businesses during the brainstorming session in the beginning. I usually tell them that they should be able to come up with at least 30 different businesses in 5 minutes (the highest numbers are usually above this). This seems to help them focus. You will also want to continue to encourage them throughout the 5-minute time period.

You will sometimes have students who try to come up with ridiculous ideas (like the key fob). These are great ones to push back on in class with regard to the value they bring in leading up to their work on this section of the exercise. You can usually show them how you can start with an idea that seems really far out there and achieve the benefits of the idea in a realistic manner.

EXERCISE: PLOTTING THE GROWTH OF YOUR BUSINESS

AUTHOR: DENNIS CERU

Description

This exercise is designed to draw out similarities and differences about how businesses grow and illuminate that not all businesses grow smoothly or in the same manner and that often a business will exhibit different growth patterns over time in response to internal and external business conditions and factors. Students will most likely find that, despite the different ways that businesses (their own or those they know) may have grown over time, many of those businesses have had to respond to the same set of external factors that have either assisted or inhibited their growth.

Growth is generally agreed upon as a worthy goal for most firms. It is widely celebrated in the media (e.g. Inc. 100 fastest growing firms), and is considered a measure of entrepreneurial success (Davidsson, 1991). While not all firms choose to grow (Ginn and Sexton, 1990; Rosa et al., 1996; Wiklund et al., 2003), analysts suggest that some growth over time is desirable for continued survival (Delmar et al., 2003). Yet it has been long recognized that the decision to grow is usually the choice of the entrepreneur, whose expectations for the size and scope of the business at start-up ultimately affect the growth potential of the business over time (Stanworth and Curran, 1976; Wiklund et al., 2003; Cassar, 2007).

Underpinning this literature is an assumption that sales of entrepreneurial ventures will gradually increase, as the business expands, creating a rising sales curve over time. In other words, growth is assumed to be normal and to follow a normal curve. For more aggressive growth strategies the curve peaks more quickly, like a "hockey stick," while for slower growth strategies it peaks later. Although there is no agreement on the number of stages, most assume that there are contextual dimensions influencing the process, especially age, size, and industry growth rate (Hanks et al., 1993).

On the other hand, most practitioners would agree that growth patterns are anything but "normal," and that the academic literature has not studied the various pathways in great detail.

Usage Suggestions

This exercise works best with a practitioner audience composed of owner-managers of their own businesses. While it may be adopted for a classroom setting with traditional students, the exercise will then be more theoretical than practical. It is appropriate for new venture creation and entrepreneurship courses, small and medium-sized business growth courses, and many workshops and programs. It may be positioned as a first class exercise preceding more in-depth exploration of the external factors and management decisions that affect business growth.

Learning Objectives

- Understand models of entrepreneurial growth.
- Recognize the many patterns of business growth.
- Learn about the external factors and management decisions that affect business growth.

Materials List

- Plain 8.5 inch × 11 inch sheets of paper
- Tape
- A whiteboard or blackboard and (ideally) projector and screen

Pre-Work Required by Students

Depending on the audience and whether this exercise is used as part of a broader class or program, selected background reading such as Churchill and Lewis (1983) (see "Theoretical Foundations") may be assigned but is not necessary for this exercise to be effective. Practical experience combined with an active interest in business growth is sufficient.

Theoretical Foundations

Brush, Candida G., Ceru, Dennis J., and Blackburn, Robert. 2009. Pathways to growth: The role of marketing, management and money. *Business Horizons*, 52(5) (September–October).

Cassar, G. 2007. Money, money, money? A longitudinal investigation of entrepreneur career reasons, growth preferences and achieved growth. *Entrepreneurship and Regional Development*, 19(1), 89–107.

Churchill, Neil C., and Lewis, Virginia L. 1983. The five stages of small business growth. *Harvard Business Review*, May–June.

Davidsson, P. 1991. Continued entrepreneurship: Ability, need, and opportunity as determinants of small firm growth. *Journal of Business Venturing*, 6(6), 405–29.

Delmar, F., Davidsson, P., and Gartner, W. 2003. Arriving at the high-growth firm. *Journal of Business Venturing*, 18(2), 189–216.

Ginn, C., and Sexton, D. 1990. A comparison of personality type dimensions of the Inc. 500 company founders with those of slower growth firms. *Journal of Business Venturing*, 5(5), 313–26.

Hanks, S., Watson, C., Jansen, E., and Chandler, G. 1993. Tightening the life-cycle construct: A taxonomic study of growth stage configurations in high-technology organizations. *Entrepreneurship Theory and Practice*, 18(2), 5–29.

Rosa, P., Carter, S., and Hamilton, D. 1996. Gender as a determinant of small business performance: Insights from a British study. *Small Business Economics*, 8, 463–78.

Stanworth, M.K.J., and Curran, J. 1976. Growth and the small firm: An alternative view. *Journal of Management Studies*, 13(2), 95–110.

Wiklund, J., Davidsson, P., and Delmar, F. 2003. What do they think and feel about growth? An expectancy-value approach to small business managers' attitudes toward growth. *Entrepreneurship Theory and Practice*, 27(3), 247–70.

Time Plan (60 minutes)

Initial prompt   0:00–0:10 (10 minutes)
The instructor should start by asking the class: "Does every business have to grow, or can a business choose not to grow?" It is anticipated that this will lead to a lively discussion that includes topics such as competition, customers, the owner's choices, family factors, and the overall economy. After about 10 minutes, the instructor moves on to the assignment.

Part 1 (plot individual growth curves)   0:10–0:20 (10 minutes)
The instructor draws a simple graph on the board with "Time" on the horizontal (*x*) axis and "Revenue" on the vertical (y) axis and asks the students to consider the following prompt: "As you think about how your business has grown over the past five years (or less if you have been in business for less time), how would you plot the growth of your business?" If this is used within a class where students do not own their own businesses, the initial prompt is modified to: "As you think about how businesses in your field or areas have grown over the past five years, how would you plot the growth of those businesses?" Students are asked to plot this simple chart on a piece of blank paper.

Part 2 (growth group discussion)   0:20–0:30 (10 minutes)
The instructor then asks the students to compare their plots with each other in small groups of four to five students and note similarities and differences.

Part 3 (growth plot sharing and class discussion)   0:30–0:60 (30 minutes)

- **Option 1**: The instructor asks each individual to post his or her growth curve plot on the walls around the classroom, and then the entire class moves around the room for a "gallery walk," observing the plots and noting similarities and differences.

- **Option 2**: The instructor asks each group to take 5 minutes to draft a consolidated growth curve plot and share it with the class by posting it to the front of the room and briefly explaining how the curve was derived and their thoughts about how growth has occurred within their businesses.

Post-Work

Follow-up work is dependent upon the audience. Within a broader class or program on business growth, this exercise may be cross-referenced in later sessions as students seek to develop their own ventures and craft a business growth and development plan. Within a practitioner-based program or workshop, this exercise may serve as a vehicle both to help the owner, manager, or entrepreneur understand the factors and decisions that affected his or her company's growth and to inform and serve as the basis for developing a tactical action plan for new business growth.

Key Takeaways

- Business growth is unique to each specific business and rarely follows a smooth normal curve of growth as has been commonly expected.
- A business may grow differently at different times in response to external factors (business ecosystem and macro-environmental trends) as well as internal influences.
- The primary internal influences affecting business growth are the impacts of management, marketing, and (use of and access to) money.

Teaching Tips

- Be explicit in the time-line instructions and tell students to plot their business growth on the horizontal axis from left (oldest) to right (current).
- Inform students that the best indicator of growth for this exercise is gross revenues (sales) plotted on the vertical axis.
- The "gallery walk" often works best to solicit the greatest amount of relevant and practical comments from the group. If electing to use the "consolidated growth curve" method to prompt discussion, the instructor may need to solicit more individual examples and practical comments.

EXERCISE: BREWSTER'S MILLIONS

AUTHOR: PATRICIA GREENE

Description

This exercise is designed to push students' thinking about what it means to grow. The students are guided in thinking about their business in the largest scope possible so that they can understand options and then pick the "right" fit for them and their business. The exercise is loosely based on the book *Brewster's Millions* by George Barr McCutcheon and the subsequent movie starring Richard Pryor. The students are given a piece of construction paper and asked to draw a quick sketch of what they want their company to look like in five years. Each student is then handed a "check" made out for $50000, told they *must* spend it on their business within the next six months, and asked to list the top five things they would do with the money. Students are next given a "check" for $500000 and asked to make another top-five list. Finally the students are given a "check" for $5 million and asked to do another top-five list. The students are then given 5 minutes to redraw a picture of their business after the $5 million investment. The session ends with a debrief to focus on questions of opportunity, resources, and leadership as aligned to the size and scope of growth aspirations.

Usage Suggestions

This exercise is quite flexible and can be used with audiences ranging from high school students through experienced practitioners.

Learning Objectives

- Understand the impact of various growth aspirations.
- Explore the various resources available through "other people's money."
- Develop a framework to support larger-scale business growth.

Materials List

- Construction paper of different colors – one piece per student.
- Colored pens, pencils, or crayons – enough for each student to easily have a selection.

- A series of pseudo-checks – one for each student (best on heavier paper for reuse). Amounts: $50 000, $500 000, and $5 000 000.
- Video clip: *Brewster's Millions.*

Pre-Work Required by Students

None.

Theoretical Foundations

Brush, C.G., Greene, P.G., and Hart, M.M. 2001. From initial idea to unique advantage: The entrepreneurial challenge of constructing a resource base. *Academy of Management Executive*, 15(1), 64–78.
Brush, C.G., Ceru, D.J., and Blackburn, R. 2009. Pathways to entrepreneurial growth: The influence of management, marketing, and money. *Business Horizons*, 52(5), 481–91.

Time Plan (45 minutes)

A 5-minute introduction, followed by a 25-minute guided set of activities, concluding with a 15-minute debrief.

Step 1 (introduction)   0:00–0:05 (5 minutes)
Open the exercise by asking the students to use the prompts below to reflect on the questions: What does growth mean to me? How big can I get? How big do I want to get?

After a few moments of reflection, lead the discussion about whether they have considered building really large businesses and what that would take.

Step 2 (drawing their current business in five years)   0:05–0:10 (5 minutes)
The crayons, colored pens, or markers and colored construction paper will have been placed on the students' tables. Each student is asked to spend 10 minutes drawing what his or her business will look like in five years. (*Note*: This is a helpful time to push the definition of "vision" as being *specifically* what students want their businesses to look like, not just a vague target of "best," "top," etc.). Prompts may include: size of revenues, number of employees, scope and scale of market (local, regional, state, national, global), and so on.

Step 3 (distribution of check 1: $50 000)   0:10–0:15 (5 minutes)
The students are each given a "check" for $50 000 and told they *must* spend the entire amount on growing their business and they must spend it

within the next six months. They are then asked to make a list of the most critical five things they would do with the $50 000.

Step 4 (distribution of check 2: $500 000)   0:15–0:20 (5 minutes)
Repeat the process for Step 3 using the new amount of $500 000.

Step 5 (distribution of check 3: $5 000 000)   0:20–0:25 (5 minutes)
Repeat the process for Step 3 using the new amount of $5 000 000.

Step 6 (drawing their business with $5 million)   0:25–0:30 (5 minutes)
Ask the students to redraw their vision of the business after a $5 million investment.

Step 7 (debrief)   0:30–0:45 (15 minutes)
The goal is to help the students envision the largest businesses they could possibly grow before they make choices that might curtail that vision. (Example: building debt to a point where an equity investor would no longer be interested.) The major point of the debrief is to look at what changes over the course of the exercise. Rather than debriefing step by step, ask several students to walk through their journey of the exercise. How did they think about their original picture? What was on the first list? Second? Third? What is different about the last picture? What are they thinking now? After a few students have reported out, the themes from their answers can be identified, either by the instructor or by the students.

One example of the board map to guide the posting of the debrief comments from the students' description of their work is to use columns (not labeled at the beginning) that will ultimately represent "money," "market," and "management." At the end of this part of the debrief the instructor can label the columns to illustrate the themes. The money, market, and management categories are drawn from Brush et al. (2009) (see "Theoretical Foundations").

The session concludes with the instructor asking the students to share their takeaways about business growth.

Key Takeaways

1. It is critical to address the concept of aspiration with all entrepreneurship groups. Where do aspirational caps come from and why?
2. The vision must be a fit between the entrepreneur, the venture, and the environment. If something doesn't mesh, it won't work.

302   *Teaching entrepreneurship*

3. Students can address their comfort level with obtaining external resources – both debt and equity that are typically necessary to achieve high-growth.

Teaching Tips

Some student groups will be less enthused than others about the idea of drawing. It is helpful to remind them that if, as teachers, we don't push them to try things about which they are uncomfortable we haven't pushed them hard enough.

Attribution

This exercise was created for Goldman Sachs 10 000 Small Businesses and is based on an earlier exercise created by the 10 000 Small Businesses UK team.

EXERCISE: THE DARK SIDE OF ENTREPRENEURSHIP

AUTHOR: ROSA SLEGERS

Description

This exercise is meant to make students think about the morally relevant consequences of entrepreneurial projects that at first glance appear to be fully in line with socially responsible business practice. It first asks students to consider a hypothetical case involving a new biotech firm that has just created a life-saving drug and then asks them to think of parallel examples illustrating the difficulty of predicting and dealing with long-term consequences.

Usage Suggestions

This exercise is best positioned as part of an introduction to entrepreneurial thinking, because it helps students become aware of the potentially very grave implications of what may seem like a wonderful entrepreneurial idea. The students will likely feel more confident discussing these issues after they have had a chance to get to know each other and the subject matter, and it is therefore recommended that the exercise be assigned in the middle of the course. It works for any audience, youth, family enterprises, adults, or undergraduate or graduate students.

Learning Objectives

- Explore how even a great entrepreneurial idea may result in suffering, whether in the short or in the long term.
- Construct scenarios to manage the consequences of our actions.
- Debate how to deal with the pressure of unforeseen consequences and the possible effects of our actions on current and future stakeholders.

Materials List

No materials are needed, unless the instructor thinks it advisable for the students to have a paper copy of the description of the biotech company. See "Step 1" under Time Plan.

Pre-Work Required by Students

None required.

Theoretical Foundations

Mill, J.S. 2001. *Utilitarianism*. Indianapolis, IN: Hackett Publishing.
Singer, P. 2001. Famine, affluence, and morality. *Writings on an Ethical Life* (pp. 105–18). New York: Harper Perennial.

Time Plan (60 minutes)

This exercise can be completed in 60 minutes, but each section can be expanded if the instructor wishes to take a deeper dive into the issues and allow students more time for discussion.

Step 1   0:00–0.05 (5 minutes)
Present students with the following scenario: Imagine a new drug company that has decided to sell a life-saving drug (antiretroviral controlling HIV infection, say) at or below the cost of production in developing countries. The decision to sell at a loss was made to show the company's commitment to social responsibility and is earning the company much praise, adding to its reputation and attracting new investors interested in corporate citizenship. Assume that there are no problems involving patent law and that the drugs are effective, prolonging and saving many lives that would otherwise have ended prematurely because of the prohibitive costs of available drugs. The company is selling the same drug at a higher price in developed countries, there is plenty of money left for R&D, and the company can afford to offer competitive wages. Additionally, new talent is drawn to the company because of its refreshing take on social responsibility. The company is taking a risk but gains much respect by breaking the focus on profit maximization: "In the twenty-first century," the company's CEO proclaims, "companies need to take into account all relevant stakeholders and not just shareholders; social responsibility is an integral part of the new way of doing business."

Step 2   0.05–0:20 (15 minutes)

- Ask students to list the pros of this attitude in general and this company's decision to cut drug prices in particular, inviting them to add to the scenario for the sake of the argument if this helps them to make their point.
- Ask students to do the same for the cons.
- Once both lists are completed, ask students to explain whether or not the advantages outweigh the disadvantages of this approach. The likely outcome will be that the company is acting for the greater good.

Student responses to these questions will likely touch on some or all of the following issues (if not, elicit these responses through follow-up questions):

- **Corporate social responsibility**: Some students will be excited about this example of good citizenship, while others will be more cynical and dismiss it as disingenuous.
- **Shareholder value**: Some may express a concern that the decision to cut prices in developing countries is unrealistic or naïve, because companies are ultimately geared toward profit maximization; others will likely make the counter-argument that public opinion and reputation are so important that even from a shareholder perspective the price cuts are worth it.
- **Distribution**: How can the company be sure that its drugs reach the right people, that there is an infrastructure in place to channel the drugs, that people from developed countries don't get the drugs cheaply on the black market, and so on?
- **Role of government**: What kind of regulations should be in place for the company to thrive?

Step 3   0:20–0:25 (5 minutes)
Once the students have made their cases and shared their opinions, draw their attention to a closely related but perhaps less obvious issue: overpopulation. Ask the students to take a few minutes to consider why this issue is relevant to the discussion – it might be a good idea to give the students a moment to figure this out by themselves and perhaps write down their thoughts on a piece of paper so that the classroom discussion is not dominated by the first ones to grasp the implications of cheap antiretrovirals.

Step 4   0:25–0:35 (10 minutes)
Ask students to share what they wrote down and allow students to reach their own (temporary) conclusions before summarizing the issue as follows:

- If indeed the drugs are effective (and we have every reason to believe they are), then more people will stay alive for a longer period of time than they would have without the drugs.
- More people staying alive for longer periods of time means population growth, especially if (as it is reasonable to expect) fewer children die at birth or at a young age.
- A growing population in a country with limited resources (remember

we are talking about developing countries) will result in increased scarcity of these resources.

- Taking the argument to the extreme (but not unlikely) conclusion, more lives might ultimately be lost as a result of the cheap drugs than would have been lost had the drugs never been introduced, owing to starvation, other diseases, and perhaps even civil war (all resulting from population growth under the circumstances common to the poorest countries on the planet). Note that what is at stake here is a simple (but terrifying) calculation: If more people stay alive, the sum total of suffering is greater when those people fall ill or die than if there had never been so many people in the first place.

Step 5   0:35–0:45 (10 minutes)

What is the proper response to arguments like this? Ask students to consider solutions to this very grim scenario. Perhaps the most obvious suggestion is birth control: Distribute not only drugs, but condoms as well – and provide instructions on how to use them properly. But what about cultural and religious prohibitions against birth control? Is it an entrepreneur's role or duty to worry about or deal with local customs and beliefs? How do we avoid being paralyzed by the possible long-term consequences of our actions? Can we justify ignoring this argument, and if so why?

Step 6   0:45–1:00 (15 minutes)

After raising questions such as these it is useful to ask the students to think of parallel examples and their proposed solutions. What are the dark sides of their own ventures? Have they witnessed other start-ups or initiatives struggle with (unforeseen) long-term consequences? A recurring question should be: Are we choosing to ignore consequences because they are unlikely to actually occur, because we have taken measures to prevent them, or simply because they are too difficult, annoying, or heartbreaking to consider?

Key Takeaways

- The importance of thinking about the short- and long-term conse-quences of entrepreneurial activity.
- The need to take into account all affected stakeholders, present and future.
- The practical and moral difficulties of acting in the face of uncertainty.
- There are productive and unproductive entrepreneurial ventures.

Teaching Tips

The topics discussed here (life-threatening disease, overpopulation, problems specific to developing countries, etc.) are incredibly complex and may therefore be intimidating to students. It is very helpful to make the students feel that they are in a "safe zone" where they can express themselves freely: It is understood that not everyone will be able to formulate their opinions in a polished way, and that people may take offense where none was intended. The goal should be open, respectful conversation, and students should be encouraged to ask their classmates follow-up questions so that they will reach a sound understanding of the different perspectives in the classroom. When these policies are clearly outlined at the beginning of the session, students overwhelmingly take responsibility for a productive discussion.

EXERCISE: ENVISIONING ENTREPRENEURIAL LEADERSHIP

AUTHOR: ELAINE EISENMAN

Description

This exercise enables leaders of growing companies to understand the critical nature of understanding their own values and using that understanding to create a values-based business. This exercise can be used to consider one's personal leadership drivers and values coupled with one's aspiration about the values for the company. By doing so, entrepreneurs are able to articulate, many for the first time, their core values and personal drivers.

Usage Suggestions

This exercise can be used in any setting where the focus is personal self-reflection as a basis for considering one's leadership style and drivers. The session is most effective when the exercise is part of a program that helps students understand their values and goals as leaders and offers them the opportunity to construct personal leadership vision statements. The exercise can be used on multiple levels including graduate, undergraduate, and executive programs.

Learning Objectives

- Identify one's key values.
- Integrate those values into a compelling vision of entrepreneurial leadership.
- Communicate the vision to others, and give and receive feedback on what is heard and its impact on stakeholders.

Materials List

- "Values Checklist" (included at the end of this exercise).
- Internet access so students can go to Google Images (https://www. google.com/imghp?hl=en&tab=wi) or Getty Images (http://www. getty images.com/) to find images that resonate with their primary values.
- If internet access is not feasible, have piles of magazines that have many pictures so students can pull out images from the magazines.
- If students prefer to draw their values, this is acceptable also.

Pre-Work Required by Students

Read Goleman (2004), Collins (2005), and George et al. (2007) (cited below).

Theoretical Foundations

Collins, Jim. 2005. Level 5 leadership. *Harvard Business Review*, July–August.
George, Bill, Sims, P., McLean, A.N., and Mayer, D. 2007. Discovering your authentic leadership. *Harvard Business Review*, February.
Goleman, Daniel. 2004. What makes a leader? *Harvard Business Review*, January.
Halpern, Belle Linda, and Lubar, Kathy. 2004. *Leadership Presence*. New York: Gotham.
Senge, Peter M., Smith, Bryan J., Ross, Richard B., Roberts, Charlotte, and Kleiner, Art. 1994. *The Fifth Discipline Fieldbook: Strategies and Tools for Building a Learning Organization*, 1st ed. New York: Crown Publishing.

Time Plan (90 minutes)

Review values checklist   0:00–0:20 (20 minutes)

- Review the "Values Checklist" and pick the top two values that answer two questions:
  a. "What values best describe my drivers for how I behave in challenging situations?"
  b. "What values best describe the way I would want others to describe the core of my behaviors as a leader?"

Identify images   0:20–0:40 (20 minutes)

- Have participants go to Google Images or Getty Images or the magazines and select the images that best symbolize their values. Print out these images.
- Tell the participants: For each image, immediately write down why you chose it, and how it defines and symbolizes your values. Create a brief story or example about each value and how it resonates in your own life.

Creating leadership vision statements   0:40–1:20 (40 minutes)
Divide the group into pairs. The group is told: "Combine these stories
into an entrepreneurial leadership vision statement that you could deliver
to your employees. Your statement should include some behaviors from
your stories so that others can understand what you mean when you
talk about your values. You are describing 'values-in-action' rather than
simply listing words and assuming everyone has a common and shared
meaning for those words. Your partner will role-play a member of your
team of the business you are now founding or lead. This statement will
provide your team with insight into what they can expect from you as their
new leader."

- **Your script**: I am delighted to welcome you to my team. As we begin,
  I want to share my vision as the founder so that you understand the
  values and principles at the core of my actions . . .
- **Your partner's role**:
  - Push back and ask questions to increase clarity.
  - Then provide feedback as to whether the vision had reso-
    nance, credibility, impact, and meaning, and how to increase
    impact going forward.
- Switch roles.

Debrief   1:20–1:30 (10 minutes)

- Ask for one or two volunteers to share their vision statement.
- Ask the group for any questions as to the clarity of the statement.
- Ask the group the following about the exercise itself:
  - Was this the first time they have clearly articulated their
    values as the basis for their company?
  - Did telling stories enhance their values descriptions?
  - Was it hard to find stories that exemplified their values?
  - How did this feel?
  - Were there any surprises?
  - Would their clients or customers be interested in knowing
    their values?
  - How can they communicate this to their clients and customers?
  - Can or should values be used as a recruitment tool? How?
  - Is it fair to expect employees to share their values?

Key Takeaways

- Owners or founders need to recognize that their values must serve as the foundation of their companies.
- These values can and should be clearly articulated.
- Stories and images about how the values are demonstrated are more powerful than simply stating the values that one holds.
- Different people have different values; the same words mean different things to different people.
- Employees need to understand the values of their companies.
- Employer–employee value differences can lead to unexpected behaviors and outcomes.

Teaching Tips

- Using images rather than words allows participants to be expansive and creative in personalizing their values. The same words do not mean the same things to everyone. Using images allows for the subtle distinctions in meaning to be highlighted.
- Participants should be encouraged to choose dynamic and rich images to visualize their values. Taking enough time to create a few stories will allow them to translate those actions into a personal statement of values-in-action.
- The process should not be rushed or the results will be superficial.
- The feedback givers who listen to the personal statement should be encouraged to provide honest and critical feedback on whether the statement and examples resonated and impacted them or if they sounded trite or superficial.

Attribution

The exercise is adapted from the work of Senge et al. (1994), Halpern and Lubar (2004), and the Center for Creative Leadership.

Values Checklist

☐ Accountability	☐ Autonomy
☐ Achievement	☐ Balance
☐ Advancement	☐ Community
☐ Adventure	☐ Competition
☐ Authority	☐ Challenge

- ☐ Change and variety
- ☐ Compassion
- ☐ Competence
- ☐ Compliance
- ☐ Connectedness
- ☐ Consistency
- ☐ Constructive dissent
- ☐ Cooperation
- ☐ Deference
- ☐ Diversity
- ☐ Empathy
- ☐ Ethical
- ☐ Excellence
- ☐ Excitement
- ☐ Fairness
- ☐ Fame
- ☐ Fast-paced
- ☐ Flexibility
- ☐ Freedom
- ☐ Friendship
- ☐ Growth
- ☐ Harmony
- ☐ Helping others
- ☐ Homogeneity
- ☐ Honesty
- ☐ Humility
- ☐ Inclusion
- ☐ Individuality
- ☐ Influence
- ☐ Innovation
- ☐ Integrity
- ☐ Intellect
- ☐ Involvement
- ☐ Knowledge
- ☐ Leadership
- ☐ Loyalty
- ☐ Meaningful work
- ☐ Meritocracy
- ☐ Openness
- ☐ Opportunity
- ☐ Order
- ☐ Passion
- ☐ Perfection
- ☐ Personal development
- ☐ Physical challenge
- ☐ Political
- ☐ Power
- ☐ Privacy
- ☐ Public service
- ☐ Purpose
- ☐ Quality
- ☐ Recognition
- ☐ Relationships
- ☐ Reputation
- ☐ Respect
- ☐ Responsibility
- ☐ Results
- ☐ Security
- ☐ Self-discipline
- ☐ Self-respect
- ☐ Serenity
- ☐ Stability
- ☐ Stardom
- ☐ Status

☐ Teamwork
☐ Truth
☐ Wealth

☐ Wisdom
Others not listed – add below:
☐
☐
☐

Table PII.1 Exercises organized by practice and content area

Practice	Exercise	Entrepreneurship content area
Play	Puzzles and Quilts	Planning, effectuation, team, leadership, problem solving, stakeholders, entrepreneurial mindset.
Play	Building the Culture of Your Business with *The Sims*	Culture, team building, leadership, resource base, founder imprinting, family business, reflection.
Play	Rainmakers	Problem solving, innovation, opportunity creation.
Play	Improvisation for Creativity	Opportunity creation, communication, fear of failure, risk, market communication, problem solving, creative thinking.
Play	Marshmallow Tower	Team dynamics, market test, feasibility, technology entrepreneurship, operations and systems, iteration.
Play	Airplane Contest	Problem solving, innovation, technology entrepreneurship, concept testing, feasibility, bootstrapping, operations, selling.
Play	Business Model Canvas Game	Business models, value creation, opportunity shaping
Empathy	The Power of Observation	Design thinking, opportunity creation.
Empathy	Negotiation for Resource Acquisition	Resource acquisition, financing, valuation, contract negotiation.
Empathy	Monkey Business	Ethics, opportunities, social responsibility, human resources.
Empathy	Sequenced and Escalated Peer Coaching Exercises	Communication, dealing with advisors, stakeholder management, opportunity shaping, concept development.
Empathy	Interviewing an Entrepreneur and Self-Assessment	Entrepreneurial strategy, start-up, market research, failure, networking, communication.
Empathy	Perfect Pitch	Raising money, acquiring resources, personal selling, communication, marketing, growth, stakeholder management.
Empathy	Who's On First?	Team building, new venture strategy and growth, family business, leadership, structure, policies.

Category	Title	Description
Empathy	Family Systems	Family business, opportunity shaping, new venture strategy, international entrepreneurship.
Empathy	Understanding the Entrepreneurial Side of Government	Public policy, customer service, entrepreneurial thinking.
Empathy	Creating Customer Personas	Market research, design thinking, international entrepreneurship, business model, sales and marketing.
Creation	Mind Dumping for Ideation	Opportunity creation and identification, problem solving, innovation, creative thinking.
Creation	Ideaspace	Opportunity shaping, market testing, feasibility analysis, new venture growth and expansion.
Creation	Future Trends and Entrepreneurial Opportunities	Entrepreneurial strategy, competitor assessment, business model shaping, market research, concept development, new venture growth.
Creation	Self-Understanding for Opportunity Creation	Opportunity search, concept shaping, team development, corporate entrepreneurship, new venture growth.
Creation	Resource Acquisition Game	Building a resource base, new venture strategy, new venture growth, opportunity search, resource acquisition, business model.
Creation	Building a Strategic Network	Resource acquisition, raising money, communication, customer acquisition, strategic partnerships.
Creation	Creating as an Artist	Opportunity creation, communication, fear of failure, risk, market communication, problem solving, creative thinking.
Creation	The Resource Challenge	Opportunity identification, resource acquisition, bootstrapping, planning versus execution.
Creation	Your Strategic Alliance	New venture strategy, goal setting, team building, opportunity shaping, expansion and growth, negotiation.
Experimentation	Feasibility Blueprint	Feasibility testing, business model development, business model, competitor assessment.
Experimentation	Competitive Cup Stacking	Operations, systems, growth and expansion, new venture strategy, tech entrepreneurship, business model.

Table PII.1 (continued)

Practice	Exercise	Entrepreneurship content area
Experimentation	Escalating Market Tests	Business model shaping, concept testing, operations, feasibility, iteration.
Experimentation	Opportunity Screening	Opportunity evaluation, concept testing, iteration.
Experimentation	Fear of Failure	New venture strategy, personal assessment, team building, opportunity shaping, risk assessment, international entrepreneurship.
Experimentation	Drawing Bridges	Entrepreneurial thinking, problem solving.
Experimentation	$5, $50, and $500 Experiments	Market testing, feasibility, business model, risk, failure.
Reflection	Developing a Reflective Practice	Self-understanding.
Reflection	Reflecting on Entrepreneurial Experience	Personal development, vision, entrepreneurial strategy.
Reflection	Cultural Artifacts	New venture creation, culture, team building, growth.
Reflection	Passion Cube	Self-understanding, team building.
Reflection	Opportunity Walk	Design thinking, opportunity creation and discovery, self-understanding, opportunity shaping.
Reflection	Plotting the Growth of Your Business	Growth, stages of growth, resources.
Reflection	Brewster's Millions	Visioning, aspirations, entrepreneurial strategy, design thinking, self-understanding.
Reflection	The Dark Side of Entrepreneurship	Ethics, opportunities, social responsibility, strategy.
Reflection	Envisioning Entrepreneurial Leadership	New venture strategy, goal setting, team building, opportunity shaping.

12. A final note: The practices support accreditation

As we stated in the opening of Chapter 1, the message of our book is quite simple. We want to advance entrepreneurship education for all types of students using an action-based method rooted in a specific set of practices. Yet this requires change on many levels. We as educators have to make some changes. As we planned the writing of this book, we openly talked with one another about the question of assessment and accreditation.

Over the past few years we have delivered many messages about curriculum innovation and change at conferences and meetings around the world. We are frequently asked about the role of assessment, often hearing the perception that accreditation requirements around assessment of learning limit opportunities to experiment with new teaching approaches and to move from more traditional pedagogical styles. That has not been our experience to date, and we are actually supporters of assurance of learning, evaluating what does work with students and what is less effective. During the time that we were writing this book, we also learned about the 2013 revision of the AACSB accreditation standards and decided to explore the revised standards. Given that AACSB is the world's largest association of business schools and has accredited 682 schools across 45 countries, this seemed worth exploring.

The AACSB revision reduces the number of standards from 21 to 15, and, while the emphasis is still placed on quality and assurance of learning, three new areas of emphasis have been added: *innovation, impact,* and *engagement.* Given our teaching interests, these words definitely caught our attention. We found three standards of particular interest:

- Standard 9: Curriculum Content: Fostering innovation with flexible guidance and clarified expectations.
- Standard 12: Teaching Effectiveness: Developing teaching skills in a changing environment.
- Standard 15: Faculty Qualification and Engagement: Elevating scholarship and developing intersections between theory and practice. (AACSB, http://www.aacsb.edu/accreditation/business/standards/2013/)

In order to go more deeply into understanding the rationale and the implementation expectations about the standards and prove that the practice-based approach we are advocating in this book is in alignment with the future of entrepreneurship education, we asked John Fernandes, President and CEO of AACSB (and Babson alumnus), if he would be willing to talk with us about the new standards and our approach. The following are his thoughts captured in an interview while we were all attending the 2013 Academy of Management meetings. We appreciate him sharing with us.

Q1: WHAT DO YOU SEE AS THE MAIN CONTRIBUTIONS OF THE 2013 REVISED STANDARDS?

A: The committee worked very hard to put together an emphasis on: 1) innovation in business schools – to create and sustain value for students, employers, and communities they serve; 2) impact – to go beyond quality to ensure that business schools are making an impact through both scholarly education and creation of knowledge, and measuring this impact; and 3) engagement – improving the level of engagement between faculty, students, and industry to foster meaningful interactions and opportunities to share knowledge.

Q2: WHY IS THERE SO MUCH EMPHASIS ON ASSESSMENT FROM THE AACSB PERSPECTIVE?

A: In 2003, AACSB was one of the first to describe a comprehensive assurance of learning set of standards for higher education. Now, in the 2013 standards, we balanced assurance of learning with curriculum in an effort to make the standards more concise, but at the same time broaden the coverage. They are still strong in assessment, but we want to avoid the viewpoint of focusing on assessment for just the purpose of assessment only. Collectively at many levels (within and outside of business schools), there seems to be a lot of collection of data out there without the purpose of program improvement. Perhaps this could be due to the fact that data reporting seems to be popular from a public viewpoint or a legislative viewpoint. AACSB believes that assurance of learning, at its core, is more than just data reporting. It is first and foremost designed to keep the wheel of continuous improvement turning, which is the foundation of accreditation. It's not to catch somebody or to audit somebody; it's to assure the continuous improvement of the school towards its mission – or even a revitalized mission.

Q3: DO YOU THINK THE NEW STANDARDS LOOSEN THE REINS A LITTLE BIT?

A: Yes, they do, in a good way. They do not loosen the reins on quality, but on perspective. The 2013 standards push management education towards flexibility in approach, in market, in focus, and in student inclusiveness – in a global sense – but also in a multidisciplinary sense. This flexibility benefits those that are interested in furthering innovation, entrepreneurship, creative design thinking – many of whom have become lead players on habits of assessment. Those that are steeped in more rigid disciplines might have to reevaluate what has been the "status quo" a little differently as a result of the new standards.

Q4: ARE YOU HEARING THAT FEEDBACK?

A: I'm actually saying that I think that's a little bit of the intent. For example, the Academy of Management is made of a cornucopia of disciplines, those with a little more flexibility in outlook, so I do not expect much push-back from AOM's members. I do wonder, though, what those in more traditional disciplines that have a lesser degree of flexibility (perhaps finance) will say when the time comes for a maintenance review utilizing the new digest of standards. With each standards revision there are always bumps along the way, and different disciplines within management education respond in a variety of ways. Historically speaking, most schools when they voted for the 2003 standards knew the two primary points of focus were globalization and assurance of learning. In retrospect – though all will agree that the changes worked well – I don't know if the membership would have voted as agreeably for the 2003 standards if they knew what assurance of learning was going to do in terms of work needed to bring about change, especially when they got to the disciplinary level. Many within the Academy of Management at that time were very disappointed with our changes, and were quite vocal in correspondence about those relating to assurance of learning. Many felt that the changes were encroaching upon the autonomy of the faculty's assessment of the individual's capabilities. Those that criticized then, of course, see the value and need now, but the change did bring about some ripples in the water. Since the revisions were just performed in April [2013], we'll process through a three-year transition window for both maintenance and initial reviews. Throughout this time we'll most likely receive feedback and opinions, towards the positive and negative, which is inevitable when change occurs.

Q5: WHAT KIND OF REACTIONS ARE YOU GETTING THIS TIME GIVEN THESE ARE THE FIRST REVISIONS IN TEN YEARS?

A: Not quite as bad, and we hope that, as schools begin to internalize the 2013 standards, they'll find strengths in and value to the changes. One that I think will bring about a decent amount of conversation will be changes made to the academically qualified (AQ)/professionally qualified (PQ) framework. As of the 2013 standards there are no longer just "AQ" or "PQ" faculty, but a matrix consisting of two academic (research or scholarly) categories and two applied/practice categories. The old "AQ" category, which is traditionally a research-defined academic in many schools, now provides a broader platform of research: basic, applied, or pedagogical. This is now called a scholarly academic (SA). The second category of academically qualified faculty is for the practice academic (PA) that might have started as a scholarly academic, very discipline-centric, but became engaged with practice, and therefore brings something different to the school. Not everybody will be a fan of these changes, but it is time to think in a more global context, and in different models.

In conversation a few years ago, one dean mentioned to me that he expected that all faculty in his school will be academically and professionally qualified. This particular school, who had strong resources, had the ability to support faculty research, their case writing – essentially everything. While many schools would like to implement this research-focused model, financially it is often not realistic. Instead most schools choose a mission and research model that's unique for them – one that highlights where they're distinctive to the marketplace. They've reinforced this distinctive brand to the market and their constituents, and if it is consistent with this new viewpoint in faculty models then they will benefit. For those institutions that have been focused primarily on trying to publish in top journals, then this flexibility might not be as welcomed, since the extensive research model was what set them apart.

I expect some extensive research institutions will eventually one day say, "These standards were in our best interest too," because they are. The 2013 standards now require that institutions place an equal value on teaching, as well as research, which will improve teaching models across management education as a whole. Even AACSB's new Doctoral Education Task Force Report (released in September 2013) says that it is important for programs to prepare doctoral students to be effective in both the classroom and in research.

Q6: INTERESTING, BECAUSE UP TO NOW IT'S LARGELY BEEN THAT WE TEACH IN THE WAY WE WERE TAUGHT. YOU DO WHAT WAS DONE TO YOU. WHAT OTHER CHANGES DO YOU SEE IN THE STANDARDS?

A: Aesthetically, we moved from 82 pages down to 50, and from 21 standards down to 15. Though it seems pretty drastic, we mostly just cleared out a lot of the verbiage and provided a broader coverage. There's a much stronger momentum towards executive education and, again, it provides flexibility – more flexibility with faculty and faculty models, and delivery models. I think that these standards are going to have a significant impact on schools, more so than the original assurance of learning standard, but again we won't see that until ten years out, as I think it takes schools generally speaking about ten years to truly make a change in culture.

Q7: IN CONSIDERING OUR BOOK, A FUSION OF THEORY AND PRACTICE THAT REQUIRES STUDENTS TO ENGAGE IN A METHOD OF ENTREPRENEURSHIP BY DEVELOPING A PORTFOLIO OF PRACTICES, HOW WILL ASSESSMENT CHANGE BASED ON THE 2013 STANDARDS WHEN YOU GET DOWN TO THE LEVEL OF THE ACTUAL TEACHING AND LEARNING?

A: I thought in 2003 we were very prescriptive on how we wanted assurance of learning done. We wanted direct assessment, and there was thinking that direct assessment by the faculty member or others in an observation format was definitely acceptable for assurance of learning standards, but assessment by practitioners in practice of the student was not acceptable because it was indirect. And now the 2013 standards say that forms of indirect assessment, like employer evaluations, are acceptable for assurance of learning. That's a big change. Remember, it's still an element of inputs to continuous improvement of the degree program itself. We are just being much more flexible. What's really affecting bodies like AACSB, which innately is like our schools themselves, is the need for constant and aggressive and quick change. And that's why you're seeing flexibility being paramount – that and tuning very clearly to a school's mission. A school must tune into its mission, and must follow that mission – after all, isn't that what is supposed to make each unique and valuable?

Q8: SO INDIRECT ASSESSMENT MEANS THAT MUCH MORE EMPHASIS OR ADDITIONAL EMPHASIS CAN BE PLACED ON CO-CURRICULAR LEARNING NOW?

A: It means that it will supplement the assessment process. I think if the school did all the direct assessment measures, they could still run into difficulties with teams of reviewers even if the team says, "We're not going to bug this school. We know that it's a great school; we're just going to let it go." To prevent this during the accreditation process, we try to make sure that people don't have an allegiance to the school, either as a graduate, former faculty member, or administrator. But we still let schools pick most of the teams, and personally I think some teams are easier than others, some people easier than others, and some people know that. That is one of the things that will have to change, as we get bigger and bigger – we will have to implement a more independent selection process of the team. This will also make the application of following the standards probably more uniform.

When a school is under maintenance review, the team report is reviewed and evaluated by the Continuous Improvement Review Committee (CIRC) for final say before going to the Board for a vote. The CIRC tries to apply a homogeneous review of schools, so that we're fairly consistent in our accreditation process. Having said that, I still think there are still sometimes differences. I think some schools in the past have gotten an easier pass, because of their name, their brand, their research prowess. But it's going to be much harder to do that with the new standards without being able to demonstrate engagement.

Q9: WHO DO YOU THINK THE 2013 STANDARDS ARE GOING TO BENEFIT THE MOST?

A: Well, if "benefit" means which schools will do well with them, who is going to shine, then for schools like Babson it's right up your alley.

However, I think it's going to be harder for a strictly extensive research institution that only values top-tier journal publications, and doesn't want to talk to faculty about tenure unless they provide those. I think it's going to be harder for them, because now they're isolating the faculty by discipline and basic research. How will that give them an environment that's innovative? Innovation comes from cross-disciplinary research and cooperation, collaboration, and working with schools outside of the business school. Innovation comes from working together more than it comes from drilling down further into one specific discipline. So I think it's going to be harder for those schools.

So that's one: innovation's going to be a stress, and then engagement. It's going to be hard for an institution if they say that all they want is for new accounting faculty to focus primarily on getting published in a top journal – so they have a chance of making tenure down the road. Think about it, that's pushing the research angle. Many schools are pushing this now, and if continued they will be pushing it down the road in a way that's preventing the school from really meeting the student/faculty engagement standards, and the value proposition of what we expect from business schools going forward.

However, for many of these schools, they're often the flagship university and a land grant institution, so they culturally move more slowly. The deans of those schools have to be pretty shrewd to make sure they're satisfying their research culture, the basic research and narrow discipline. This is when the question will come, what else are they doing to foster innovation and engagement and therefore demonstrate impact? You need to show us how your approach is having impact on your mission.

Q10: IS THE IMPACT ON PRACTICE IMPORTANT?

A: Yes, the impact on practice is important, but that's not the only measure of impact – here's where the flexibility comes into play. AACSB is not saying the impact must just be in practice. Certainly applied research must be on practice. Pedagogical research must be on practice. Basic research does not necessarily have to immediately have impact on practice. But what we want schools to be able to do is at least point backwards and say, what we were working on a few years ago, remember that, and now here it is where it's starting to impact practice. They're going to have to build a reputation. And some of it's going to be a "look back to show what we did in the past" to demonstrate that they have had impact.

Q11: IT'S NOT JUST THE PHYSICAL CLASSROOM?

A: No, not just physical. From a personal perspective (not necessarily an AACSB approach), I'm thinking of the "classroom" definition in its broadest sense, long-term. To be a great school, an institution must able to source and service its students globally, and to do so it might not have the capability of doing so in a full-time classroom setting. Schools really have to engage in upping their electronic delivery methods. That's when I think a lot of the innovation will take place.

In August [2013] AACSB is doing a program on MOOCs and will be exploring many of such questions. I'm not one that thinks that movements like MOOCs are the end-all be-all, but I think providers and academe will get to the point where they will find some way of validating online performance. Then, I think schools will have a better chance and capability of reaching out globally.

Q12: IF WE ASKED FACULTY TO EVALUATE THEMSELVES, FROM ONE TO TEN, WITH ONE BEING THEORY-BASED TEACHING AND TEN BEING PRACTICE-BASED TEACHING, WHERE DO YOU THINK THEY LIE ON AVERAGE? WHERE WOULD YOU SAY BUSINESS SCHOOLS MOSTLY ARE TODAY ON THAT CONTINUUM, AND WHERE DO YOU THINK THEY SHOULD BE?

A: Well, I think some are ones and twos, and some are nines and tens. So it's unfortunate, you know. I'd like to say everybody's a six or a seven, but it's a really broad spectrum.

Q13: IT'S REALLY INTERESTING THAT YOU SAY THAT. IT MEANS THAT NO ONE HAS STRUCK THAT BALANCE YET.

A: Exactly. The mode is – let's say, it's really those that haven't done much of it at all, and those that have stayed close to practice and maybe are much further along. I just have a hard time saying what the average would be, but let me be fair and say a lot of ones to threes and a lot of sevens to nines.

Q14: SHIFTING JUST A BIT, WE'D ALSO LIKE TO ASK YOU ABOUT ANOTHER VIEWPOINT ON ASSESSMENT. SOME CRITICS DO SAY THAT, OR DID SAY THAT, ASSESSMENT STIFLES CREATIVITY. HOW DO YOU RESPOND?

A: I think there's some truth to that, though *stifle*'s a little strong. But I do think it constrained creativity in that we were very prescriptive in our model about how to do assurance of learning, and we were trying to change a mindset that this is to be done to improve the program. As a result we discovered that we need the engagement of cross-disciplinary faculty in the setting of learning goals, assessment measures, and finding out what's working and what's not. So, by turning down completely indirect measures, you could say that it was constraining. Before the 2003 standards, indirect measures were permitted. Then they were not. Now indirect measures are back. Given that they were permitted, then taken away, and are now coming back, it seems to me that having no flexibility in developing assurance of learning techniques or measurement techniques makes them less likely to be well done. You need to remember that in 2003 there were not many operating models of assurance of learning. From 2003 to 2013, there have been a lot of items that schools have changed and, as a result, assurance of learning is now really embedded in the schools.

What's important is that through the standards we set stretch objectives for schools to achieve. Schools then pursue these objectives through their own planning and design, and come up with really innovative techniques or strategies. During the review process, or even in conversation, schools are excited to share (or brag about) these strategies or results with AACSB review teams or staff. When found, we bring these new ideas or processes to conferences to share as best practices, include them in our best practices database, and highlight them in our research reports. True innovation and growth occurs on-site at our schools – AACSB serves as the conduit to bring it together in a way that everyone can learn from, and as a result the industry moves forward. Best practices and innovative ideas can only move forward when they are shared and built upon.

Q15: WHAT WOULD YOU LIKE TO SEE AS THE RESULT OF ALL OF THIS?

A: Well, I know that assessment will just be part of the everyday toolkit of schools. It probably is much more in that state now than it was even a couple years ago. What I think it will do, and I hope it will do, is continue to improve programs. What I fear is that the disruption coming into the industry now is coming so quickly . . .

Q16: DISRUPTION, MEANING TECHNOLOGY?

A: Yes, technology is one, but also globalization, funding constraints – even shifts of where students are coming from. The really good faculties are in one or two regions (largely in North America and Western Europe), and then the students are in others (largely the Middle East and Africa, South America, and Asia). So now what are we going to do? We have good faculties that we are not accessing – technology has to help that situation out a bit – but we need to establish new ways where we can better leverage faculty talent to meet the needs of students at the global level.

Much of this thought process has developed from the work that our Latin America and Caribbean Advisory Council has been doing. As a result, I often am focusing on emerging regions, and, I'll tell you, it's really tough out there. In emerging economies, schools are about 8 percent of the traditional "AQ" level. It is pretty impossible for an institution to earn AACSB accreditation with such a low level of AQ faculty. In Latin America/Caribbean, we have about 15 or 16 schools that are accredited – such institutions are able to fund an adequate faculty level. But those that are outside the "major" institutions find it hard to recruit and support academic faculty.

Q17: HOW ARE YOU GOING TO WORK ON THAT?

A: Well, we are researching the state and well-being of management education in "emerging economies" across the globe, not just in the Latin America/Caribbean region. One of the things that we've invested in over the last ten years is the breadth and depth of knowledge found in our knowledge services database and internal files. We've made a concerted effort to try to learn as much as we can about all regions of the globe. If we don't know something or have something in our database, we go out and find it from other sources. We are really trying to beef up what we know, to be able to understand where the industry is going, almost to the country level.

Q18: IF YOU LOOK AT IT BY COUNTRY, BUT AT LEAST BY REGION, COULD YOU BRIEFLY DESCRIBE HOW YOU THINK NORTH AMERICA'S GOING, WHERE YOU THINK LATIN AMERICA'S GOING, WHERE YOU THINK AFRICA'S GOING, WHERE YOU THINK THE EUROPEAN UNION IS GOING?

A: Sure, let's start with the Baltics.

Baltics. Unfortunately, right now, the Baltics are experiencing a significantly low birthrate, and as a result you could almost say they are essentially shutting down. I'm not sure what is going to happen, hoping for the best and will watch and wait.

Europe. More broadly, Europe will experience growing economies in Eastern Europe. Western Europe's economies are not growing much anymore, and with that tends to go the population – right now there is a decline in younger and higher education age individuals. But on the flip side there are actually more drivers in Europe to improve, because of dwindling higher education population. A number of years ago (maybe 2005 or 2006), I spoke at a conference in Spain, where the discussion was focused on many items, but one key element was global sourcing and global placement. It's pretty evident some of the schools really listened – some of our healthiest programs now are in Spain. They were one of the first to see the markets dwindling, and made a concerted effort to source both locally and globally.

Latin America, Asia, and the Middle East. The positives are there is economic growth in all areas – Latin America is growing, Asia is growing, and the Middle East is growing. As a result, each have become regions where higher education is at the highest point of need. Lucky for those in our industry, the most popular higher education genre is business – particularly for the one in five international students who study outside of their own country.

North America. The good news for North American schools is that there's a higher propensity of students from emerging regions who would like to come to North America (to a school like Babson). Much more likely than there is for a kid from Swampscott to be going to CEIBS in China. As a result North American schools will have a much bigger pool to recruit from, which of course is a good thing. In addition, the U.S. higher education age population will grow until 2025, but then it begins to decline. So, I think for the next 10 to 12 years, the U.S. is in pretty good shape. But until then U.S. schools must learn from our colleagues in Europe – they can't stay stagnating when it comes to international recruiting. They can't say,

"Oh, we got these big pools and have lots of students coming in, so we can just focus on where we are." For U.S. schools to continue to be the higher education leader in business, they will need to search out the best students in the world, and have ways to accommodate their presence. We've also got to be more aggressive with recruiting students locally and then placing them globally.

Q19: WE HAVE ONE LAST QUESTION, AND IT'S REALLY JUST ASKING FOR YOUR WORDS OF WISDOM. OUR BOOK AGAIN IS ON TEACHING ENTREPRENEURSHIP AS A METHOD USING A PORTFOLIO OF PRACTICES. THE MAJOR EMPHASIS IS ON THE EXPERIENTIAL, WHILE BASED ON A SOLID INTEGRATION OF THEORY AND PRACTICE. GIVEN THIS APPROACH, WHAT ELSE SHOULD WE HAVE ASKED YOU ABOUT ASSESSMENT?

A: You know, I think to be an effective entrepreneur you've got be a reasonable risk manager, meaning you can't be risk averse, but you can't be too risk embracing to the point of making a lot of mistakes. I think entrepreneurs must know how to take opportunities, examine the risk – managing the bad ones while optimizing the positive likelihoods. Identifying threats and successfully managing them, during the emergence of the creative endeavor, is really important to increase the likelihood of success.

For schools, I think they need to do all they can to inspire creativity, and the inquisitiveness in the student, though the institution cannot do it all. For true success, there must be an innate level of creativity or curiosity that comes instinctually to students. As a dean or director of an entre-preneurial program, I would want to try to determine a way of how we could tap into the creativity quotient of students coming into a program. Knowing such an item would be valuable to be able to develop successful curriculum(s), and to be able to really provide what students need to learn.

It's going to be an exciting world in higher education, but at the same time I see significant changes coming – like the tenure system, or even discipline decentralization. Certainly the latter must be evaluated for consideration, if not by combining departments of schools, then by pro-viding the means for faculty from one school to know faculty from other schools within the university (at the minimum). Different "schools" within academic institutions need to work together. In the long run I can foresee higher education overall becoming a game of finances, necessities, and ultimately elimination. Families will begin to look at their pie of finances, and will begin to allocate around the necessities. Even though higher education should be a number one priority, it becomes a factor of overall economic development, and individual development of families. I wonder where people will place higher education in terms of priority, if they will settle for a more economical approach, and if they will begin to significantly limit their willingness to spend. If they do, then that's going to put increasing financial pressures on schools. So schools need to be really fit about how they manage their funding model.

Q20: TO CLOSE, IF WE ASKED YOU TO GIVE US ONE WORD TO DESCRIBE THE 2013 STANDARDS, WOULD IT BE FLEXIBILITY?

A: Yes, that could be one. Considering the changes coming through AACSB's 2013 standards, suggestions made through our new Doctoral Education Report, and the AICPA's Pathways Commission for those in accounting, I think it would be appropriate to utilize a couple of words. The focus on many levels for business schools is now to improve innovation and engagement, and to get there you need application and flexibility.

Thank you, John Fernandes, for sharing your thoughts with us. The future of education will certainly require educators around the globe from various disciplines to think and act more entrepreneurially than ever before.

Index

reflective frameworks 90–97
role of theory and practice 85–8
theories and models 91–2
types of 93–5
see also Brewster's Millions Exercise;
    Cultural Artefacts Exercise;
    Dark Side of Entrepreneurship
    Exercise; Developing a
    Reflective Practice Exercise;
    Envisioning Entrepreneurial
    Leadership Exercise;
    Opportunity Walk Exercise;
    Passion Cube Exercise;
    Plotting the Growth of Your
    Business Exercise; Reflecting
    on Entrepreneurial Experience
    Exercise
reflection-in-practice/reflection-on-
    practice 89, 90, 271
reflexive dialogue 76
Reik, T. 44
Reis, E. 80, 81, 116, 133
relaxation theory 27
research techniques, empathy
    development 48–50
resource acquisition exercises 146–51,
    168–72, 214–18, 219–23, 229–33,
    295–8,
Resource Acquisition Game 214–18
resource base exercises 110–13,
    214–18
Resource Challenge Exercise 229–33
Rhenman, E. 31
Rice, G.E.J. 45
Rich, S.R. 56
Richardson, V. 71, 72, 73
Rieber, L.P. 26
risk assessment exercises 254–9
risk exercises 118–24, 224–8, 264–9
Robinson, R. 56
Robinson, Sir Ken 58
Roffey, S. 31
Rogoff, B. 12
role play 35–6, 50, 222, 266, 310
Rorty, R. 74
Rosa, P. 295, 297
Rosenberg, N. 47
Rouse, J. 13, 14
Ruben, B.D. 35
Ruef, M. 153

rule-based play 28
Runco, M.A. 61
Ryle, G. 7, 8

Salaff, A. 220
Salen, K. 28
sales exercises 131–5, 168–72, 188–93
Sandberg, J. 13
Sander, Jil 58
Santinelli, A. 135, 168–72, 220
Sarasvathy, S.D. 6, 7, 47, 55, 56, 58, 71,
    98, 106, 116, 211, 213, 229, 230,
    260, 261, 264, 266
Sawyer, B. 31
Sawyer, J. 45
Schein, E. 111, 112, 281
Schell, J. 25, 28, 30
Schiller, F. von 26
Schlesinger, L. 6, 7, 106, 116, 159, 161,
    211, 261
Schlesinger, P. 224–8
Schlossberg, N.K. 89
Schmidt, H.G. 91
Schön, D. 16, 89–90, 91, 139, 141, 271,
    272, 277
Schooley, C. 31, 35
Schraw, G. 88
Schumpeter, J. 54, 58
Schwartz, P. 206
Scott, L.R. 290, 291
Seelig, T. 229, 230, 232–3
Seidel, V.P. 140, 141
self-assessment exercises 254–9
self-understanding 55, 56, 61, 63
self-understanding exercises 271–5,
    285–9, 290–94, 299–302
Self-Understanding for Opportunity
    Creation Exercise 209–13
Senge, P.M. 309, 313
sensemaking 73, 76–7
Sequenced and Escalated Peer
    Coaching Exercises 159–63
serious games 31–8
Sexton, D. 295, 296
Shane, S. 5, 54, 290, 291
shareholder value 305
Shaver, K.G. 290, 291
Shepherd, D.A. 54, 71
Shubik, M. 31
Siegel, R. 116

Teaching entrepreneurship